DESPERADOS of NEW MEXICO

by

F. Stanley

New Foreword
by
Marc Simmons

SANTA FE

New Material © 2015 by Sunstone Press. All Rights Reserved.

No part of this book may be reproduced in any form or by any electronic or mechanical means including information storage and retrieval systems without permission in writing from the publisher, except by a reviewer who may quote brief passages in a review.

Sunstone books may be purchased for educational, business, or sales promotional use. For information please write: Special Markets Department, Sunstone Press, P.O. Box 2321, Santa Fe, New Mexico 87504-2321.

Library of Congress Cataloging-in-Publication Data

Stanley, F. (Francis), 1908-1996.
 [Desperadoes of New Mexico]
 Desperados of New Mexico / by F. Stanley ; new foreword by Marc Simmons.
   pages cm. -- (Southwest heritage series)
 Originally published: Denver, Colorado : World Press, 1953, with title Desperadoes of New Mexico.
   Summary: "The lives, and often deaths, of seventeen New Mexico desperados" --Provided by publisher.
   Includes bibliographical references and index.
   ISBN 978-1-63293-078-1 (softcover : alkaline paper)
 1. Outlaws--New Mexico--Biography. 2. New Mexico--Biography. 3. Frontier and pioneer life--New Mexico. 4. New Mexico--History--19th century. I. Title.
 F801.S73 2015
 978.9'04--dc23
                                 2015022925

Sunstone Press is committed to minimizing our environmental impact on the planet. The paper used in this book is from responsibly managed forests. Our printer has received Chain of Custody (CoC) certification from: The Forest Stewardship Council™ (FSC®), Programme for the Endorsement of Forest Certification™ (PEFC™), and The Sustainable Forestry Initiative® (SFI®).

The FSC® Council is a non-profit organization, promoting the environmentally appropriate, socially beneficial and economically viable management of the world's forests. FSC® certification is recognized internationally as a rigorous environmental and social standard for responsible forest management.

WWW.SUNSTONEPRESS.COM
SUNSTONE PRESS / POST OFFICE BOX 2321 / SANTA FE, NM 87504-2321 /USA
(505) 988-4418 / ORDERS ONLY (800) 243-5644 / FAX (505) 988-1025

CONTENTS

THE SOUTHWEST HERITAGE SERIES / I

FOREWORD TO THIS EDITION / II
The Controversial F. Stanley
by
Marc Simmons

A MAN'S REACH / III
from
The F. Stanley Story
by
Mary Jo Walker

TRIBUTE TO F. STANLEY / IV
by
Jack D. Rittenhouse

1953 EDITION / V

I

THE SOUTHWEST HERITAGE SERIES

"The past is not dead. In fact, it's not even past."
—William Faulkner, *Requiem for a Nun*

The history of the United States is written in hundreds of regional histories and literary works. Those letters, essays, memoirs, biographies and even collections of fiction are often first-hand accounts by people who wanted to memorialize an event, a person or simply record for posterity the concerns and issues of the times. Many of these accounts have been lost, destroyed or overlooked. Some are in private or public collections but deemed to be in too fragile condition to permit handling by contemporary readers and researchers.

However, now with the application of twenty-first century technology, nineteenth and twentieth century material can be reprinted and made accessible to the general public. These early writings are the DNA of our history and culture and are essential to understanding the present in terms of the past.

The Southwest Heritage Series is a form of literary preservation. Heritage by definition implies legacy and these early works are our legacy from those who have gone before us. To properly present and preserve that legacy, no changes in style or contents have been made. The material reprinted stands on its own as it first appeared. The point of view is that of the author and the era in which he or she lived. We would not expect photographs of people from the past to be re-imaged with modern clothes, hair styles and backgrounds. We should not, therefore, expect their ideas and personal philosophies to reflect our modern concepts.

Remember, reading their words and sharing their thoughts is a passport back into understanding how the past was shaped and how it influenced today's world.

Our hope is that new access to these older books will provide readers with a challenging and exciting experience.

II

FOREWORD TO THIS EDITION

The Controversial F. Stanley
by
Marc Simmons

As a professional historian, I've often been asked my opinion of the author who wrote under the pen name, F. Stanley. According to his 1996 obituary, he published 190 books and booklets on New Mexico history, quite a record by any standard. The problem is, F. Stanley has been almost universally condemned for the innumerable flaws that litter his writings. However, behind the man and the work lurks a curious story.

He was born Louis Crocchiola in New York's Greenwich Village on October 31, 1908 to Italian immigrant parents. After receiving a Bachelor's degree in English at Catholic University in Washington, DC, Louis entered the priesthood in 1938. On that occasion, as was allowed, he formally added the new names Stanley and Francis to his birth name, Louis Crocchiola. Thereafter, he was called simply Father Stanley.

Shortly after his ordination, the young priest was diagnosed with the beginnings of tuberculosis. Following medical advice of the day, the Church sent Father Stanley to Hereford, Texas in the Panhandle, hoping the arid climate might cure him. It did! Something else occurred at the same time. Father Stanley fell under the spell of the Southwest, leading him to become one of the most prolific historical writers of his day.

In 1940 he applied for pastoral work in New Mexico, since he was fluent in Spanish and thought he could be most useful there. The Archbishop of Santa Fe accepted him, assigning Father Stanley first to the Guadalupe church in Taos and then to the San Miguel church at Socorro.

During the 1940s, he served six or so different parishes in northern or eastern New Mexico, thereby becoming familiar with rural and small town life. It was while stationed at Taos, though, that Father Stanley caught the writing bug through mingling with local authors. But later as he was transferred by the Archbishop from one parish to another, he would begin looking into the history of his temporary residence and compiling a file of notes.

His first book, *Raton Chronicle*, appeared in 1948. Then in rapid succession F. Stanley published full-length histories on Cimarron, Socorro, Las Vegas, and the Maxwell land grant. Soon to his line of books, F. Stanley added an on-going series dedicated to a single small town or fort that other writers had ignored. These little booklets remain easily recognizable with their canary yellow covers and crimson red lettering, plus the New Mexico state emblem, the Zia sun symbol. Eventually, these small works alone numbered 123 titles.

One of the earliest treatments of the historic and controversial Maxwell Land Grant was published by F. Stanley in 1952, titled *The Grant That Maxwell Bought*, also published in a new edition by Sunstone Press. Although other books on the subject have appeared since, serious readers still need to go back and examine what Father Stanley had to say. Otherwise, small nuggets buried in his pages, and nowhere else, may be missed.

Remarkably, F. Stanley personally financed all of his publications, often going deeply into debt. The several printers he used were generally tolerant of the delay in paying his bills.

Even more stressful for Father Stanley was the harsh criticism his writings received from historians and book reviewers. They unmercifully picked apart his unedited and untidy prose, pointed out frequent mistakes, and condemned the neglect of standards in the composition or format of his books.

For one example, a serious slip occurred in the naming of F. Stanley's longest work, a history of the New Mexico state capital in three volumes, titled *Ciudad Santa Fe*. Under the old Spanish system, Santa Fe in reality never achieved the rank of a *ciudad* (chartered city), but retained the status of a town (*villa*). The author had missed that pivotal fact and thus launched his three volume set with a conspicuous error on the covers.

In 1985 Mary Jo Walker, a librarian at Eastern New Mexico University, Portales, published a sympathetic biography, *The F. Stanley Story*. The book contains quotes from interviews given by Father Stanley in which he defends himself and his methods.

His main plea was: "Pardon the mistakes, but say a kind word for my effort." Painfully aware of his failings, he claimed that his intent was merely to assemble fugitive information from obscure courthouse records, old newspaper files, and archives so that others more able could pick up the thread where he left off and carry on.

After publication of Walker's biography, some historians, myself included, began to look more charitably toward Father Stanley Crocchiola. The fact is, despite his deficiencies, he managed to make in his own quirky way a not insignificant contribution to our regional history.

Today, F. Stanley books and booklets are worth collecting. I'm always happy when I can add another one of his to my personal library. I just wish he was still around so that I could tell him that.

Sunstone Press in choosing to include F. Stanley books in its honored Southwest Heritage Series is wisely making many of these books available again to the reading public.

III

A MAN'S REACH
"Take him for what he is worth"
from
The F. Stanley Story
by
Mary Jo Walker

It is difficult to say to what extent negative criticism and neglect may have personally affected Father Stanley. Some of his works in the 1970s showed considerable care in preparation, but no more so than his major efforts in earlier decades. He knew his own limitations as well as any of his critics did, but he believed quite sincerely that the flaws in his work were largely literary in nature and therefore of little overall significance; or alternatively that they represented realities over which he had little control, such as his limited time or the cost of typesetting footnotes. His first reactions may be surmised from comments in the foreword to *Dave Rudabaugh*.

> *I used to apologize for my mistakes. Come to think of it, why should I? I tried; that's more than my critics did. I investigated to the best of my ability, often going sleepless and hungry in order to attain the facts. No patron has come along the way. I had to rough it alone.... The book may not be literary, but it is factual. In the long run, truth survives.*

Two years later, in *The Duke City*, he confessed from a somewhat different perspective:

> *I am grateful for all criticism--constructive or otherwise.*

And in *Satanta and the Kiowas*, 1968, he pled:

Let my mistakes be my Calvary, and let my readers be my confessors from whom we hope to obtain pardon and forgiveness.

Simply and with a kind of humble determination, he persevered for many years, his principal resources being his formidable drive and his eagerness to help preserve the history of the region he loved so well. No doubt he attempted too much; probably, as with so many of us, his reach exceeded his grasp. His hope, which he stated over and over again, was that his books would provide guidance for others and "prove a... contribution to Western Americana." That purpose and his dedication to it do not serve to be lightly dismissed.

Taken as a whole, with all its human flaws, F. Stanley's work stands as a unique contribution, as much a part of the written record "as Coronado's visit." Even Ramon Adams acknowledged that "he deserves a full measure of credit for supplying hitherto unpublished information," for putting something into print about obscure places and people, for adding to the body of recorded knowledge about the Southwest. Whatever the final evaluation may be, however, it is certain that F. Stanley has earned a place in southwestern history in his own right.

F. Stanley (circa 1953). Photograph courtesy of Golden Library, Eastern New Mexico University.

IV

TRIBUTE TO F. STANLEY
by
Jack D. Rittenhouse
from
The F. Stanley Story
by
Mary Jo Walker
Albuquerque, New Mexico / March, 1984

Some historians write because they hope their writing will bring them money or promotion or tenure. Some write to espouse a cause. A few write because they must, because it is the only way they can quench an inner thirst or scratch an itch of curiosity. The last class is the happiest, and F. Stanley is in this group.

The term historian has many shadings. Among academic people, a historian is a certified scholar whose commission of rank is a degree of Doctor of Philosophy in history, and whose income results from full-time teaching or writing history. Some of these go on to glory and excellence in their work; some gain renown as researchers or as teachers, become a historian's historian, but find writing a difficult task. Many bank their inner fire when they don their doctoral robes and are content to plod along as routine teachers, living as comfortably as a toad in a puddle of buttermilk, looking upon their diploma as a union card.

The grass roots historian is another type, curious about people and places around them. Their writings are their only certification. Some become antiquarians, with a dilettante interest in ancient things and more curious about precision in minutiae than in the social significance of their subject. The term antiquarian has a different meaning among historians than among bookmen.

Still another type of historian is the buff, an individual who is an enthusiast or devotee of a specific subject. When it comes to sheer bulk of knowledge about a subject, or even to accuracy on a point of information, I have seen many buffs who outclassed PhDs. I personally know only three individuals who have their own microfilm readers at home, and all three are buffs. They travel great distances to look at a gravestone or a courthouse record, which is not to say that professional historians and grassroots historians also do not do this, of course.

We owe much to the grassroots historian and the buff. They are the prospectors who discover new lodes. They are curious about people and places and customs, combining the interests of the folklorist and the historian, and if they are good at what they do, they find their work accepted and even honored.

F. Stanley is one whose curiosity and inner fire has drawn him to the study of people and places and events that had gone unnoticed until he saw them. He advanced knowledge in many directions, lit many candles to dispel darkness.

His works are only beginnings, and he knows this. In a sense, history writes itself merely by occurring, and thus there is the axiom that history is not written but rewritten. Another New Mexico local historian, Fray Angélico Chávez, once spoke to El Corral de Santa Fe Westerners and said that history is not a static, pure thing that can be discovered once, written down, and preserved intact forever. Instead, he said, history is a living, growing body that must be nurtured...and which occasionally requires surgery.

F. Stanley has wandered across the Southwest like a Johnny Appleseed of history, planting seedlings in the form of booklets and leaving their later nurturing to others. Later historians will convert these seedlings into trees, by pruning, fertilizing and grafting. The work will require more research, more verification, correction and amplification. But F. Stanley planted the first seed.

The historian who uses only *one* source for his work is a fool, but the historian who refuses to review any source is an idiot. Any source may have errors caused by lack of information, or poor proofreading, or hasty writing. But some questionable bit of old-timer's lore may raise the possibility of truth; it is then up to the later historian to prove or disprove the fact. Once, when I was gathering information about the New Mexico ghost town of Cabezón, I read an old-timer's memoir that mentioned a stage line running through the town. Nowhere else did I find any mention of this, and I sought to verify the story. A usually reliable professional historian scoffed at the notion that the town had ever been on a commercial stage line. Then a museum curator found a printed timetable of the Star Stage Line, listing the route and showing Cabezón as a stop. Although many dissertations do not list F. Stanley works as sources, the padre's booklets have nonetheless been studied for similar possible clues. Given the time and resources, F. Stanley himself would have gone farther; he leaves that to others.

His severest critics often have been people who never wrote a recognized book, or whose books themselves are not without the flaws of typesetters and human errors, or whose dyspeptic nature made them discard a sculpture because of a chip.

The body of work produced by F. Stanley will become part of the vast lore about the Southwest. It will remain as long as libraries stand and will be consulted and used by generations as part of the grassroots literature. Future writers will correct its errors, just as their mistakes will be corrected by still later scholars. But someone had to start it, and F. Stanley was the man.

V

1953 EDITION

DESPERADOS OF NEW MEXICO

DESPERADOES
OF
NEW MEXICO

by

F. STANLEY

Copyright 1953

Registered at the Library of Congress

DESPERADOS OF NEW MEXICO

DEDICATION

To the little known frontier marshalls of New Mexico who helped make the Land of Enchantment a better place to live in.

CONTENTS

Foreword: ix

Book One
    Coe's Last Crow (William Crow) / 1
Book Two
    Cimarron Playboy (David Crockett) / 23
Book Three
    Regular Regulators (Dick Brewer) / 41
Book Four
    A Midnight Snack and Death (Billy the Kid) / 67
Book Five
    Headless in Parral (Dave Rudabaugh) / 103
Book Six
    Anton Chico Express (Jim Greathouse) / 129
Book Seven
    Last of the Kid's Gang (Tom Pickett) / 143
Book Eight
    Blood Money (J. Joshua Webb) / 153
Book Nine
    19, 20, 21 and Death (Porter Stogden) / 167
Book Ten
    Wheel on My Neck (Clay Allison) / 185
Book Eleven
    Big Shot, Small Town (Rattlesnake Sam) / 203
Book Twelve
    Incident in Raton (Gus Mentzer) / 213
Book Thirteen
    Murder for Christmas (Baca of Socorro) / 221
Book Fourteen
    Affair in Springer (Dick Rogers) / 237
Book Fifteen
    Moon Over Socorro (Joel Fowler) / 261
Book Sixteen
    Man with the Red Beard (Vicente Silba) / 275
Book Seventeen
    Train Robbers, Inc. (Black Jack Ketchum) / 299

Bibliography / 317

FOREWORD

Truth is so much stranger than fiction that we are inclined to look with askance upon what is known to be a fact in order to accept the quasi-miraculous in the life of a desperado or a frontier marshall. Like the Emperor Jones it seems that the bullet could not be molded that would annihilate men like Pat Garrett, Wyatt Earp, Jeff Milton, Doc Holliday, Tom Pickett and others good and bad who are part of the history, if not the folk-lore, of the West.

Gather around at a party and strike up a conversation about famous generals and you drift into names like Caesar, Napoleon, Hannibal, Lee, Grant, Washington, and, in this our day, the leaders who marched our Allies to victory in both World Wars. More knowing ones will bring up such odd names like Alexander, Cincinnatus, Bolivar, the Iron Duke, Belisarius and others of lesser note but leaders nevertheless. All will have at least a nodding acquaintance with Washington, Napoleon and Caesar.

If, at the same party, the conversation swings to outlaws, Billy the Kid, Clay Allison, the James boys and possibly the Younger brothers will make the rounds. Very few will give you the truth about them any more than they will give you the truth about Napoleon, Washington and Lee. Tall tales they have read about cutting down a cherry tree, twenty-one men, one for each year in the Kid's life, and on and on, until you begin to wonder if they know what they are talking about, and if you want to be a wet blanket as well as to silence them ask them how much real research they have done on the subject. Not just Raine, Burns, Forrest and others who are considered authorities, but the actual court proceedings, eye-witnesses (if any still survive), newspaper accounts of the day, diaries and other such material.

No one who has ever written about badmen has exhausted the subject any more than others have about Shakespeare, Luther and Napoleon. By badmen readers of Western Americana understand that the term is applied not in the sense of evil but to desperadoes armed with a six-shooter, as much a part of his dress as a tie to a businessman or a compact to a lady. There are men of evil in the world who taint everything they touch; men sick in mind as well as heart who belong in mental wards but who contrive somehow to receive the sympathy of the public while the men we write about received the fear.

Newspapers are mostly responsible for the glamor that seems to accrue to murderers, desperadoes, bandits and rustlers. Years ago deeds of trigger-happy bad men were relegated to page two and sometimes to a corner of page six so that the modern research student has to go over the old files with a magnifying glass and a fine tooth comb. Two lines about the man he is studying might be the reward for his efforts to say nothing of the dirt, eye strain and headache. In the Southwest Victorio, Geronimo, Nana, Coloradas Mangas, political speeches, new Territorial laws, new gold discoveries and the colonizing of new towns were of more importance to the editor than the exploits of Rattlesnake Sam, Clay Allison and Billy the Kid. Indeed, Billy the Kid was not discovered until a reporter came in from the East to drink in the New Mexico sunshine for his health and ended by vomiting "Billy the Kid's Exploit" for the National Police Gazette in New York on May 21, 1881. Pat Garrett of course had to get on the band wagon and from that day to this there has been no cessation.

The turn of the century brought the glaring headlines that made murder a front page "must" in journalism. Illiterate or educated a nobody today has just to go out and commit a nice juicy murder or two and even a brilliant victory in Korea will be thrown off the front page. Recently a dishwasher by the name of Cook, unknown outside of his own immediate family which he later proved knew him very little went on a spree and left a trail of blood from Missouri to California. Not one girl in America would marry such a man.

After he was electrocuted bus loads of girls of marriageable age went thirty-five miles out of their way to see the corpse. Thirteen thousand people that only read about the death of President Roosevelt insisted on visiting the remains of the desperado Cook. Why? What is there about outlaws and killers that makes everybody say its wrong yet they eat it up in pulp magazines, comics, movies, television, radio scripts?

We have selected seventeen desperadoes of frontier days not because the list is complete or because New Mexico was particularly more cursed with such men than Kansas, Texas or Arizona but because for the past eighteen years we have been working on New Mexico history and we give this phase of her growth. Of the number we have selected only two are natives but that does not mean that there were not more in the days when this State waved the Spanish, Mexican and Confederate flags. The latter but for a short time and by conquest.

Desperadoes of frontier days command a certain amount of attraction. No one ever made a movie or wrote a story of the killer who snuffed out the lives of five people on the corner of Bleecker and Minetta Streets in Greenwich Village, New York, one hot summer day in the year 1921. He killed four people to get at a fifth. Newsboys hawked the paper on the spot three hours after it happened and more papers were sold in that area that day than ever before or since. After that: silence. It was nothing new. It happened every day on Mulberry Street, Chatham Square, Mott Street, Elizabeth Street. All of them produced toughs as rugged and mean and surly as William Antrim, Clay Allison, Rattlesnake Sam but somehow they never captured the public fancy. The frontier outlaw wore a six-shooter and at times carried a Sharps buffalo gun or a Winchester; these went around with tommy-guns and sub-machine affairs that were productive of massacres rather than of individual deaths. Little danger, big danger, it really doesn't matter. All it takes is one bullet in the right direction.

One explanation perhaps was that in frontier days rifles and guns in the hands of civilians were common sights and everybody was a marksman after a fashion especially in cowboy camps, buffalo-hunters camps and railroad towns. Then there were the ever-menacing Apaches, Kiowas, Comanches and Plains Indians that were hazzards along the Santa Fe Trail; Loving and Goodnight Trail and the progress of the railroad. Even rustlers and desperadoes didn't count the Indians they killed. Pioneering in those days wasn't in the fields of atomic energy, vitamins, science and education. People were mainly seeking to prove the theory of the survival of the fittest whether it was a mule skinner, a freighter, a settler, cattleman or a gunfighter. This book isn't seeking to explain how gunfighters operated, their method of drawing, "buffaloing", and trigger action. Others have already placed such books before the reading public.

The frontier desperado was a rugged individualist stamped and marked not by environment but by circumstance. Unlike our modern gangster he faced his enemy squarely and always gave him a fighting chance. No true desperado ever shot his enemy in the back, or, as we say in modern parlance, "took him for a ride." He had no paid cronies to protect him. The members of the gang were all aware that in fighting the law it was each man for himself. As far as they were concerned they were fighting for a cause even if that cause proved only a matter of pride as in the case of Poncho Griego, Gus Mentzer, Chuck Colbert. Our modern mobster kills to protect an investment. Sometimes he kills as the result of an attempted bank robbery. But how many of the tellers at the bank are armed? In the case of the frontier desperado how many of the passengers of the Wells Fargo Express were not armed? Somehow there is nothing clean or fresh about the modern gangster who always seems to rub his personality with grease or something slimy. He certainly hasn't the outdoor look that characterizes so many of the outlaws of the 80's. Besides it takes one generation to write about another. Contemporaries make such a fizzle of it. Perhaps because time places these things in focus and gives the proper prospective. Our modern bandit carries about him the palling odor of alleys, dens, unlight streets. Now many of these men, while not personally clean, such as Rattlesnake Sam and Dave Rudabaugh, still they walk about with an air of the great outdoors so that their gunsmoke fades away leaving something in the aftertaste that proves them to be men, even if outside the limits of the law. Something of the vast unconquered wilderness permeates their being if not their deeds. Their killings were feats of personal bravery and strength; those of our modern mobster of cowardice and personal weakness.

No killer is such by heredity. Had William Antrim, or Bonney, as many prefer to call him, lived in Brooklyn where he was born all his life he would have died virtually unknown, unsung and unheralded. He no doubt would have shied away from a gun as from a deadly reptile. Had Rudabaugh remained a bartender his ashes would not now be sand-swept on foreign soil. With desperadoes it was the survival of those who were quickest on the draw. Today usually the victim of the gangster doesn't know who his enemy has paid to kill him any more than when he will be "taken for a ride." His enemy doesn't say: "Well, Bill, I guess you and me must have it out. Have you got a gun. If not I'll wait until you get one; then we will face each other and draw."

Mind you I don't say that all did this. But those who did not were rather the exception than the rule. When it comes to killing we all do it—not with a knife or a gun or a blunt instrument of any sort but with the little destructive organ called the tongue. Has anyone recorded the number of deaths brought about by Gossip? Gossip puts even the mobster to shame. The tongue has been as effective a noose as a hangman's rope. "Good fences make good neighbors" wrote a modern bard, but because the fence is there curiousity is born on the other side of the barrier that gives rise to such yappity-yap that our poor neighbor is dead long before he suspects his demise. Perhaps it is this same curiosity about the past that accounts for the popularity of outlaws of frontier days. There is something about a six-shooter that every red-blooded American tot likes. How many toy guns were sold last Christmas? How many kids have you heard say: "Bang, I shot you. You are dead?" After we grow out of those days we want to read about them. It's in our blood. Let's face it. For every private home library that has a copy of Shakesphere there are probably ten with a Billy the Kid either in a pocket edition, comic strip or regular edition. One more won't hurt.

Some of these men face the public for the first time having been pushed off the pages of their day by Billy the Kid, Clay Allison and Dave Rudabaugh. We have tried to tell the truth in all instances and list conversations as they actually took place. Once I went to see a movie called Texas Rangers. In it Dave Rudabaugh, a member of Sam Bass's gang is killed during an attempted train hold-up five years before he was actually killed hundreds of miles from the place, and five years after the death of Sam Bass the leader. And to make it even rougher at the same time that he was State's Witness in Kansas for the Kinsley robbery. Never before has anyone attempted to verify the facts of Rudabaugh's life following his escape from the Las Vegas jail. This arousied my curiousity. Because one authority called Rudabaugh a "killer of jailors" everybody else followed suit. No one dared to disagree. Dave Rudabaugh never killed a jailor in his life although we might call him an accessory after the fact. I am not trying to prove anything by writing this book. I merely want to tell the truth.

We in no way condone the action of any desperado herein portrayed. In some way they have contributed to New Mexico's history. That is the task we have set out to do. We accept them as much as we accept a weed on our green lawn. No matter how you pluck a weed it has the habit of growing in again. No matter how we write about sheriffs, railroads, cowboys, buffalo, settlers, colonists, cattlemen—these weeds are necessary evils to fill in the picture. Weeding these men was a painful task—Garrett, Milton, Gillette, Hixenbaugh and Earp would have told you that. On the other hand because there were men like Billy the Kid we have men like Pat Garrett.

A work of this sort is never complete without co-operation. We wish to thank all the old-timers interviewed, all newspaper editors who helped me with old files—the late Mr. Vandale of Amarillo, so generous with his library; the staff of the New Mexico Museum; the library staff of Texas University at Austin; the Highlands University staff; the Bishop of Amarillo for the use of his valuable collection—all and any who have in any way contributed to make the truth as exciting as fiction.

F. Stanley

Canadian, Texas—January 3, 1953

Grand Central Hotel, Socorro, N.M., scene of Joel Fowler's last killing

Book One

COE'S LAST CROW

A young man in a battered, torn uniform of rather questionable allegiance slumped rather than leaned against an equally battered unpainted gate that led to a dilapidated hut once called home in the pre-war years. The faded blue pants he took from a Union prisoner. The apology for a gray coat that might have filled broader shoulders than his gave him the appearance of a scare-crow. He picked it up at the State prison where clothes were made during the war and might have fared better had not Texas-loving Colonel Baylor confronted the spoilers with his "over my dead body" act and reminders that they had just come from fighting for the Texas they now sought to rob. The only thing about the place that had a nourished look were the weeds, flanked by droves of cockle burs. The rank grass and undergrowth stood as tall as he was and he would not be classified as short in any language. But he wore the weeds of mourning as much as the weeds about the place were a symbol of grief for the glory that had been. Flowers once bloomed from the gate to the door as a sign of the life within very much as the bloom of youth but a few years before once gave him the hope that his was anything but a lost cause. Now he came back to this.

Shutters were more off than on hinges. Everything was so drab, so crisp and dry under the vaulted, blue Texas sky that he felt akin to the naked look as if in losing a war he had erased all that was bright and hopeful about the old homestead. Within, the emaciated looking woman he called mother, bit her lips and went about preparing the same meal that had been hers during those barren years; black eyed peas, potato-bread, beans. Yet this was a plentiful supper compared to the many nights of just beans. There were times when you just had your dreams that filled you so much you couldn't sleep. Those were the best suppers, those dreams. All the steaks and gravy you wanted. The soldiers on the battle front were not the only ones worn thin as a result of war. This was not her only concern. The war did something to William. He seemed so restless. There was a shiftiness about his eyes that was not there when he left home. It was as if he had defiled and uncleaned himself in some way she could not quite understand. He went around with a smirk as if all things were to be ridiculed and nothing sacred. Discontent. He carried it around with him like a bird on wing. Try as he might he just could not reconcile himself to things as they stood in an effort to claim back things as they were. Nor did he walk alone. There were so many other young men in Texas returning home from the conflict seeking to fit themselves into the puzzle that confronted them. Peace came only to the land.

There out in the fields, four legs against the wind—lean, stringy, scrubby, destitute of flesh to cover their bones—were the longhorns bellowing away their swan song as the gentle breezes carried it along to bury it on the lone prairie. Neglected from want of care it is a wonder that any survived at all. Now that the boys were back they would be driven to the river banks where the grass was lush and be driven northwards to the markets to be the new eyes of Texas that these boys might see new hope in the cattle industry and awaken from the dead to bring glory to the Lone Star State. The quick and the dead. How quick such men like Loving, Goodnight, Chisum, Pierce and others were to see that if Texas were to survive the aftermath of the struggle it would be through the re-birth of the cattle markets dead for so long. Men who refused to be licked by what they came home to, who did not sulk and fret like this William Coe, and became richer if not better men for it. Out of the ruin, smoke, drought and disaster they arose like mighty bulwarks that pulled the Iron Horse to them as they trailed the longhorns to meet the rails and won greater glory on the cattle trails than all the years of vain fighting in the war between the States. Thus they cemented East-West relations far quicker and more solidly than any other single factor in the history of the nation, gold discoveries included.

As the young man leaned there feeling sorry for himself he kept repeating:

"Is this what I came home to? Is this what I fought for? This shack? I've seen hogs housed in better quarters out near Waco."

"Supper is ready, Billy," called out his mother in that squeaky, high-pitched voice of hers.

"Coming."

She watched him toy with the food for a moment.

"What do you plan to do, son?"

"First thing, get out of this outfit. I guess there are fences to be worked over. And those weeds out there. . . ." His voice trailed off. He continued to eat. After a pause he looked up and said: "Don't fret about me. I'll figure out a way."

So the days passed with nothing accomplished except a more intense restlessness, a more sour disposition and bitter complaints.

"I think I'll take a look around Fort Worth. Something might be stirring there."

"Whatever you think best, son."

There was plenty of excitement around Fort Worth. The name Charles Goodnight was on everybody's lips. A thirty year old cowboy who refused to be licked. A dreamer some called him. He had the craziest idea that he could trail a herd of cattle all the way to Denver. Plumb loco. But he had spunk and guts. Had to admire a man for that. Might get himself killed but no one would say he didn't have nerve. Just the man I'm looking for, thought Coe.

Goodnight himself was seeking out men of courage, nerve, stamina. Men not afraid of thirst, heat, hunger, Indians, death. He would guarantee none of his hired hands that they would ever see Denver. Certainly he doubted if any would make the return trip. But there was no way of finding out unless you tried. Nor were Indians the only death distributing riders of the plains. There were drifters, rustlers, guerrillas who refused to recognize that the war was over. They killed for gain. And quite a success they made of it too. The undertaking was risky at best. This, Goodnight sought to impress on his men. Even with the combined forces of Oliver Loving, a veteran trailer, the outlook was as insecure as it was hazardous.

So on June 6, 1866, William Coe convinced Charles Goodnight that he was everything the stockman expected a cowboy to be and became one of the hands that followed the longhorns out of Texas to change the history of the West. After more vicissitudes than even Loving thought possible despite his vigilance they were fortunate enough to reach Denver with half the herd they started with. Whether William Coe was aware of it at the time, all the country this side of Rabbit Ear all the way to the very gates of Denver was to be a map of the scenes of his depredations and desperado feats. Rabbit Ear—that landmark near the present town of Clayton in New Mexico so dear to the heart of the Santa Fe caravans as they wended their way like so many prairie schooners over the semi-arid wastelands to bring the East to the West. And Coe noted in that trip how easy it would be to despoil the Santa Fe trader of his goods at this spot and go off into the void without leaving a trace. In mapping this out in his own mind he also fingered the writing on the wall that was to spell his death. This very year he was to become the first of New Mexico's more notorious desperadoes as we know them during these years of the rise of the cattle industry, the gold rush and mining camps. The railroad had not quite made its appearance when Coe got his head caught in a noose.

Perhaps it was all the suffering encountered by the trail blazers on this eventful trip in 1866 that steered Coe on his course. All that danger and just a few dollars to throw on whiskey and women to show for it! "That nice looking fellow named Coe" as his friends said had no difficulty mixing in with the women of Denver who enjoyed his attentions as well as his money. He had more of the former than the latter. Of all the outlaws to trample New Mexico's Land of Enchantment, he was by far the handsomest. Blonde hair, blue eyes, six-foot two-inches tall, one hundred and seventy-five pounds, evenly distributed, teeth white and even, he was a heart breaker. But he was not a parlor crasher; he would rather crash in the strong boxes of a stage and instead of seeking to burn women into desire he desired to burn brands into stock he appropriated as easily and readily as he might have appropriated the women of Denver, Fort Worth, Las Vegas or Folsom.

Beauty exacts its toll even from uncaring hooligans who are receptive to its charm without being conscious of the fact. Thus when the handsome Coe made the rounds to the bars and dens of frontier day Denver a host of cowboys attracted to him painted the town red with him and had the habit of gathering around him so that talk soon converged around the idea of a quicker way to get rich than trailing cattle. To this many were agreed. Others maintained allegiance to Loving and Goodnight. Rustling seemed about as good a way to start as any. So rustling it was. The Coe Gang was to be the scourge of Southern Colorado and Northern New Mexico. Soldiers at Fort Bascom, Fort Lyon, Fort Union said they would rather chase Navajos, Apaches and Comanches from Santa Fe to Independence than go out on those fly by night excursions after Coe and his men which usually ended up in the loss of more government horses and mules than if they had remained at home.

Coe built his headquarters in No Man's Land in the Oklahoma Panhandle a few miles across the New Mexico border near the present site of Kenton. It was a field-stone structure about thirty-five feet long, fifteen feet wide on a promontory commanding a view of the Carrizo and Cimarron valleys. From this vantage point he could hold up Santa Fe caravans at will as well as make forays around Fort Bascom, Fort Union and Las Vegas. The number of government animals he made away with has so embarrassed the commanders of these military posts that they have been as tight lipped about it as an atomic scientist at Los Alamos. He would have had to look far and wide for a more strategic hideout. For a man with Southern sympathies this was the ideal spot for preying on government camps. That he hindered Indian warfare and thus brought about the deaths of many of his own people never dawned on him. The government made him poor; the government would make him rich. So he reasoned. He had to be within striking distance of Forts Union and Bascom if he were to keep a fresh supply of horses and mules on hand. In his line of work this was important.

It was a veritable fortress he built with the aid of so many willing hands. It had two entrances, one from the north end and the other from the south. Windowless for reasons that need no explanations, the only ventilation came from the port holes high up in the walls—nine of these faced east; the same number faced the opposite direction. Above the south entrance were four more. The north entrance had five. Near each entrance rose a deep, wide chimney which solved the problem of heating and cooking. The water situation was solved by bringing it in by the barrels-full from the nearest creek. Basins were stacked outside and each morning the men took a dipper filled a basin and washed. If they were in jeopardy of attack the washing was done inside and the water pitched into the dirt floor. They had from the fortress to the horizon to relieve themselves. While soldiers from Fort Union often thought of attacking the place it was agreed that discretion was the better part of valor. The desperadoes would sell their lives dearly and the military post was understaffed as it was in the effort to stamp out the hordes of Comanches and other tribes who succeeded too well in making life miserable for travelers along the Santa Fe Trail. Which were the worse depredators, the Indians or Coe's Gang? The soldiers didn't think there was too much difference. Both had to be exterminated.

And the way he crowed about it! He went around as if he were not less a personage than General Grant or General Lee. The brass of the fellow. He would come up to them at Loma Parda several miles from Fort Union as they were having a glass or two on their day off, and boldly tell them the mistakes they made in trying to capture him. Of course, the military were not allowed to go around the bars armed. There he stood in the middle of the barroom floor, his men encircled about him, on his feet very much like a rooster all set for its early morning brag, and mockingly pity the boys in blue who would have enjoyed disobeying orders about a tavern brawl and bashed his handsome head in. When the Negro troops came in there was no stopping him. He was the cock of the walk. If before he crowed in plain chant; now he went up and down the scale. "Flap those wings, boy. Flap those wings. Some day we'll clip them," said one.

One devastating effect of the war on these frontier posts was the scarcity of horses and mules it produced. Comanches, Kiowas, Navajos and Apaches didn't relieve the situation any. Such marauding on the part of Coe and his men was bound to over-stock his own needs. Thus when he and his followers would ride to a ranch with a string of horses the owner rarely questioned the freshly made brand over the government brand on the left shoulder of the animals. Then the commissary would come riding in from Fort Union or Fort Lyon and ask if the rancher had any horses to sell. Of course he did. Over the third brand which the rancher put on the animal he bought the soldiers tortured the animal by putting on the fourth which was the first to begin with.

Coe's Raiders became the scourge and the bane of their existence. All along the Goodnight Trail, the Loving Trail, the Santa Fe Trail, the Fort Bascom-Fort Union Road, the Santa Fe Pass at Glorieta, the Raton Pass, Pecos, Madison, Las Vegas, Rayado the word was be on the lookout for Coe and his riders. New fields of endeavor were opened with the rise of Elizabethtown, Virginia City, Baldy, Cimarron and other mining camps. Much of the gold from these camps found its way to Robber's Roost as Coe's fortress hideout was called. Over in Las Vegas he found a muchacha whose dark eyes, raven blue-black hair, olive complexion, slender body, attracted the desperado and stirred his blood. Golindrina, he called her and was the nearest person akin to love in his life. She consented to be the cook and general factotum at the hideout. Steaming plates of red-hot chili she served much to the dissatisfaction of the men but no one dared complain. She made no attempt to conceal her own love. Several settlers at Madison, now non-existent, seeing the pair together riding in a buckboard, remembered how striking the couple looked. "As handsome a pair of young'uns," said old timer Butler one day before he died, "as y'd ever beholden anywhere..' She was the apple of Coe's eye as long as he lived. Following his death she returned to Las Vegas and obscurity.

Trinidad, Colorado, was a small adobe ridden community in those pioneer times, bursting at the seams with prospectors, teamsters, bull-whackers, merchants, mule-skinners, drifters, gamblers, lawyers, scouts, Indians, cowboys, gamblers, Cyprians and desperadoes. Into this heterogeneous mass of floating humanity rode Coe and his entire squad one fine day to "hurrah" the town. They were bent on fun and merry making. Up and down the dusty street of the bewildered village they rode wiping out their six-shooters, firing over the conical sombreros of the natives, shooting as close to dudes as they could without hitting them, taking out their large bowie knives and cropping the hair of gamblers, blowing kisses to Cyprians and spilling bottles of whiskey over them as a perfume, bending down from the saddle to sweep up a gay señorita who attracted their fancy, doing their love making on horseback, much to the distraction of the dons and dueñas whose daughters seemed to enjoy the caresses from the gringos although they pretended resistance. Up and down the main street they rode making everything in sight a target either for their guns, gibs or horses. Into the cantinas they rode picking up all the bottles they wanted, smashing those they couldn't use, forcing spectators to drink from hats, dance a jig, stand on their heads and anything that struck their fancy. A six-shooter was a good persuader. They enjoyed mule-skinners dancing to the tune of exploding revolvers. The fiddlers of one dance hall they forced into the street where they rounded up all the women they could find and danced, drank, caroused, shot, bullied, kicked, punched, fought, loved, spat, smoked, cursed, laughed, robbed anything in sight, pulled the clothes off the Cyprians, relieved the sheriff of his guns and emptied them at this feet as he danced in the dust, put him on a horse and headed him out of town, gambled, took over the astonished village and elected Coe king. This they called the spoils of war.

The sheriff was in a quandry. No one would unite forces with him to oust the invader. He rounded up a few men but they timidly told him that life was too valuable to lose it at the hands of an outlaw. Hearing that Charles Goodnight was bringing in a herd of cattle to the north, he dispatched Deputy Sheriff Tafoya to seek him out for aid. Forty miles away on the Apishipa the deputy steamed into camp as excited as his horse was sweaty and jumbled a tale to the stockman who couldn't quite make out what it was all about. After quieting him down a bit the trail blazer decided to take all the men he could safely spare and investigate the disturbance at Trinidad. This could be a trick. If he left the cattle completely unprotected it would mean bankrupcy for him. But the excited deputy seemed honest enough. He would chance it. Cutting out a fresh horse he told the deputy to ride back and spread the news that he was coming with a large force to restore law and order. News soon reached Coe that Goodnight was on his way to block his rule.

The news rather flabbergasted Coe who counted many friends among Goodnight's cohorts. If a pitched battle were to be fought it would mean the lives of many of the followers of both sides. Indeed several of Goodnight's riders were so impressed with the idea that an outlaw could take over a town at will that they decided then and there to join forces with Coe. Goodnight told them to collect their pay and check out since they preferred the way of a transgressor to law and order. Besides in such a frame of mind they presented a threat to him. His cattle empire was still in the cradle stage and he had no intention of seeing it die in infancy because of some faithless followers. Coe decided that he would not pit forces against Goodnight and left Trinidad as suddenly as he had come much to the relief of the citizens glad to see the end of his reign of terror.

After this relations between the stockman and the desperado were strained. One thing lead to another and Coe threatened to kill Goodnight on sight. The cattle baron had respect for Coe's trigger finger and aim and avoided the meeting. Not that he was afraid to face it if necessary but he wanted to live a while longer. He was not one to court danger any more than he was for running away from it. There were better ways of dying than at the hand of an outlaw. Coe just wasn't worth fighting as far as Goodnight was concerned. Frustrated at Trinidad Coe returned to Robber's Roost rather dejected and morose. He busied himself with cattle rustling and horse stealing on such a scale that the government sat up and took notice. While before he was given a wide berth, now Washington insisted that the frontier posts crack down and eliminate him if possible. There seemed no way of stopping him. More men were detailed to capture him and large rewards posted for his capture dead or alive. Coe answered the challenge by increasing his allotments from Fort Bascom, Fort Lyon and Fort Union. He would ride to the corrals on a day that was particularly inclement, defy the guards, force them to put down their rifles, cut the best animals and tell them to send his regards on to Washington. Indians did not molest Coe for the more horses and mules he stole the less the number of soldiers sent out to chastise them and off they would go to the settlements — Anton-Chico, Chaparito, Las Vegas, La Questa, Rio Colorado — raiding, plundering, running off farm stock with carefree abandon sometimes taking children as captives to be sold in Mexico at five dollars a head.

Juan Bernal was an influential citizen of Las Vegas. His sheep roamed the fields out to far horizons. Fort Sumner, Anton-Chico, Taos, Tres Ritos, the lush bottom lands of the Little Cimarron and the Cimarron. He treated his herders better than most therefore had more herders than many. Some of his flocks grazed in the vicinity of the future 101 Ranch where his herders set up winter quarters. Coe swooped down on this camp killing three men and running off five hundred head of sheep. Skirting Trinidad he grazed the sheep along the Greenhorn and steered them up to Pueblo where he found a ready buyer. Bernal rushed to Fort Union for help but by the time the soldiers caught up with the desperado the animals were disposed of as well as the profits. Coe spent his money as quickly as he got it. Pueblo offered possibilities so the outlaw pillaged the area, burnt fences, barns, crops fought off pursuit and left Pueblo in such a state of excitement that the ranchers decided to band together for their mutual protection. They appealed to the commander of Fort Lyon. A troop of soldiers was called out and the trail lead south later on to be infused into what appeared to be an Indian trail. It wasn't until Coe was a prisoner at the Fort that the commander found out that the outlaws changed their boots for moccasins to throw the soldiers off the trail. Discouraged and considerably baffled the soldiers returned to the post empty-handed and none the worse for wear. Coe back tracked over his trail continued his depredations and even killed two ranchers who objected to his running off their stock. He was a holy terror. The people of Pueblo called together a vigilante meeting and planned how best to trap the slippery critter. A committee was chosen to meet with General Penrose of Fort Lyon and demand immediate results. Another committee was dispatched to Colonel Lane at Fort Union. Surely there must be some way of stopping the outlaw. The colonel promised to see what he could do.

Santa Fe merchants and freighters sent a representative to Washington to investigate the inactivity of the men they had sent out to track down the marauder. All to no avail. Coe, elusive as he was daring, continued on his merry way killing, rustling, stealing, holding up the stage, demanding tribute of Santa Fe caravans, burning and destroying. The government dispatched a special messenger to military headquarters at Santa Fe making it imperative that Coe be seized and his followers wiped out. He must be stopped. General Carleton would be held fully responsible if such depredations continued. The commander of the military district was still smarting under the fiasco at Fort Sumner that the Navajos call "The Long Walk" to this day. If General Carleton were not capable of breaking up the Coe gang they would have to send a man who could. The general made a personal visit to Fort Union and Fort Lyon. What he told them must have burnt their ears. Capturing Coe became an obsession. The success of the cattle industry, peace treaties with several tribes of Indians, the development of new settlements, the progress of the Santa Fe Trail—all depended on the capture of the outlaw. Bring in Coe dead or alive.

Several years before Coe's raids began, the Sumner family came in from Missouri and decided to settle the Little Cimarron country between the sites of the present communities of Folsom and Clayton. The whole tribe moved in and homesteaded. A town mushroomed. The settlers decided to call it Madison in honor of Madison Emory one of the settlers who acted as sort of peace officer, judge, mail clerk, grocer and organizer. One of the big affairs in town was the gala day he took to wife one of the Sumner girls, widow of a fellow by the name of Butler. She had a half grown son who took the name Emory. Coe attended the wedding and brought his dark-eyed consort and many agreed they were the best dancers and the best lookers on the dance floor that night. Coe was rather taken up with the Emorys and stayed with them often. He never took anything belonging to them. At first he came alone; at times he brought his girl friend. One time he brought in one hundred and twenty five mules from Fort Union and invited the people of Madison to witness his changing the U. S. brand to one of his own making. He was never obnoxious and had a gay smile for all. The people of Madison really liked his charming ways.

That Madison became one of Coe's regular haunts was not lost on the soldiers from New Mexico and Colorado in search of him. Fort Lyon was particularly determined to capture the desperado. The soldiers set up quarters near the village determined to camp there indefinitely in the patient game of waiting. One evening word came that Coe had slipped into town with two of his men. He sat down for a drink at the only bar in town, discussed his exploits and crowed to the bar tender how good he was at dodging the military. The bar tender was rather nervous. At any time now the fireworks would begin and he would be in the very center of things. Suddenly the door swung open and Coe found himself looking down the barrels of eight Winchesters.

"You are under arrest," said the lieutenant in command. "I wouldn't try to act smart right now, if I were you. Just stand still and let one of my men take your revolver. Good. Now follow me quiet like."

Coe obliged.

Not having any orders concerning the others, they were given their liberty with an admonition about trying to liberate their leader. The capture of Coe didn't seem to impress the public as the commander of the fort thought it would. Fickle public. For three weeks General Penrose awaited orders as to the disposal of his prisoner. No one seemed interested. Meantime Coe chatted with the soldiers, played cards and made himself generally well liked. No one could believee that this handsome fine figure of a man was all the ranchers around Pueblo claimed him to be. Coe was looked upon as a martyr and scrapegoat for all the killings and rustling along the Arkansas, the Greenhorn, the Rio Grande and the Cimarron although it was highly probable that other gangs were responsible. The soldiers were not of the opinion that he was to blame for everything he was accused of by civilians, consequently they relaxed their vigilance. This Coe realized; this he played up to.

Meantime his cronies were not idle. Under the guise of wood cutters several of them visited the fort to see if the commissary would sign a contract for firewood. They familarized themselves with the layout of the post and managed to see their leader. A plan of escape was chosen. Revolvers were smuggled to Coe and a spot selected where a horse would be placed in readiness. The date, hour, manner all perfectly timed. Coe had a thorough understanding of the program and routine of the fort. He knew when the men were busiest, when parade was held, when there were the least number of guards. The plan of escape was simple.

The men were to purchase a quantity of goods from the sutler's store and spread abroad the idea that they were going in quest of new grass with a view of bringing in stock for grazing. This was as good a place as any to out-fit themselves —food, clothing, blankets, tents—all the articles necessary for such an expedition. With everybody seemingly engaged in some duty or other Coe, who had the freedom of the post, came to the store for a slug of tobacco. He lingered about the place watching the men load the chuck wagon. He even offered to help load several sacks of flour. The sutler was glad to get the extra help. Coe slipped into the wagon, was immediately covered up and the loading continued as if nothing unusual was taking place. The driver joked with the soldiers at the gate, waved goodbye, and urged the mules into a slow trot. Out of sight of the garrison the team was halted, supplies readjusted and Coe sprang on the waiting horse down to the Greenhorn over to Trinidad. The supplies were taken to the hide-out. No use wasting them. No one seemed concerned over Coe's escape, much less the soldiers who hoped they wouldn't be pressed into another trip to Madison.

But the ranchers set up a hue and cry louder than any group of coyotes at night. The soldiers had no choice. They knew that Coe would investigate Madison thoroughly before entering the town. They resorted to strategy. It was noised abroad that a supply of mules was being shipped to Fort Union by a bunch of ignorant freighters who were novices at the job. Because of a Kiowa insurrection very few soldiers could be spared to protect the caravan. Coe thought this a good opportunity to replenish his resources and decided to appropriate the animals. That the teamsters ran off without putting up a fight failed to arouse his suspicions. Settling down to change the brand he was surrounded and had no choice but to surrender. As Coe was the man they were after the others were let go. Coe cheerfully returned to Fort Lyon and greeted everybody as long lost friends. A game of cards here, a throw of the dice there—drinking, joking, laughing and kidding his way into the good graces of the soldiers, a month passed before he began plans for a second escape. Mind active, eyes open, thoughts alert, he watched for an opening. One day a band of Cheyennes came to the sutler's store with some pelts they offered in exchange for a bolt of goods and other commodities. Coe lingered about the place. It seemed that the Indians were intersted in procuring some firewater but the sutler told them that it was against the law.

"If you want firewater," said Coe, "There is no reason

why you shouldn't have it." He had a gallon of Taos Lightning stored away in his bunk. The potency of this fiery drink has been attested to by that reckless breed of men who first opened this frontier shortly before the Black Hawk War as they followed the streams in search of beaver. Mountain Men they were called. Trappers set apart in frontier history from all other good men and true to take their places in the dance of life that meant the winning of the West during those frontier times to focus the eyes of the nation on the possibility of a coast-to-coast America. A swig of Taos Lightning more than fortified their spirits. It made them hate the haunts of men and kept them in communication with nature. It converted them into a way of life that was more Indian than the Indians themselves. They, in their own outdoor way, made definite contributions to the Americanization of Americans. It was at Don Fernando de Taos, their headquarters, where they learned to stir and foment this exhilaration known as Taos Lightning that made giants of little men and strengthened the weak. It took a body to hold what it embodied. Indians thought as much of it as the Mountain Men. There were severe penalties attached to selling it to them.

Coe, gifted with the facility for making friends, acquired this potent brew as the result of a card game. It was against the stern discipline of the post to keep it but men are more fruitful about the forbidden things. Coe was also a student of Indian whims. He knew that they knew that liquor was where you least expected to find it. They were not surprised when he told them that he had some for them at no cost to themselves. All he wanted in exchangge was a pony. When nature formed the Indian she omitted resistance to alcohol in their make-up. One drink was enough to make them glassy-eyed. And if that drink happened to be Taos Lightning it might result in anything from a massacre to just plain passing out. The rate of exchange was rather one sided. In those days a man valued his pony as he valued his life. It was as important to him as eating and sleeping. Stealing a man's horse often resulted in hanging. An Indian valued his horse as much as the next man with this difference: A raid on the next wagon train would replenish his loss. To Coe it was a fair bargain. The price of his freedom. Drops of forgetfulness and bliss for liberty. Before long several of the Indians slouched against the wall into a deep sleep. Coe relieved one of his blanket, grunted past the sentry as he spurred on his pony and was off.

Knowing that the search would spread from Madison to the Vermejo, Rayado and Cimarron, he remained in the Pueblo area pillaging, barnstorming, horse-stealing, rustling, gambling as in days of yore when prisons hindered not. At times he was seen in Elizabethtown, Willow Creek, along the Apishipa, the Greenhorn, the Cimarron. He was ever one jump ahead of the menacing troops who always showed up where he had been, never where he was. Resentment against him by stockmen and ranchers became bitter. Again he rode to Fort Union, ran off a string of horses and mules, sold them along the Santa Fe Trail, called for his señorita and took her dancing in Trinidad. There were enough prices on his head to make somebody a pretty rich man.

The commander of Fort Lyon fussed and fretted. Why was Coe permitted to escape? The citizens of the country asked him that and he in turn asked his soldiers. Why wasn't he hung? A sad state of affairs this when such a desperado was permitted his liberty at will. A body just wasn't safe any more. Wasn't it the duty of the military to protect the people? It was bad enough what they had to suffer from the Indians? But this raider! He was worse than Quantrill. By George, if they ever got their hands on Coe they would make sure he wasn't pampered. They had a tree and rope ready.

Over at Tiptonville, near Fort Barclay later to be the site of the village of Watrous, a lad not much over eleven years old, listened to the gossip at the boarding house where his mother cooked and cleaned. He had heard so much of Coe. He swaggered, aimed a gun and bragged about his hero. Coe stood for the boldness and daring of his own life. Some day he hoped to be like him, become rich and take his mother from this drudgery that was the bane of her existence. But it didn't work out according to his dreams. Within the next year Coe was dead and his mother packed off to the new mining town of Silver City. He was known as William Antrim. Lovers of western folk lore know him better as Billy the Kid. Twice the boy missed seeing him as he came in for a meal. Once when he helped himself to some horses as the Fort Barclay trading post.

General Penrose, face red with anger that seemed to be bursting out all over, fist banging on the oak desk before him, shouted at the lieutenant standing at attention:

"Find him. Put him in chains. Don't come back without him."

"Yes, sir."

He saluted, made a soldiery exit although the name he had for the commander was far from soldiery. Somewhere in the vast expanse between Southern Colorado and the Mexican border, if not already across the border, was William Coe. What an order: Find him! You might as well go out and hunt for the pot of gold at the end of the rainbow. Where do you begin to look for such a man? Madison? Elizabethtown? Baldy? Trinidad? Robber's Roost? Pueblo? El Moro? There were so many other things he would much rather be doing. Then word came that Coe made a raid on some stock in the vicinity of Fort Bascom. At least this narrowed down the search. He could pick up the trail from there. Coe was bound to pan off the animals on some unsuspecting rancher. Hot on the trail the lieutenant came upon the outlaw's camp near Willow Creek. So, that was it. He was going to sell them to prospectors. Keeping out of sight, he awaited a favorable opportunity. When most of the outlaws were asleep in the hills, he pounced on the camp, clamped chains on Coe before he could quite get the sand out of his eyes, and, peacock fashion, presented the prisoner to his commanding officer.

"This is getting to be a habit," said General Penrose. "I am afraid there will be no escape this time."

He called for the orderly.

"See that this man is confined in the guard house. Keep the chains on him. Under no circumstances is he to have visit-

or. Nor are his chains to come off save at feeding time. That is all."

"Yes, sir."

Coe said nothing. A shrug of the shoulders, a bow to the general, a smile for the orderly and the doors of the jail closed on him. A week passed. Two soldiers guarded him, guns ready for action, as he quietly ate his meals. Twenty-four hours a day someone was outside his door standing guard. He was led out for an hour a day to exercise around the parade ground. The weeks stretched into a month and still no orders as to the disposition of the prisoner. Vigilance relaxed. The chains were taken off more often. He was permitted no razor for shaving nor water for washing. Now he could be called anything but handsome. One night the sentry dozed. Just for a moment. What was that noise? He jumped up, looked in on the prisoner. He was fast asleep. What a scare! The prisoner just a moment before had a revolver thrown in at him from the little window high up in the cell. He was mothering it in his sleep like a tender parent. Several weeks passed. A lone soldier brought him his grub now. One evening as the jailor placed his supper on the floor he found himself staring into the muzzle of a six-shooter. "Just you be quiet and nothing will happen. Unlock these chains." The jailor had no choice but to comply. Coe would not hesitate to kill him; he knew that. Coe was out of the fort before the alarm was raised. The commander was fit to be tied. All he could do at the moment was to telegraph Fort Union that Coe was on the loose once again.

Coe took advantage of his natural disguise. His matted hair, bristling beard, soilly appearance were all to his advantage. He had always been pretty dapper about his appearance. Outside the fort he stole a pony and avoiding main traveled roads as much as possible made his way back to Robbers Roost. His men had just sacked a freight wagon headed for Fort Union.

Over at Madison, Sergeant Pat O'Brien stood at the bar, one foot on the rail, looking into the glass before him. What did he see there? Did it tell him that in a few short years he would die of T. B. at the Fort Union hospital and be buried in the post cemetery? That over his grave would be built a pig sty? Who knows? Outside came the tramp of horses approaching. They stopped. The door opened.

"It's Coe and his men," said the man behind the bar.

"And, bejabbers, who might Coe be?" He knew only too well. He had orders concerning his man.

"I ain't a-wearing a monkey suit," laughed Coe from behind the soldier. He came close to the bar.

" 'Tis not me uniform ye be liking, now, is it?" The soldier smiled back at him.

"The uniform and the man in it."

"No trouble, please. We want no trouble in here." The bar tender had a ring of alarm in his voice.

" 'Tis no trouble ye'll be getting," said O'Brien. "My friend here will be getting the trouble." He pointed to Coe.

"Why you . . ." He reached for the six-shooter. A cheery voice called out:

"I wouldn't do that if I were you."

Private Birkmeyer stood in the doorway, an army rifle poised for immediate results. He had been at Mrs. Emory's arranging for dinner. She told him that she thought that Coe was in town. Looking over the men, the private said:

"All of you, turn around and face me. Keep your hands where I can see them and dont' try what you can't finish. Sergeant, take a look at those horses outside. Appear to be Fort Union stock. Bartender, come around and take the boys' guns. Thank you. We will leave them at Mrs. Emory's."

Sergeant O'Brien came in. "Looks like more men coming. Our men be too far afield at the moment. I must bid ye farewell at the moment."

"We will meet again," said Coe.

"Ay. 'Twill be a pleasure." O'Brien made a mocking bow to Coe. The soldiers left, none too soon.

"I think we ought to pay a visit to Fort Union," said the leader of the outlaws. All agreed.

They raided the corrals at the military post and rode over to Cimarron. They had loads of fun shooting up the place, making the rounds, and trying their luck at poker with the profits from their latest escapade. It was so easy. They had slept at Loma Parda, breakfasted on hard liquor and sourdough, hid out in the hills until evening. At dusk five of them entered the fort. It was an easy matter, for the government had hired so many civilians at the time to help with the freighting that no one questioned five more. Brooms in hand, they went over to the corrals as if to clean them out. They overpowered the guard. The rest was easy.

Meantime, Sergeant O'Brien rode with his men to Robbers Roost. Empty. He suspected that Coe was out on another raid and would eventually turn up at Madison. He rode over towards the present site of Springer. A lone rider approached him. It turned out to be Buddy Emory. Coe was at his mother's place alone. His mother knew that they couldn't be too far off so she sent him in search of the soldiers. Coe was still asleep when the soldiers arrived.

A knock at the door.

"Did ye sleep well, now"? came the voice of the sergeant. "If ye did, kindly come out wid your hands above your head."

Silence.

"No pranks, mind ye. Look out the window." The house was surrounded, all rifles pointing his way.

Coe surrendered.

"That horse has been ridden hard," Coe said to Mrs. Emory. The sergeant noticed the look of fear that stole over her features.

"Never you mind, lady. Ye will never be disturbed by the likes of him again."

She never was.

Again a committee came to Fort Union. Did the commander have any orders concerning Coe? No. Would he turn the outlaw over to them? He saw no reason why he shouldn't. The desperado was taken to Pueblo. News of his arrival brought in ranchers from far and near.

"He is a murderer," said the vigilantes.

"Away with him," said the mob.

The mob ruled.

They formed ranks like Crusaders of old banded together

for a common cause. The rope and the tree so long promised received Coe unto its own. Years later a rancher along the Greenhorn decided to dig a well. Several feet down he struck iron. It proved to be a ball and chain. Then he uncovered the skeleton to which these articles were attached. Handcuffs were still about the boney wrists. "Whoever the poor devil was, I'll give him a Christian burial," he told his son. Later he asked a neighbor.

"Oh, that. That was Coe. The vigilantes stormed the jail at Pueblo one night, brought him down here and hung him. And from what I heard about him he deserved it."

David Crockett's grave, Cimarron, N.M.

Courtesy of Philip J. Rasch

Grave of Wm. Antrim at Alma, N.M.

Book Two

CIMARRON PLAYBOY

(David Crockett)

David Crockett of Alamo fame is enshrined in the hearts of Texans and symbolizes, not only for him, but other Americans as well, the spirit of Independence, freedom from oppression and courage. In his day and at the height of his political glory he was known in Washington as amusing the high-brows with his quaint utterances and accentric dress. He weaved a homespun philosophy that smacked of honesty, thus endearing himself to those who loved honesty as a virtue so long as it was practised by others. The straight-shooting Tennesseean walked about the streets of the nation's capitol with a flamboyant air of freedom and a tolerant heart. His life was not much different from other frontiersmen of his day and age. He married, served a second term in Congress, was defeated on the third try, after which he decided to migrate to Texas where a man could breathe. Sometime before leaving he had married a second time. It was decided in family council that he go alone, investigate the truths of the reports and if he liked it he could locate there and return for his loved ones. He liked it fine. But he never returned for his family.

Hemmed in the web of rebellion, Texans had no intention of conceding that theirs was anything but a holy cause. Independence was a consummation devoutly to be wished and they were doing something about it. Whichever way they looked at it they would never be happy under the flying eagle of Mexico and while they would prefer the bald eagle of the Stars and Stripes, they were content for a time to live under the protection of the Lone Star. Men like Crockett made this possible. As David Crockett was an honest man, no matter what his other failings, he was sincerely convinced that the shedding of his blood before the firing squad as he stood up against that field-stone wall of the abandoned mission of San Antonio de Valero, better known as the Alamo, that his death was not in vain. Another David Crockett was to be shot from behind a wall several decades later up at Cimarron in New Mexico not too far from the Alamo but not because he was a hero.

Founded on December 7, 1816, San Antonio de Valero was a noble experiment. Christianized Xarame Indians were taught the fine arts, the domestic arts and the art of Christian living at this mission center and had time and events deemed otherwise the Alamo (Cottonwood) mission would have emulated Santa Barbara in California and San Geronimo de Taos in Mexico. The cornerstone of the church attached to the mission was laid on May 8, 1744, and the project, staffed by Franciscans, reached the peak of its glory in 1761, with a convent for friars, a porter's lodge, refectory, kitchens and enclosure for the Indians. Due to an epidemic, the padres were constrained to take in Zanas, Yprandes, Cocos, Tojos, Payayae and Carancaguases. But one disaster fell upon the heels of another. By 1793 the Valero mission records were transferrerd to the Villa de San Fernando. The church of the mission had never been completed. It was of rather rough Tuscan workmanship, cruciform in shape. The mission was abandoned and turned over to the Flying Company of San Carlos de Parras as a protection against Indian attacks on San Fernando, San Antonio and other settlements. The Company subsequently followed the example of the friars and abandoned the place. At the time it became the cradle of Texas Independence it was in the process of decay even though its stout walls withstood the onslaughts of General Santa Anna y Lopez and his troops. On March 6, 1836, David Crockett immortalized his name at the Alamo. As he faced the firing squad did he think of that little baby in Tennessee, who was given his name but not his heritage?

Because he fell in the struggle for Independence there is

a certain sacredness attached to his name that no misdeeds by namesakes can ever tarnish. Indeed the tombstone stolen from the grave of desperado Crockett at Cimarron by relatives was not because they wished, as they said, to sanctify the place by a more lasting and appropriate marker. They wanted to kill the legend of a second Crockett. To nip it in the bud before it spread on the wings of popular fancy and the outlaw become more popular than his martyred namesake. We only have it on hearsay that the desperado buried in Cimarron was his nephew. It is possible that it was his grandson.

In the office of the county clerk at Dandridge, Tennessee, is the marriage bond of David Crockett and Polly Finley, and the record of an earlier license issued to Crockett and Miss Margaret Elder on October 22, 1805, returned unused. Polly died shortly afterwards and was buried near Maxwell, Tennessee. David, who was the marrying kind, next took to wife Elizabeth Patton and settled down in Gibson county. After his death at the Alamo the Republic of Texas awarded his widow property near the present site of Canadian, Texas. She decided to sell it later on to H. C. Forester and she was awarded other property more to her liking. William H. Harris was called to witness for Texas and he testified at the Gibson county courthouse that he knew Crockett's widow and that he was also well acquainted with the children of the hero of the Alamo, giving their names as John W. Crockett, Robert P. Crockett, George Kimbron the husband of Rebecca Elisera Crockett. Forester testified in Texas on July 28, 1883, that: "David Crockett died at the fall of the Alamo in San Antonio, Texas, in 1836, and that he left surviving him his wife, Mrs. Elizabeth Crockett, and also three sons: John W., Robert P., and William, and also three daughters: Mrs. Matilda Tyson, Mrs. Kimbron and others whose names he did not then recollect. (See Hemphill County Land Claims, Vol. 2—1879-1887.)

The grateful State of Texas never forgot the elder Crockett's part in the fight for her Independence. And since he had come to her domain for the purposes of settling there, her citizens deemed it no more than just that his widow be granted three hundred and twenty acres of land consecrated by his blood.

This land was in John county, later divided into Hood county after another Texas hero of Civil War fame. Mrs. David Crockett was sixty-eight years old when she received the grant. At that age one would hardly expect her to begin farming and stock raising. To work this land she brought with her a married son by the name of Robert and his wife and children. It is highly probable that one of these was the subject of our sketch for none of the others of Crockett's brothers came to live in Texas. And David Crockett the desperado, although born in Tennessee, grew up in Texas.

Robert Patton Crockett had always been interested in seeing the country where his father shed his blood for a cause. He was old enough to accompany his father when he came to Texas to look over the prospects, but it was decided that he remain in Tennessee to keep the family together. Robert had married Matilda Porter, managed a small farm in Tennessee and in 1854 dumped his worldly possessions into a covered wagon, collected together his mother, wife and brood and steered for the Texas skies. He first settled in Ellis county and became fairly successful as a stockman. Two years later he sold his ranch and moved his cattle to the grant the State gave his mother. The land was directly east of Granbury in present Hood county at Acton where Elizabeth Crockett lies buried and where one may see her statue reaching out of the earth in a spirit of independence. David Crockett as the black sheep of the family is never mentioned in any of the accounts of the more illustrious member of the family. Any of Robert's sons now living were too young to remember young Davy. Until it can be proven otherwise, I will maintain that Davy was rather the grandson of the hero of the Alamo rather than the nephew. Young Davy came to Texas when he was four years old. Having the name of a famous forebear did not mean that there wasn't work to be done. He learned how to read and write, chop wood, milk cows, ride horses, shoot guns, follow the plow. Being brought up during the Civil War years he developed an intense hatred for Negroes, even though his father never owned a slave, nor did he ever have any formal contact with that race. He had a receptive mind as a half grown young one when Texas threw in her lot with the South and the propaganda he heard against Negroes and Yankees made such an impression that he carried the date to his grave. He was partisan to the core and in complete sympathy with anything that downed a Yankee or hindered a negro.

Tall, slim, with brown wavey hair, light blue eyes and high cheek bones, riding the range made him wiry if not muscular. He had the habit of flapping back his head to the right reminiscent of the days when a wild unruly lock would plunge down over his eye every time he took off his hat. He would flip it back with the shake of his head although his mother often threatened to cut it off because it reminded her too much of an unbroken bronco. While he learned that the man after whom he was named played a prominent part in the history of Tennessee and Texas he was not overly impressed by it. He had to work as hard as the next. Being related to the great or near great was no relief from chores, sweat and tears. Cattle trails were opening up from the Brazos to the Arkansas and markets boomed. With money he saved young Davey became a successful stockman in his own right. He was a shrewd bargainer, a careful buyer and a hard worker.

Robert Crockett took charge of the old toll bridge across the Brazos near Granbury put up by the citizens on a co-op basis. Later on when the State of Texas put up a new bridge it was named the Robert Crockett Bridge in commemoration of many years of faithful service. Much of the ranch work devolved on young Davy as Ashley was too young for this type of work. In return Robert gave him cattle. Added to what he already owned, he stood in the way of becoming another Charles Goodnight. It was about time he branched out on his own. Another young cattleman in the area, also a native of Tennessee and a rabid Southerner, was a fellow by the name of Clay Allison. He was older than Davy and had followed several trails north into the Pecos and Cimarron country. He was quite impressed with the lush grass of the Vermejo, the Red River and the Cimarron. "If ever you want fat meat bearing cattle,' said Allison, "take them up to New

Mexico. You will be closer to the markets. You won't run the meat off them. And they thrive."

Being close to the market meant much to the cowboy. It saved pounds and consequently meant more money. It saved work. Best of all it opened new horizons. The cowboy was a rambler at heart and he could hitch on to this excuse for being on the move. Allison decided to go up and try it first. If it worked out for him he would advise Crockett. Allison was quite successful. Crockett cut out his cattle, took them to Granbury, sold them at a profit and introduced himself to Lucien B. Maxwell's town of Cimarron. This was to be his final resting place.

The discovery of gold on Willow Creek on the Maxwell Land Grant brought such an influx of people into the area that cattle men by the dozens were coming to supply these camps with beef. The meat markets of Baldy, Rayado, Prairieville, Elizabethtown and Ute Park offered as much to the stockman as Denver, Pueblo and the rising markets of Kansas without the labor and struggle of riding trail to those markets. Crockett bought up cattle of Anton-Chico, Las Vegas, La Questa, Costilla from natives who did not place as high a value on the beef as Texans did, thus ending up with more of a herd than if he would have brought his cattle up from Texas. He purchased property near the Clay Allison place and took as his foreman Gus Heifner who cowboyed for him in Hood county. The two were inseparable. Very little is known of Heifner's antecedants and less of what happened to him after Crockett was killed. He disappears from the scene completely.

When the vigilantes of Elizabethtown banded together to hang Charles Kennedy in the doorway of his own cabin, the man selected to help Clay Allison was David Crockett. After hearing the tales of horror that poured forth from the lips of Kennedy's common-law wife, Crockett would permit none other than himself to put the noose around the killer's neck. Kennedy was not a desperado, a gunman of the frontier type, he was rather a killer such as we know killers today. He worked at the game for a profit. He never looked a man in the eye and said: "Draw." Rather he fed and bedded his victims, taking care of them as they slept. When Parson Tolby was killed Crockett worked with that arch-agitator O. P. McMains and Clay Allison to bring his murderers to justice. Although the wrong man was hanged, Crockett paraded the streets of Cimarron defying the sheriff, the soldiers from Fort Union and the Maxwell Land Grant and Railway Company, waiting for them to commence the action so that he could bring his Winchester into play. It especially irked him to see that with the exception of the officers the soldiers that confronted him were Negroes. The officers were just as bad. They were Yankees. Those were hectic days. With Allison he had two hundred cowboys under his command and it looked like he would fight the Civil War all over again. The murder of Parson Tolby is an unsolved mystery to this day.

Citizens of Cimarron soon realized that second to Clay Allison, David Crockett was the man most to be feared. He was a master of the unexpected. Gus Heifner was usually with him and when the citizens least suspected action, the pair would ride in, take over the main street, announcing their arrival by shooting off their guns, aiming through windows to hit lamps, wash stands or whatever struck their fancy. They rode into bar rooms shooting holes through hats, the tops off bottles and if anyone raised an objection he was usually carried out. They rode their horses into stores, bought the best outfits in the establishment and told the clerk to send the bills to the sheriff. As the sheriff had been in the employ of Lucien B. Maxwell and collected many fines he was bound to have enough money to cover their expenditures. Once the sheriff objected. Crockett hunted him up, forced him to pay the bill, took him over to Lambert's bar and at gunpoint made him drink until he babbled like an idiot.

Sometimes Dave and Gus came across a fellow they didn't particularly like. Especially if it happened to be someone who objected to his losses in a poker game. Awaiting their chance they would suddenly spring out at him as he passed a cantina. They took off his gunbelt, marched him to the bar, where Gus kept him in custody while Crockett went up and down the street rounding up everybody and anybody old enough to hold a glass in his hands and the procession halted at the bar where the victim was told to buy a round of drinks for all. No one dare refuse to drink any more than to buy. This happened one time to John McCullough, the postmaster and brother-in-law to Frank Springer, an enterprising young lawyer for the Maxwell Land Grant Company. The town of Springer in New Mexico is named after him. McCullough got in touch with the sheriff and told him that he ought to arrest Crockett. The sheriff told him that the arrest of the playboy might have its repercussions in another cowboy war. They had just gotten over one and were lucky to come out of it alive. However, if he thought he could do it without arousing the enmity of half the county he would commission him deputy sheriff. Crockett found out about it.

"I hear you are going to arrest me, John. Now ain't that a hot one." He marched the postmaster to the nearest bar, put him on a table and made him dance a jig. After this he drank to the postmaster's health, made him ride his horse up and down the main thoroughfare while he held the bridle as Crockett yelled out: "Look, everybody, I'm under arrest. The new deputy has placed me under arrest. A peace loving citizen like me." Behind the deputy rode Heifner and in back of Heifner rode Henry Goodman. They passed the sheriff's office. All the sheriff did was to give his deputy that "I told you so" look.

Heifner was standing near the stage station. The sheriff and a rancher by the name of Joseph Holbrook seemed engaged in earnest conversation. He could catch a snatch or two of what they said. It had something to do with Crockett. He went to his buddy with the tale that Rinehart and Holbrook were cooking up something that didn't sound too good for Crockett. In customary fashion the cowboy hunted up Holbrook.

"Joe, I hear you are interested in arresting me."
"Who told you that?"
"A little birdie."
"Well, you tell that little birdie he's a d—m liar."
Crockett pulled out his six-shooter.

"I want the truth. Didn't you sign up with the sheriff as deputy for the express purpose of arresting me?"

"I have no quarrel with you. Why should I want to arrest you. I've got a ranch to look after. I have no time to be worried about arrests."

"See that you look after it and leave well enough alone."

He put his gun away much to the relief of the accused man.

"No, I don't think you will arrest me," said Crockett. "There isn't a peace officer brave enough to do it. At least not in Cimarron." He turned his back on Holbrook.

At this time several companies of Negro troops came into Cimarron from escorting a caravan along the Santa Fe Trail. It was a standing custom that troops coming in along the Trail would rest up a day or so at Cimarron rather than exerting themselves for the extra push to reach the fort, not too far away, but far enough to make it tedious. Besides, it was rather rough on the horses. They usually put up at the Beaufort Corral & Livery Stable owned by A. G. Bushnell, who later sent his bill to the quartermaster for feeding men and horses. He quartered them free of charge. Whenever such troops arrived in town Crockett would hie off to Lambert's and drink and gamble until word came to him that they left. He would have enjoyed killing them all but he was sensible enough to see that it was the government that he would have to answer to. Apart from the soldiers the men he killed at Elizabethtown and Cimmaron were Northerners. Sometimes he went over to Mat Crosby's ranch where his girl friend lived. She was interested in Davy but was rather reluctant to marry him until he reformed his wild ways. She knew that he pleaded self defense in his killings and got away with it, but there would come a time when he wouldn't. She did not want to become a widow right after marriage. She was two years younger than Mrs. Crosby, her sister.

Crockett, Heifner and Goodman spent the evening at Lambert's bar. At nine o'clock Crockett said to Heifner:

"Gus, ask Henry for a quart to take along to the ranch.

We'll settle the account later. I want to get home. Too many people in town I don't like."

He walked towards the door, turned the knob to open it. The action was simultaneous with someone's turning it on the other side. Exerting more force Crockett managed to open the door and for a moment stood staring face to face with a Negro soldier. But just for a moment. He pulled out his gun and before the other could be aware of his action, shot him dead. He was in a bad mood. All evening long he had been throwing hints to several soldiers playing cards in the same room that their company was not appreciated. These soldiers were just north of the door in the northwest corner of the cantina. Two were playing and a third looking over their shoulders kibitzing. All had checked their guns at Bushnell's place. As Negro troops had been stationed at Fort Union since 1866 Crockett should have been accustomed to seeing them. They were to be stationed there until 1882. Angered because these soldiers persisted in remaining in the same room with him and drinking at the same bar, the urge to kill reached its pinnacle when he opened the door to see another ready to join his comrades.

Lambert and everyone else in the room stood frozen to the spot as Crockett swung around, sending two shots at the trio who had suddenly lost interest in the card game. They had not been expecting this action or they would have hurried to the other exit. Perhaps they would not have made it anyway as Heifner would probably have polished them off anyway. Two slumped across the table. Each was shot through the brain. The kibitzer propelled into action but got as far as the door leading into the dining room where a fourth bullet dropped him. Four shots—four deaths. One might ask why he didn't give them a fighting chance according to the code of the West. The only answer is that Crockett did not consider them as human beings.

"Let's get out of here before all Cimarron wants to know what the shooting is about," cried Goodman. His face was pale. One could see that he was very much in fear of being mistaken as the culprit. He shot past the other two as he bolted for the exit and threw himself behind a pile of lumber stacked up close by. This belonged to Frank Only Crocker. It was rather a stupid selection since this would be the first place the posse was likely to look. Not only the posse but the enraged soldiers who would be on the lookout for the slayer of their comrades. Goodman was fortunate that nobody seemed concerned at the moment. There was shooting every day and night in Cimarron and people sort of got used to it. Whenever they heard shots over Lambert's way they shrugged their shoulders and said: "Look's like Lambert will have another man for breakfast," and let it go at that. Mrs. Crocker, hearing a noise behind the woodpile, got up to investigate. She opened the door and peered out. Nothing. She would have liked to circle the wood pile but decided that discretion was the better part of valor and returned to bed. Goodman sighed with relief when he saw the door close. Mrs. Crocker had a Winchester in her hands when she hesitated on the threshold. He soon made himself scarce.

Lambert sent word over to the commanding officer that four of his men lay dead in his place and would he be so kind as to empty the place of their remains. This announcement caused a good deal of excitement at the livery stable. It was a tremendous barn surrounded by a high adobe wall. It was originally built by Maxwell to house his racing horses. When he sold the Grant, Sherwin, manager for the new Maxwell Land Grant & Railway Company, used it more for stabling the company's mounts than for the few race horses that remained. He rented it to Beaufort and after a shakeup in the company it was acquired by Bushnell.

Crockett and Heifner stuck close together. It was inadvisable to procure their mounts as oddly enough they were stabled in the same place where the soldiers were quartered. They left town on foot, avoiding contact with anyone. Outside of town the pair separated, Crockett making his way to the Dick Steel ranch, the present Springer outfit. At dawn the leader of the soldiers gave orders for a complete search of Cimarron and the surrounding area. Crockett was to be brought to him dead or alive. Every home was entered and every square inch turned upside down. They were leaving nothing to chance nor oversight. They beat every brush with the butt of their rifles and prodded through anything that looked like it might hide the body of a man. There was never such a search in Cimarron before or since. No one was permitted to enter or leave Cimarron until he answered questions to their satisfaction. Martial law took over. The sheriff was ignored as incompetent. A twenty-four-hour watch was kept at Lambert's over the protests of the highly incensed Frenchman who saw nothing unusual in the affair. The ceiling and walls were full of bullet holes. Someone was always shooting or being shot at Henry's. Besides, he said, he was not in the habit of harboring criminals. The captain responded that he was leaving nothing to chance. Four of his men had been shot down in cold blood. How would he answer his commander at Fort Union if he reported that he did nothing about it? When the commander of the garrison found out what happened he sent several more troopers to aid in the search.

John Baptist McCullough and Joseph Holbrook went to Sheriff Rinehart's house in Block A 3 S.W. Holbrook heard of the killings and decided that this was as good a time as any to show Crockett that he wasn't afraid of him. "I think I'll take that badge you once offered me," he told the sheriff, "if the offer for the arrest of Crockett still stands."

"More than ever now." The sheriff had hoped that the soldiers would find the killer and save him the trouble of hunting him down. He wished now that he had accepted that offer to open up a flour mill in Old Town, Las Vegas. With Holbrook sworn in, the sheriff decided to work independently of the military. For one reason too many of the cowboys in and about Cimarron had fought for the South during the recent war between the States. They offered Fort Union no cooperation. The sheriff would hardly hope for help if he threw in his lot with the soldiers. Besides, he was better acquainted with Crockett's habits than the men in uniform.

The road going to Urraca (present Cimarroncita) passed by the old stage barn used by Whitman, the freighter. Near it was a well-curb and behind this Rinehart, McCullough and

Holbrook decided to lie in wait for Crockett. They knew their man. He was nervy enough to defy all the soldiers, the posse, the sheriff, the world. He would pass this way either in going to Crosby's place or if already there, in coming from seeing his sweetheart. There was quite a scene between the lovers. News of the killing reached Miss Howard's ears.

"How can you possibly expect me to marry you after this," she said in a tearful voice. "Every time I look at you I will think of the number of men you killed. It's no good." Crockett agreed.

"You better stay here tonight," said Mat Crosby. "No telling what will happen if you try to get to town." The sheriff was aware that Crosby harbored Crockett. Why didn't he go out to the Urraca ranch and arrest the desperado? Many have maintained that Rinehart was not the type of sheriff to go out of his way when he expected trouble. He had come to Cimarron as miller for Maxwell and lived in those days in the grist mill still standing. He was well liked and got along fine until Maxwell sold out. Maxwell had only one falling out with him. That was the time when he acted as witness with his wife to the marriage of his daughter Virginia against his wishes. She married a captain from Fort Union, the ceremony taking place in the grist mill. Rev. Thomas Harwood, the Circuit Rider, performed the ceremony. Rinehart was elected sheriff not on his merits as a marksman but on his popularity as a miller. Hiding behind a wall to trap a desperado may not have placed the sheriff on the list of famous frontier marshalls, but it prolonged his life. And that was what he was interested in. He would not even be out there losing sleep had it not been for Holbrook. One would judge from watching the three that Holbrook was the sheriff.

Crockett managed to slip into Cimarron without detection. He knew that a trap was set for him, but he was not planning to fall into it. What nettled him mostly was the news that Holbrook was now a deputy. He wished that he had killed him when he had the chance. It made his blood boil remembering how Holbrook cringed before him in his denials that he had any intentions towards eliminating the outlaw. Above everything else he wanted to meet Holbrook once more.

"I should have killed him when I had him begging for mercy," he told Heifner who had joined him.

"Better be careful.'

"Of Holbrook?" He laughed scornfully. "If I bared my breast and pointed to my heart, he wouldn't have the guts to shoot."

"You never know," said Heifner prophetically.

But Crockett was not aiming to be surprised if he could help it. He knew that the law was in waiting somewhere along the road. If any man ever went about courting danger that man was Crockett. Already in Cimarron he decided to go from house to house, knock at each door and ask if the sheriff was in. He was mighty fast on the draw. This was to his advantage if the men hunting him did not decide to shoot first and ask questions afterwards. The soldiers had relaxed their search for the night. Had Crockett gone over to Elizabethtown, up to Taos and over to Colorado, he might have lived a long time. Perhaps. The way he flirted with danger he might not have lived another week anyway. Men like Crockett are attracted to danger like a moth to a flame. It is hard to speculate just what his position would be in relation to Billy the Kid, Clay Allison and other more widely known desperadoes had he lived. Cimarron would have enjoyed a nice juicy gunfight had Crockett been a mite more patient.

Crockett knocked at Frank Only Crocker's door. Mrs. Crocker came to the door. The outlaw asked for her husband. She said he was away on a business trip. He next asked for Jess Wheeler who boarded at the Crocker home. He was with her husband.

"Appears to me they are both in," said Heifner out of humor, "but are hiding behind a woman's skirts."

"Shut your mouth, Gus. If the lady says they are not in, they are not. Mind your manners."

Mrs. Crocker thanked him. Crockett tipped his hat and said he was sorry to disturb her but that he was looking for the sheriff. The next stop was Chittenden's close by. They woke up the rancher and made inquiries as to whether the sheriff was there and if not did the rancher know where he was? Chittenden did not. The sound of the voices alerted the sheriff. Chittenden's was close to the old stage stop.

"I'm going from house to house till I find him," said Crockett.

"That's rather dangerous," commented Chittenden. "No use inviting trouble."

"I guess it's trouble either way. If I have to go I'd like to take the sheriff and his deputies with me."

Chittenden had no answer for that.

"Crockett," said Heifner years later, "had no idea that the sheriff was behind the well-curb. His idea was a man-to-man showdown. When we came parallel to the old well, from behind the curbing came a voice we instantly recognized as Holbrook's:

" 'Hands up.' "

The surprise of the pair could only be imagined. They were riding horses loaned them by Crosby. They jerked the animals to a halt and Holbrook jumped up pointing a double-barreled shotgun at Crockett.

"It's loaded and the order still holds: Hands up."

Instead of complying Crockett laughed in his face.

"Holbrook, of all people," he roared. "And hiding behind a well-curb. Ain't that a laugh. Go ahead and shoot. I dare you to shoot." He pulled open his shirt. This is the spot."

"Holbrook let him have it. Both barrels. Heifner didn't wait to see his companion fall off the saddle to the ground. He dug in his spurs and did not let up until he breathed the air of the Vermejo country. Crockett was carried over to Lambert's.

"Get word over to the captain at Bushnell's that his search is over," said Holbrook to Henry.

Crockett never knew what hit him. They buried him next to Parson Tolby. Carey, who ran a hardware store in town, was asked to make a marker for the grave. The citizens agreed that Crockett deserved death for the murder of the four soldiers. But one murder was not solved by another and they decided that Crockett was murdered. The four soldiers were not buried in Cimarron as many believe. They were taken to Fort Union for burial.

Heifner, ashamed of his mad dash from the well-curb, procurred a Winchester and all day long the next Sunday rode up and down the streets of Cimarron looking for Rinehart and Holbrook. They were out of town. Not finding them he left town for good. Meantime the vigilantes decided to arrest those implicated in the death of Crockett. It must be said to their credit that they had no intentions of lynching the trio. But to prevent such a possibility Morley, Springer and Sherwin sent to Fort Union for soldiers. No doubt if the soldiers had not arrived lynchings might have taken place. The sheriff and the two deputies were in jail facing trial for the murder of Crockett. Said the Santa Fe New Mexican in its April 13, 1878 issue:

"Joseph Holbrook, Isaiah Rinehart and John McCullough were indicted by the grand jury and arraigned before the court for the killing of one David Crockett; to which they pleaded not guilty. They were admitted to bail in the sum of $25,000. Judge Parks is complimented by the Cimarron paper (Cimarron News and Press) for his fairness, integrity and ability; and the paper expresses a desire to have him retained permanently in the First District."

Judge Parks eventually ruled that there were extenuating circumstances and the prisoners were freed as "Not Guilty." Holbrook testified that not only did Crockett refuse to obey his command to put up his hands but reached for his gun so that it became a matter of self defense. Someone who knew both Crockett and Holbrook real well once remarked: "It wouldn't have made much difference to Holbrook whether he put up his hands or not." But this fellow was not friendly towards Holbrook as they had had a falling out over a piece of property.

Sheriff Rinehart seems to have had no say-so at all in all the proceedings. He sold out eventually and moved to Tascosa, Texas.

Cimarron settled down to law and order after this and not as many killings took place there as before 1878. Robert Crockett came up from Anton, Texas, and asked to see the grave of David Crockett. He was not impressed with the headstone. Could he take it down and have a fine granite one made? The people of Cimarron thought it was all right. So the marker was taken down but the granite one never arrived. Was David his son? In destroying the marker he did not destroy the legend of David Crockett any more than the memory of what another David Crockett did for Texas in the Alamo.

Identified as Dick Brewer. The man whose place Billy the Kid took in the Lincoln County War.

Said to be Jim Greathouse. He befriended the Kid only to see his home go up in smoke. Fowler ended his career.

BOOK THREE

REGULARS AND REGULATORS

(Dick Brewer)

Over in Bavaria a young man with cold blue eyes that reminded one of a fish out of water, and close-cropped, dark blonde hair, sat listening intently in the best sitting room of his well-to-do mother to a glowing account of General Fremont's First Expedition. Although he was a young nobleman connected with the court he was forever buying German translations of the feats of frontiersmen in America. Kit Carson's name had a certain appeal and time and again he begged leave to go to America to see all this for himself. Time out of mind he wanted to become a fur trapper, a trail blazer and as his mother's voice droned on he wished that he could leave all this pageantry to become a Mountain Man and roam the Sangre de Cristo Mountains that guarded Taos. His mother glanced up from her reading, ordered hot chocolate and asked the family to retire for the night. She was a buxom matriarch, that one, with fine feathers and ambitious plans for her sons and daughter and treking off to America was not among them.

"Really Emil," she said. "We are not barbarians. I can't see why tramping through an unbroken wilderness and living the life of a savage should appeal to you."

"Perhaps a man is free there," he said.

"Is doing without the finer things in life freedom?"

"It depends." That was all he said.

The next morning when she came down for breakfast she found a note on the dining room table. Emil was tired of the sham of court life, parade, gossip, pretense. He preferred the buckskin of a trapper to the uniform of the army. The freedom of the woods, a bed under the stars—that was the life for him.

In America Emil von Fritz found that he had been too well trained in imperialistic ways. Try as he might he could not live without rule and system. He joined the army. As much as he rebelled against his life in Bavaria he felt naked out of uniform. Manual labor degraded him. The melting pot of the Knickerbocker City could not hide the shame he felt at the utter contempt in which he was held and classified as another "foreigner." Only his pride made him hold on. The Civil War found him a captain with the army in California. When New Mexico was threatened by Confederate invasion General Carleton called for volunteers to save the Territory. Captain Fritz was given a company of recruits to drill. By this time he had come to love America.

The soldier gave a good account of himself as we gather from the Memoirs of one who rode with him: "On the day of our arrival (in Tucson where the California Column also stopped to dispute the authority of the Confederates) May, 1862, Captain Emil Fritz, Company B, First Cavalry, dashed through the town at full speed and in five minutes it was surrounded. Shortly after, the prisoners were marched to the guard house and later sent to Fort Yuma. They are a set of bad men who had scorned the law and had their own way. Affairs had taken a turn and I think their jig is up. General Carleton has taken hold with a firm hand and not one of these outlaws against the civil or national authority will escape his authority." (In the Alta California San Francisco newspaper for July 10, 1862 in possession of the Bancroft Library.)

At Fort Union Fritz became acquainted with Captain Laurence G. Murphy. Later on at Fort Stanton he got to know two other army men by the names of Riley and Brady. Soon they would be mustered out of the army. They didn't want to go back to California. Years of service in the New Mexico posts built up a host of friends for them. If only they could open up a chain of sutler stores like that fellow Moore at Fort Union! That was it. A trading post at Fort

Stanton. Brady felt he would much rather be a rancher. Murphy, Riley and Fritz pooled their resources but found that they did not have enough capital. They went to see another friend who had been in the Army with them but who was now on his way to fame and fortune in Santa Fe. He had been a sergeant in Fritz's Company of California Volunteers and like his captain decided that New Mexico was the land of golden opportunity for him. His name was Rynerson. As a lawyer he had become acquainted with another outstanding attorney in New Mexico by the name of Thomas Catron, whose star at the moment was in the ascent. He loaned the money to launch the venture and had he foreseen the bloodshed that was to result he probably would have changed his mind. He was not aware then that the Lincoln County War would result. His insistence on payment even during the fray was in keeping with his cold blooded nature.

Now Fritz was a good man excepting of course when he went on a mad tantrum. He was a good soldier too, having the rank of major when mustered out of the service. Murphy liked him for his business acumen and even prior to his discharge he had property in his own name near Fort Stanton. With the formation of the Bonito area as the new Lincoln county and the placita del Rio Bonito reconverted into the village of Lincoln the county seat the partners decided that here would be the best place to carry on their mercantile business and expand in wealth in the health of the glorious New Mexico sunshine. To Lincoln also came McSween, Dolan, Brady and Tunstall. Dolan was taken in as a junior partner. Brady became sheriff of the new county. McSween took up the practise of law becoming for a time the firm's lawyer. Tunstall, the Englishman persuaded McSween that he would do better if he left the Murphy employ and entered into partnership with him. This arrangement seemed satisfactory to the lawyer who liked the sound of McSwen & Tunstall. As Fritz wished to be identified more with the cattle and ranch part of the partnership, his name was left out of the sign above the mercantile store of Murphy, Riley & Dolan.

In Bavaria Matriarch Fritz continued to rule the roost

and now that Emil had proved to be quite a businessman he was held up to the others as the epitome of success, greatness and emulation. Younger brother Karl tired of being considered the less important member of the two, decided to come to America to see this wonder-worker brother of his. But the Southwest was far from New Work and as he had no money to make the trip he joined the army for a while. But being in the American army was quite different than being an officer in the army of the Archduke. When his term of enlistment was up he settled among the German farmers of Pennsylvania leaving the visit to his brother for another day.

Meantime young sister Frieda blossomed into womanhood. The boys, although a success in America, were a disappointment to Ma Fritz. This much she was willing to admit. But Frieda was the apple of her eye. In her she placed the hopes of a good marriage and a high position at Court. All was going along nicely until after Vespers one evening when Frieda kicked a heel off her shoe upon leaving the church. She stumbled into the arms of a tailor's apprentice and romance. The virago heard from her daughter's own lips that she could not go through with the marriage to the baron. She was in love.

"And who is this object of your affection may I ask?"

When she heard it was a tailor's apprentice she fainted. The girl was confined to quarters until she changed her mind. One night a ladder was placed against the window and the last of the children flew the coop. This happened before Emil's discharge from the army.

Major Fritz was staying at the St. Nicholas Hotel in Las Vegas. He was on a holiday and as he had some business to conduct at Tecolote nearby, this was as good a place to stay as any. He was also concerned with how Browne & Manzanares ran their mercantile store at Las Vegas since he and Murphy had already discussed the possibility of a sutler's store at Fort Stanton. There was a timid knock at the door.

"Who is it?" He asked.

"A young lady here to see you," came the reply.

His sister had travelled all the way to Fort Stanton and finding out that he was at Las Vegas pushed on in the hopes of seeing him there. It was a delightful surprise for the brother who had left her a baby to see her now a grown woman. He was also impressed with his brother-in-law. It has been said that he died not many years after and Frieda returned to her brother's New Mexico ranch and married Dolan who fell heir to the Riley, Fritz and Murphy fortunes. Be that as it may Emil, Karl and Frieda are the back drop to the story of Dick Brewer, Dudley, McSween, Dolan, Murphy, Brady, Tunstall, Billy the Kid and the Lincoln County War. Would big brother Emil help her and her husband? Of course. He was hoping to open a little shop in Lincoln town that would be a combination saloon, restuarant and saloon. Her husband could run this while he took care of business at Fort Stanton. After he was mustered out of service he would see what could be done. Since the soldiers insisted on spending their money in town, Emil was going to see that he got a good slice of it, hence the need for someone to look after his interests eleven miles from the fort. All went well until a letter arrived from the home country. In it Ma Fritz said in no uncertain terms that Frieda was a disgrace to the family honor. She was a perverse child carried away by the promises of one who was a tailor's apprentice. His hand shook as he read the letter. He dashed out, saddled his horse and went to town to kill his brother-in-law. His sister told him that her husband had gone to Las Cruces for supplies. Emil said he would return.

Alarmed at this turn of events, Frieda told her husband that the major would kill him if he were still in an angry mood by morning. Not waiting to find out, they harnessed up the chuck wagon and with all their worldly goods set out for Pennsylvania in the hopes that Karl would be more amendable. Quartermaster Bolton saw Major Fritz going about like an old war horse.

"What's biting you," he asked? They were old friends and Bolton did not think it a presumption to talk to a major as an equal.

"I'm going to kill my brother-in-law." And off he rode. Quick to catch the drift, the quartermaster saddled the fastest horse on the post and rode to overtake the fumming major. Four miles out of Fort Stanton he caught up with him.

"Are you going to throw over your fine army record because of a brother-in-law? And your honorable discharge with the rank of major coming up so soon! Calm down. Think it over. Come on back with me and let us talk it over with Murphy and the others." This seemed like good advice to the major who decided that two wrongs could not make a right, so he turned back. On the other hand if the major refused to turn back and carried out his plan, the world would never have heard of Dick Brewer, Billy the Kid, Dave Rudabaugh, Tom Pickett. Nor would have Roberts, Brewer, Tunstall, McSween, and a host of others met their violent deaths. But in turning back Emil Fritz was not aware of this.

In due time the major was discharged from the army. He calmed down considerably and wrote his sister that all was forgiven. He acquired a ranch or two in addition to his other interests. At the moment he was a dealer in hides. But he did not feel too well. He coughed incessantly and a slight droop rounded his shoulders. Once in a while he spit up blood. If he could see the Fatherland perhaps he could get well. Nostalgia. In Pennsylvania he called on Karl and Frieda. He did not look a bit well. Overworked, he said. But they had a different name for it.

"Why don't you take out some insurance," said Karl. "Everybody is doing it and it's a good investment."

"Perhaps it's not a bad idea." He was not too sure that the insurance company would be interested in a man who spit blood. But he would try. In Philadelphia he took out a $30,000 policy naming his sister as beneficiary. He sailed for Europe. There he was given a royal welcome and a shroud. Hopes of a cure by returning to his place of birth proved but a shimmering shadow. His bones were interred in the family vault and a letter sent to Karl. After a suitable period of mourning Karl came to New Mexico to wind up his brother's estate and find his will. He went to see McSween at Lincoln town and unfolded the drama of the Lincoln County War.

"Emil had a policy with an insurance company in Philadelphia. I wish you would investigate it. The rest of his business is so tied up with Murphy and Riley that I am afraid I shall have to stay here a long time."

"It looks that way," said the lawyer.

Several months went by. Karl stood confronting the lawyer who had sent for him. Open before him on the oak desk was a letter from the insurance company. They refused to pay. Karl could not believe his ears.

"But they must," he yelled loud enough to be heard all the way to Fort Stanton. He inherited his brother's temper if nothing else.

"If Emil had T.B. at the time he drew out the policy the company is under no obligation to pay," explained McSween.

"But they knew. Anyone could see that Emil was a sick man. In spite of his condition they issued a policy. You are a lawyer. Force them to pay."

"I'll see what I can do."

"You'd better."

McSween could not tell whether that was a threat or a result of an upset state of mind. He made no comment and Karl left in a huff. McSween was clever enough to get $10,000 out of the company.

That was in 1876.

Ten thousand dollars! Everything has its price. So did this policy. The lawyer had written to friends of his in Philadelphia to handle the case for him there. When the Philadelphia lawyers returned the bill for services rendered the ten thousand dwindled down to one thousand. They had arranged with the company that this one thousand reach New Mexico. The other nine thousand never left Philadelphia. When Karl came to claim it McSween refused to give it to him claiming it as his fee. The fury of the claimant knew no bounds. He denounced McSween as a crook and took his grievances to Murphy, Riley and Dolan. He sought aid in bringing McSween to justice. As they were also on friendly terms with the lawyer they thought they could persuade him to turn over something to Karl and his sister. He refused to comply and one thing lead to another to erupt into the Lincoln County War. The amazing thing about this war was that not one of the parties concerned was a native of Bonito, or Lincoln as it was now called.

Alexander A. McSween was a native of Prince Edward Island. He migrated to the United States in pursuit of his law studies but mostly to escape his parents who had singled him out for ordination in the Presbyterian ministry. Law degree tucked under his arm, he decided that Eureka, Kansas, was the best place to begin his practise. He hung out his shingle but no one seemed to notice it so he moved to Atchison where he met Susan Hummer, formerly of Gettysburg. Her family had lost all in the famous battle that took place there so they decided to march on to new frontiers opened by the influx of buffalo hunters and the railroad. Threatened with T. B. he went on to New Mexico taking his bride with him. Perhaps this explains his sympathy for Emil Fritz and why he would not consciously skin him or his relatives. Besides, he was deeply religious and still not averse to the idea of the ministry.

He had heard about the blue skies and dry climate from Santa Fe traders and decided to give it a try. He had no definite place in mind. He would worry about that when he got to New Mexico. Near Las Vegas a chance meeting with Miguel A. Otero, a citizen of importance in the financial and political scene, resulted in a letter of introduction to Laurence Murphy, well known to Otero. Murphy gave him as his first client Emil Fritz. Mrs. McSween noting that all the men about Lincoln wore guns as part of their dress, urged her husband to do so. But he insisted that he would live by his wits and the Bible.

Lincoln, one of those timeless towns of New Mexico, looks today very much as it did in McSween's day, except for the highway of asphalt cutting through it. Adobe structures made up the homes, stores, saloons, warehouses and other edifices very much then as they do today. What is shown visitors as the Lincoln County Courthouse was the original Murphy Mercantile store. Here Karl Fritz, Alexander McSween and Laurence Murphy discussed the terms of Emil's will and the disposal of his estate. Karl decided not to press the matter of the insurance money for a while because there were a number of unpaid bills to be collected and attached to the value of the estate. McSween was elected to pay a visit to all the creditors for the purpose of closing these accounts. Karl thought he was rather slow about it and again broke out with threats. The lawyer succeeded in collecting one thousand dollars which he turned over to his client.

But Karl Fritz was not satisfied. He insisted on the full amount that accrued to him and again brought up the matter of the policy. He asked Murphy to back him up. The merchant became a little too bold and overbearing and for this and other reasons not directly connected with the Fritz estate, especially over the John Chisum affair regarding the rustling of cattle by Murphy or his hired hands, McSween severed relations with Murphy, Riley, Dolan and Fritz. He transferred three thousand dollars more to the Fritz estate claiming that in fees and other costs he was entitled to reserve for himself the $5,800 that he did. But he was a righteous man. He did not deny that over and above his fees there was still $5,000 coming to Karl Fritz and his sister. Karl asked him to pay it. The lawyer stalled. Why, he never quite explained. It is my contention that he had it tied up in his partnership with Tunstall and in order to pay Fritz he would have to dissolve the partnership which at the moment he was not disposed to do.

The break with Murphy was complete. The merchant had asked him to represent him in the case of Murphy vs. Chisum. It was on open secret around Lincoln that the cattle under discussion once carried the Chisum brand. McSween was aware of this and refused in no uncertain terms. Along came J. H. Tunstall a wealthy Englishman who had bought a ranch on the Rio Feliz about thirty miles from Lincoln and decided that he would like to open an mercantile store in town but as he could not be at the ranch and the store at the same time he was looking for a man he could trust to enter into partnership with him. Hearing about McSween he approached him on the deal and it was no sooner discussed than done. Where would a poor lawyer get the money necessary for this venture? It was a well stocked store and only the best could be obtained there. Even if McSween had sunk five thousand dollars that did not belong to him in the deal the business flourished to the extent that he could have paid him back without feeling the loss or pinching pennies. Added to this he opened a bank in the store. Why he stalled in paying Fritz is a secret he carried to the grave with him. Even Mrs. McSween who lived at White Oaks for many years following the Lincoln County War and who became the Cattle Queen of New Mexico was not aware that there was a reason. To make matters worse, Frieda came to New Mexico.

Karl Fritz and Mrs. Frieda Fritz Scholand insisted that McSween show them their brother's will. The attorney said that the will was in Murphy's custody because he stoutly maintained that Fritz had turned it over to him as security for debt owed the Spiegelberg Brothers, merchants of Santa Fe, who trusted Emil who was vouched for by Murphy who was vouched for in turn by Thomas Catron. The debt stood at $900. McSween paid the merchants at Santa Fe and brought the will to Murphy who explained that there was the little matter of the debt to Tom Catron to be settled. Murphy's private debt was paid but he insisted that there was still the matter of $10,000 due Catron through him as he had made himself responsible to the Santa Fe attorney for Emil. Murphy then declared that Chisum, McSween and Tunstall were ganging up against him to put him out of business and to make him responsible for a bill that should come out of the Fritz estate. The Cimarron News and Press scoffed at the idea and ridiculed Murphy who wrote the editor some scathing letters. The only reason he did not send one of his gunfighters up to Cimarron to finish off the editor was because he was suffering acute pains that turned out to be cancer and he was now spending his fortune running from doctor to doctor in quest of a cure as cancer was an unknown quantity in those days as it is today. The editor of the paper, Frank Springer, was a lawyer and naturally took up for his confrere.

Many stories have been circulated concerning the much disputed will in order to make good copy for the tall tales that made the rounds concerning the whys and wherefores of the Lincoln County War. Actually all the Fritz heirs were interested in was the $5000 due them. After that they would be content and whatever the dispute between Murphy and McSwen other than the estate would not interest them in the least. Such was the state of affairs in 1877 when McSween decided to take the wife to St. Louis for the Christmas holidays. With them travelled a Negro man servant who had been with the family for years. Actually he had been the heritage of Mrs. McSween's father who turned him over to his daughter upon her marriage. He had been offered many an opportunity to strike out for himself but he refused to leave the McSweens.

Murphy's spies, ever on the alert, reported to their leader that the McSweens were moving out—taking a powder—as we say in modern parlance. "Over my dead body.", roared the merchant. He ran to where Karl was boarding and informed him that he would be out $5000 if McSween ever reached St. Louis. Fritz went to Judge Warren Bristol who was conducting court in Lincoln at the time and asked him to issue a warrant for the arrest of McSween on the charge of embezzlement. The sheriff and his posse caught up with McSween near Tecolote this side of Las Vegas. He had no trouble finding him as spies kept on the trail and were able to keep him informed. McSween was surprised that his carriage should be stopped and asked Sheriff Brady if his wife at least and the servant would not be permitted to continue on as the injunction was not against them. The sheriff believed this to be a ruse and between them they would smuggle the money out of New Mexico. He thought it best that they all come back to Lincoln town.

The first question asked the crestfallen lawyer was: Why was he fleeing the country? Was it an admission of guilt? McSween denied that he was fleeing. If Murphy wanted the money why didn't he seize his share of the Tunstall & McSween store? It was valued at more than five thousand dollars. Murphy thought it a good idea. "Whatever I am," cried McSween, "I am not a thief."

"Does that mean that I am one," asked Murphy?

"That depends on how you live with yourself."

Turnstall was next placed on the stand. He swore that

he and McSween were partners; that he carried on the business under the firm name of J. H. Tunstall & Co.; that McSween's interest in the business was worth at least $5,000. This satisfied the judge who bound McSween over to the administrators Murphy, Riley and Dolan. They sued out a writ of attachment and placed it in the hands of Sheriff Brady of Lincoln county. He was told to attach McSween's interest in certain property, and among other property, the sheriff was directed to attach the interest of McSween in the partnership property of J. H. Tunstall & Co. The sheriff levied this writ upon the stock of goods, but he was compelled to take possession of them by force since a mob had gathered in the store who were in sympathy with McSween and more so with Tunstall who they felt was imposed upon and the innocent victim of Murphy's greed and Fritz's anger. Turnstall took exception to all this maintaining that none of this had anything to do with him. It was between Murphy and McSween. By impounding the goods at the store it was the effrontery to the Englishman who reasoned that as partners what was taken from McSween was also taken from him. He brought in a number of his cowboys from the ranch to protect his property; hence the collision between the sheriff and the mob at the store. This measure taken by the partner placed Tunstall in the same category as McSween as far as Murphy was concerned—an enemy.

Every account ever written of the murder of Tunstall places it as a cold-blooded murder without motive or any connection whatsoever with McSween. A study of the case shows very clearly that Murphy reasoned that Tunstall stood in the way of his collecting money he badly needed despite the fact that his business was a fairly successsful one. Tustall believed that there ought to be other ways of settling the Fritz-Murphy case without dragging him into it. In levying McSween's goods, his goods were levied, too. No one could convince him otherwise. The leader of the mob at the store who directed the action against the sheriff was a Dick Brewer, formerly a cowboy for Chisum and now foreman of the Tunstall ranch.

If ever there was a trigger-happy foreman who led a group of trigger-happy cow-hands, that man was Richard

Brewer. One of the lesser known hands at the moment was a youth by the name of William Antrim better known as The Kid. Brewer was a big, burly, swathy complexioned individual who handled a gun from the time he was big enough to carry one. A native of Waco, which was then no more than watering place in Milam county, he learned to ride and shoot before he could write his name. He came to know New Mexico when he rode with Baylor's Babies to capture Mesilla, Fort Fillmore, Fort Bliss and Tucson. Discharged from the service following the Civil War he herded cattle from Fort Worth and Red River Station up to Abilene, Kansas along the Eastern Trail sometimes called the Chisholm Trail. In those early days of cattle trails as an out growth of an ever increasing demand for new markets to stabilize the needs of a fast growing industrial East, and a web of iron rails, Texas made her bid for fame to corner the meat market of the nation. Each herd that moved north was usually directed by twelve men with six horses per man. To realize the extent of this industry from 1866 to 1895 ten million cattle were driven from Texas in 4,000 herds averaging 2,500 head. The herds moved at the rate of speed of from ten to fourteen miles a day. This took a total of 48,000 men if we do not count those who made several drives. It certainly helped the employment situation of the Lone Star State in the days prior to the advent of oil.

Brewer later trailed for John R. Blocker and R. T. Driskill. In Kansas he joined a bunch of toughs at Abilene, hurrahing the town, plundering merchants and building up his reputation as a gunman with a killing or two, not a strange pass time for the era. He was a good rider, an excellent cowboy and a handy man with a six-shooter. He drifted into New Mexico to cowboy for John H. Chisum. He would have liked becoming sheriff of Lincoln County and had no use for Brady which was why he was so vindicative when the Lincoln County War burst wide open. He was the killer behind the gun until his death, and not William (Bonney) Antrim who did not assume leadership until after the death of Brewer.

Judge Bristol would never admit that he was influenced by Murphy in attaching Tunstall's property. It never occurred to him that in harming McSween he was also hurting Tunstall. On the other hand Murphy was rather elated. To close down a competitor would be to replenish his fast dwindling resources. A deputy named Matthews was sent with a posse to attach certain cattle and horses belonging to J. H. Tunstall & Co. since the company was so reluctant about the goods in the store. The posse was surprised to learn that Tunstall had called in a U. S. Marshall by the name of Wilderman to take over his affairs. The marshall insisted that a Federal officer was above a county official so if he said the horses and cattle were not to be touched he was talking in the name of the United States Government. Matthews would have to obey him. Said the marshall to the posse:

"If any of you so much as lifts a finger to take a steer or a horse, you oppose the government which I represent. You become Federal violators."

The men milled around Matthews waiting to act upon his answer.

"And you, Matthews, if you attempt to go through with this, I'll deputize these very men to arrest you."

Matthews glanced from the men to the marshall. He had never been up against a case like this before. Wilderman he knew from working with him at Las Cruces. He was a money grasping, cold blooded individual who would just as soon turn over to Murphy if paid more as work for Tunstall.

"These horses and cattle are placed in the charge of the U. S. Government under my care. You can't fight the whole U. S. Government."

"I'll be back with more men. Whether you represent the U. S. Government, or Wilderman, or Tunstall or McSween is for the courts to decide. All I know is that I have a court order to pick up these horses and cattle. As an officer of the law I must take them in tow. I'll be back. Come on men."

That was how the Lincoln County War started.

All the glowing accounts of all the writers of the world cannot change the facts. The most accurate account is given in the Santa Fe New Mexican for May 4, 1878. The most romantic account written in verisimilitude is found in Walter

Noble Burns' book *The Saga of Billy the Kid*. But no matter what Garrett, Poe, Otero, Burns and a host of others have to say about the character known as Billy the Kid and the Lincoln County War, it remotely began with Emil Fritz and actually opened up the morning that Marshall Wilderman refused to comply with the court order as handed to him by Matthews.

The University of New Mexico Press, in the fall of 1952, published a paper covered booklet entitled *Billy the Kid, the Bibliography of a Legend,* by J. C. Dykes. The author chooses as his first item Billy the Kid's Exploit, found in the National Police Gazette, New York, May 21, 1881. But this is not the first time the Kid appeared in print. The first reference made to the Kid in print is in May, 1878 when he lines up with Tunstall in preventing the sheriff from taking goods, half of which belonged to the Englishman no matter what McSween's debt to the Fritz estate.

When Tunstall hired Dick Brewer to take over his ranch as foreman he was aware that he hired a fighter and gunman as a cowboy. In those balmy days of cattle rustlers it was mighty important that your foreman be quick on the draw as well as a leader of men. Cowboys attached themselves to such a man with loyalty unto death. Tunstall was in a stew. Beset by court order, mocked by Murphy, placed in an embarrassing predicament by his partner, defensive because of Matthews, he was now approached by Marshall Wilderman, who told him that he would certainly have to pay through the nose if he wanted the marshall to continue to stick his neck out for him. Not knowing where to turn next, Tunstall rode out to the range and sought out his foreman. He explained the situation. This was a little different than fighting rustlers, but Tunstall had hired him and Tunstall interests he would protect as he did against Sheriff Brady in the store at Lincoln town. The hired hands were of the same opinion.

"You see how it is with me," he explained to Brewer. "With Wilderman making claims and demands and the deputy making claims and demands, I don't know who to turn to to protect my interests. I wish the regulars (meaning the soldiers at Fort Stanton) were here to take over. I am afraid there will be bloodshed."

"We will be the Regulars," smiled Brewer, as he turned to his men for confirmation. They were all in accord. And their number was twelve.

Over their protests Tunstall left the range to ride back to Lincoln to look for Wilderman and inform him that his services were no longer needed. At Lincoln he was told that Wilderman had ridden to the ranch house in search of him and for an answer to his demands. Wilderman had left a message that he was expecting Matthews back and felt that the deputy would not be denied. Which of course meant a fight. At the ranch Tunstall induced Wilderman to turn over the horses and cattle that were supposed to pay the McSween debt. He next rode the range to pick up Brewer and his men, dividing the cattle and horses he took from the marshall. The cattle he left in the care of a trusted cowboy; the horses he wished to take to Lincoln.

The next morning Matthews arrived with his men to settle the dispute and found that Wilderman had left but was informed that the cattle in question were close by. The horses were on the way to Lincoln. He divided his men. He would round up the cattle; Morton and some other men would go after the horses. Tunstall, the better to think out his thoughts and present a plea to the court, separated from his men full of confidence that if anything happened they would be close by to protect him. Thus when Billy Morton caught up with the lone rider he was too far away for any of the men to be of any assistance. Besides they were so intent on driving in the horses that none of them knew of the disturbance behind them until it was all over. None of them witnessed the affair so that when the news was brought to them it was Morton's version.

The arresting party present at the time say that Tunstall was told that he was under arrest for obstructing justice. They maintain that he resisted arrest and that he fired at the posse twice before he was brought down. Two chambers in his revolver were empty when he was found. The amazing thing is that two shots are supposed to be fired at close range and no one was hit. It has happened. Many gun battles were fought in which men fired at their target five or six times within fifteen feet and missed every time.

"As no one else was present at the time, the other men with Tunstall having left," says the reporter for the Santa Fe New Mexican, "the statements of the parties are uncontradicted and will have to be taken for what they are worth."

The next day Dick Brewer gathered his men about him at the McSween residence in Lincoln. While all this was happening Murphy realized that he was too sick to carry on his business and sold out to Dolan who promptly had the sign across the false front of the store to read: J. J. Dolan & Co. But Murphy controlled all his actions and Dolan had no freedom until Murphy's death which was not long in coming, although it was not a violent one as was to be McSween's and many others. Dolan eventually branched out to become a wealthy, respected citizen and owner of a chain of dry goods stores all over New Mexico.

The men Dick Brewer gathered about him as the Twelve Regulars were: Billy (the Kid) Antrim. He was not known as Bonney until some time after these events. Charlie Bowdre, Doc Skurlock, Henry Brown, Jim French, John Middleton, Fred Wayt, Sam Smith, Frank McNab, Sam McCloskey, Tom O'Folliard, Bill Scroggins. These were the original twelve. Later were to come: Frank Coe, George Coe, Stephen Stevens, Tom Pickett and Dave Rudabaugh. There was not one who wasn't a desperado. Gunfighters one and all they were veterans in the art of cattle rustling, hurrahing towns, killing Indians and just plain killing.

Brewer marched his Regulars to the Dolan store only to be confronted by a stalwart line of blue. Soldiers from Fort Stanton! Believe it or not, this was the work of Marshal Wilderman. Peeved because Tunstall had refused his demands for more money, he consulted with Dolan and told him that Tunstall was coming to town with a bunch of cowboys.

"You represent the U. S. Government," said Dolan, "And in this very town are outlaws wanted by that government. Now who close by also represents that government and must work with you in arresting men wanted by the Government?"

"Commander Dudley. Why didn't I think of it sooner?"

Thwarted in his design to burn Dolan out, Brewer marched his men back to the McSween residence. Commented the Santa Fe New Mexican:

"The estate of Emil Fritz was indebted to the firm of J. J. Dolan & Co. (Murphy-Riley) and also they excited themselves to recover the money collected by McSween; hence the enmity of the firm. McSween and his friends still wanted to take the goods attached from the sheriff (who had succeeded in taking over the Tunstall store) and knowing that it was dangerous to attempt to do so with their force they resorted to strategy. Among other property attached belonging to J. H. Tunstall & Co. was some hay. It was the only hay in the town of Lincoln. Some soldiers had been sent to town to protect the place from violence, and the sheriff let them have a small quantity of hay but before doing so had it accurately weighed. Wilderman was acting as deputy U. S. Marshall and had in his possession writs for the arrest of several outlaws; among the number were Evans, Baker and Davis. So Wilderman was sent to Fort Stanton for soldiers to help arrest these men. He obtained the soldiers for the purpose of representing to the commanding officers that he knew the men to be in town and at the house of J. J. Dolan & Co., then in the possession of the sheriff (who had gathered together a posse when he heard that Tunstall was coming in with his cowboys and decided to protect the place against the violence of the Twelve Regulars. He had his men hidden inside just in case Brewer decided to break through the soldiers if they got there before he did, and to give the Regulars a warm welcome if they did not).

"While he was gone, McSween's friends caused warrants to be issued against the sheriff and every man in the Tunstall & McSween store upon the charge of stealing hay. When the soldiers came from Fort Stanton under the direction of Wilderman (after first protecting Dolan's) they surrounded the Tunstall store building and took possession of the same to search, as Wilderman pretended, for the outlaws" (Santa Fe New Mexican, May 4, 1878).

McSween did not like the spilling of blood any more than he enjoyed being hounded by the sheriff and his men. Brewer's presence with the Regulars annoyed him. Yet the Dolan faction was in an ugly enough mood to necessitate the presence of Brewer. It would be better if Brewer had something to go by. McSween had him sworn in as a constable. Get a picture of the new constable. Tall, stocky, lantern-jawed, green-eyed, as swarthy as a Latin, he presented a sinister appearance with his dark, thick curly hair, handle-bar mustache, bristling whiskers stunted in their growth and weaving a pattern of darkness about his face. He didn't look like a man you would ask to escort your daughter home after a dance. "When in doubt," he would say, "Shoot first and ask questions afterwards."

As desperate and lawless as they come, he had a sense of loyalty which did much towards molding the character of a young fellow who worked under him and was soon to outrank him in Western folk lore and legend. His philosophy was to beat the other fellow to the draw if you did not want to be a deadbeat. Just how many men Brewer killed is not definitely known, but from his reputation as a gunfighter you may bet your bottom dollar it was more than one. Tunstall has been pictured as a jovial, laughing-from-the-belly, hearty Englishman, but that is because we have stereotyped Englishmen of the day as small, rotund Pickwicks laughing their way through life like so many country squires out of Dickens forever feasting on ale and mutton. Actually no accurate description of Tunstall has come down to us, and his picture at the Lincoln County museum shows anything but a rotund, jovial Briton. Accounts of the day did not describe men, they related events. But we do know that the Englishman had qualities that endeared him to his men. When men of such stamp as Bowdre, Brewer, Antrim, O'Folliard are bent on loyalty "unto death" to a man who was not even a citizen of their country he must have had qualifications that inspired.

"At the same time," continues the editor of the Santa Fe

New Mexican, "The Constable (Brewer, acting in collusion with Wilderman and McSween) entered with warrants for the arrest of the persons left in charge of the store by the sheriff. The outlaws were not found, but the men in charge of the store were disarmed and taken prisoners, and the store was then taken from the possession of the sheriff and turned over to McSween and party, which was the real object of the instigators of the plan. Warrants were then sworn out before Squire Wilson against the persons who composed the posse of the deputy-sheriff Matthews when Tunstall was killed. Then warrants were placed in R. M. Brewer's hands and he took a posse of twelve men and went after Morton, Baker and others. He arrested these two men and started for Lincoln . . ."

When Morton started after Tunstall's horses he had no idea that he would precipitate the Lincoln County War. It is the concensus of opinion that he killed Tunstall more to curry favor with the Dolan faction than for his own benefit. Baker was with him when he pursued the Englishman. Settling with them was not part of Billy the Kid's party although he was in on it. Brewer was the leader. It was under his direction that the men were taken prisoners. McCloskey, who had known Morton for many years, berated him for shooting a defenseless Englishman. Morton told him that he had no right to talk that way to him for it appeared to him that Brewer was taking him out to kill him. McCloskey told Brewer that Morton was his friend and if any harm came to Morton, Brewer would have to answer to McCloskey. McCloskey had taken Morton's gun and tucked it in his belt at the waist-line. As Morton and McCloskey rode together the killer of Tunstall decided that they would exact his death in payment and was willing to gamble on a chance in a thousand. His game was to side up against McCloskey as if to slap him for his taunts, reach down quickly for the gun sticking out of McCloskey's belt, bolt ahead and put McCloskey in the line of fire between himself and Brewer's men. In doing this, for some reason known only to himself, he turned the gun on the only man in that group that would have fought for him, and fired twice. Actually it happened in his favor. The others were so stunned that they halted their horses, frozen into immobility. Morton, quick to react from their surprise, spurred his horse into a fast gallop. Baker grasped the situation and in a split second was fleeing his captors to join Morton. But Brewer thawed out as quickly as he froze and as fast as Morton and Baker were riding they rode right into the Great Beyond.

"Brewer's party say that Morton, when riding with McCloskey, snatched his pistol and shot him and then started to run, when he and Baker were shot by the posse. McCloskey had stated to persons the morning of that day on which the men were killed that threats had been made to murder the prisoners but that it would not be done as long as he lived; and on the same day Morton posted a letter to a friend in Virginia in which he calls McCloskey his friend, and says he expects to be killed before he reaches Lincoln. He was shot in the breast with eleven balls, the exact number of men in the posse, and Baker was shot in the same manner." (Santa Fe New Mexican—ibid)

This of course quite changes the story that Billy the Kid did away with the two men. Any one of the eleven bullets would have proven fatal. But there were thirteen men in all. The paper is of the opinion that McCloskey was killed by his own men anxious to avenge the death of their employer. McCloskey stood in their path. Eleven bullets were found in each, possibly because Brewer was busy taking care of McCloskey. It was the visa-versa plan of Morton with the death of Tunstall.

"A portion of the same men," continues the account we are following, "Who had killed these three men (the third being McCloskey) on the night of the first of April, entered the town of Lincoln, concealed themselves in the corral in the rear of the Tunstall & McSween store and murdered Sheriff Brady and his deputy, George Hindman, shooting them in the backs (as a jesture of scorn and insult) as they were quietly walking down the street, and when down fired another volley into Brady and then shouted like madmen. Two of the assassins (one of them was William Antrim) then attempted to rob the dead and were only prevented from getting off with their arms by being fired at after they picked up the guns of the murdered men, when they dropped them and ran. It is also said that Hindman, who did not die for some minutes, asked for water and his murderers threatened to kill any person who should attempt to give him any. The same men and some others killed Roberts a few days after this at the Indian Agency. The particulars of this case are well known and the manner in which the brave man died, killing one and wounding four others after he had been shot down had become the talk of the town. But it is not generally known that the men who had shot Roberts had gone to the Agency to look for the Court (Judge Bristol) that was expected from Mesilla, as it is believed on good authority, for killing the judge and district attorney. They had made their threats that no court should be held in Lincoln county, and when it was held it was with a guard of soldiers to protect the court and officers.

"We are also informed that the Grand Jury was terrorized and frightened into doing just as these outlaws dictated. That they were told that one hundred men were in arms in the mountains and would deal out vengeance upon those who did not obey their dictates. In this way the court was practically a farce. Only three of the men who murdered Brady and Hindman were indicted, and they were going to leave the country, although the others were well known. Five men swore to Wilderman's being present with the assassins at the time, and before the shooting with a Winchester rifle. He himself admitted being there but he says he went out to feed his dog. Yet he was not indicted. Not one of the eleven men who killed Baker, Morton and McCloskey were indicted. One of the fourteen who killed Roberts was indicted, although it was well known that several of them fired at him and that they tried to have the owner of the house into which he ran after being shot to bring him out of doors so that they could kill him and threatened that if he did not do so, they would burn the house to the ground. The Grand Jury in their report say that McSween is a much abused man, notwithstanding the fact that he holds on to every dollar that he has ever collected for the Fritz estate, except the $300 above referred to.

"Dolan (Murphy was in the hospital in Santa Fe) was indicted for killing Tunstall when he was thirty miles away at the time, and had eight men with him as proven. Everything goes to show the existence of terror, and the determination to override the law by McSween and his friends. It is openly stated by them that neither Dolan, Riley or Murphy can live in that country.

"All was quiet during Court, but it was the quiet that precedes the storm. Several bodies of armed men were at last accounts said to be seen in the woods looking for each other with the avowed purpose of killing on sight. Other parties are trying to prevent this and to have the parties disband and go home . . ." (Ibid)

"On Monday, April 1 (1878), at Lincoln, Sheriff Brady, while walking toward the courthouse in the plaza, was fired upon by a party of men posted in the McSween house and instantly killed. George Hindman was shot and killed at the same time.

"When Brady fell he dropped his rifle; Antrim (this is the first reference made to Billy the Kid in print), who it appears was one of the attacking party, ran out to secure it. He was fired upon by Matthews and wounded. McSween, Robert Wildman and W. P. Shields were subsequently arrested and taken to Fort Stanton where they were held as prisoners." (Ibid. April 13, 1878)

"On Thursday, April 14, a party of fourteen Regulars under the command of Richard Brewer rode up to the Indian Agency at Blazer's Mill, dismounted and asked for food. Major Godfroy, the Agent, told them they might have dinner which they partook of, leaving two or three of their party outside. While they were still inside a man named Roberts, whom they were in search of, rode up. He was evidently unaware that the party were inside. On enquiring (of one of the men who happened to be sitting outside) if the posse had been there he immediately discovered that he had committed a fatal mistake and indicated a disposition to sell his life as dearly as possible. Frank Coe came out and sat down by Roberts, outside of the house, and engaged him in conversation.

"In the meantime the balance of the party scattered out and disposed themselves so as to obtain a cross fire on Roberts. Suddenly, Coe sprang to one side, leaving Roberts standing alone, and firing commenced.

"It is not positively known who fired the first shot. Roberts was shot in the side, the ball traveling through the bowels, inflicting a fatal wound. He, however, shot one of the attacking party named Middleton, through the lungs. George was shot through the head and Bowdre slightly wounded.

"Roberts then took shelter in Dr. Blazer's room, barricaded the doors with mattresses, etc., and made a desperate fight, not for his life, for he was already a dead man to all intents and purposes.

"Brewer, who was very much enraged, ordered Dr. Blazer and Major Godfroy to turn Roberts out. This they refused to do. Brewer then threatened to burn the house unless the wounded man was turned over to him. Mrs. Blazer pleaded with Brewer for the life of Roberts who was a stranger to her, but to no avail. Finding that the inmates of the house could not be persuaded or intimidated into turning Roberts out, Brewer proceeded to the sawmill about one hundred and twenty-five yards from the door of the room in which Roberts had taken shelter, getting behind a saw-log and glancing over it at the door. Roberts caught a glimpse of the top of Brewer's head and fired, the ball entering Brewer's eye and killing him instantly.

"The band left shortly afterwards, taking with them Middleton who was perhaps fatally wounded, and leaving Brewer's body which was buried by Dr. Blazer and Major Godfroy the next day. Roberts died on the following day." (Ibid—April 14-15)

"Dick Brewer and twelve men called themselves The Regulars and swore to protect McSween and property." (Ibid Aug. 10, 1878)

Shot by a dying man. That was how Dick Brewer passed out of the picture and made way for Billy the Kid. No marker was placed over his grave. Next to him lies Roberts an unknown. All because of an insurance policy.

Brewer was gunning for Roberts and Roberts knew it. Roberts was not the innocent by-stander that many authors would have us believe. He had come into the country to ranch and needed money. Large rewards were posted for Brewer and his men. Roberts spread it over the area that he was out for that money. Despite his crippled condition he was a dead shot. He had nothing to lose, everything to gain. When Brewer heard of Roberts' intentions he decided to add his name to the list of his victims. So they lie side by side waiting for Gabriel's horn.

Following the death of Major Brady (Civil War rank) lawyer Thomas Catron called together a meeting of the Masonic Lodge as Brother Brady was a member of that organization. He gave the eulogy and explained to the assembled Brothers how the sheriff met his tragic end and pleaded that something be done to pour oil over the troubled waters at Lincoln. Copeland was appointed sheriff in his place. He made his home at the McSween residence. For shameful neglect of duty as well as for failure to give bond as Collector of Taxes, Governor Axtell removed him and appointed George W. Peppin as sheriff.

Major Murphy died at Santa Fe at St. Vincent's Hospital established by the Sisters of Charity. Sunday, October 29, 1878, he gave up the battle against cancer. "Billious fevers," said Dr. Longwell. He had been bedridden for three months. Like Brady, he had been a member of the Masonic Fraternity and was buried with honors by the Lodge. Major Laurence Gustave Murphy was forty-seven years of age at the time of his death. He was born in Wexford county, in the south of Ireland. He studied for the priesthood at Maynooth College in his native country but at the approach of Minor Orders realized he had no vocation. Rather than face his parents who evidently really had the vocation, he made his way to the United States, drifting to Independence, Mo., where he obtained a job as a teamster on the Santa Fe Trail. He settled for a time at Fort Union in the employ of W. C. Moore, who ran the sutler's store at the post. When the Civil War broke out he was one of the first to enlist in the New

Mexico Volunteers (July 17, 1861). He was sworn in as First Lieutenant, Regimental Quartermasters, First New Mexico Volunteers. He joined his regiment at Fort Union and was assigned his duties by Col. St. Vrain, Mountain Man and trapper of note. Murphy had served some years in the regular army as sergeant-major of the regiment. Upon the re-organization of the New Mexico Volunteers he mustered out of the army in 1862 but was soon recommissioned a First Lieutenant and in 1863 was made a captain. He was brevetted a major for gallant service in the line of duty. In 1866 his regiment disbanded and he received an honorable discharge at Fort Stanton. He then established himself as a sutler at that post and later on at Lincoln. Acquainted with Fritz through the army, they decided on many business ventures together. Perhaps there would have been no Lincoln County War if he had not been involved with Fritz. Quien sabe? McSween and Tunstall stood in his way as competitors. McSween became his enemy as a result of a cattle rustling charge brought by Chisum. It is possible that McSween refused to pay the Fritz estate because he knew his one-time friend was involved and he wanted Murphy to stew awhile, without foreseeing the consequences.

Brewer, the first leader of the desperadoes in the Lincoln County War, would have stopped a bullet in any case, whether at Dodge, Abelene, Caldwell, Deadwood, Tombstone. He was a roving spirit kept alive by the smell of gunsmoke. It also choked him. From the time of his first killing he was riding for a fall. He died with his boots on. Clay Allison would have enjoyed that. He was the type of man who would have left the employ of Tunstall & McSween if it had not offered the excitement of a battle or two.

William Bonney (Antrim), whose youthful appearance won him his nickname, The Kid.

William Antrim, stepfather of The Kid. He fiddled his way through life but never into the Kid's heart.

Courtesy Philip J. Rasch

BOOK FOUR

A MIDNIGHT SNACK AND DEATH

(Billy the Kid)

The old man walked up the ancient street, kicking up dirt as he dragged his feet. His eyes were pinned to the road. He reminded me of a hawk ready to swoop. He was in the hopes of picking up a stray two-bits that might have fallen out of the pockets of a drunk as he staggered home last Saturday night. The old man was lucky that way. It meant a bottle of beer if his search proved successful. Here in this adobe village twelve miles from anything that looked like pavement he gave ninety-four years of his life very much in the same pattern in his old age as in his youth. It was a small village of four hundred souls, ancient when General Kearny's men marched through it in the year of Manifest Destiny to surplant the Mexican flag with the American. Here without electric lights, running water, bath rooms, the people dreamed their dreams and had their visions.

Old Francisco saw many things, lived many tales, watched many changes surround his village without ever entering. Here he found life. Up the village's only street in the campo santo he would one day rest his weary bones. Coming to the corner of the plaza, hands behind his back, fly open, nose running, he stopped at my door. Without knocking he walked in, placed his skinny old rump on a stump, for chairs were a luxury in that old village hidden away in the Sangre de Cristo foothills, that never severed its links with the past, and gave out a rumbling noise to attract my attention. He sat with an air of importance as if he had a secret he wished to share with me. He pulled out a dirty old rag that had once been a part of a shirt, wiped his watery eyes, ran the cloth along his handlebar mustache, put the rag back in hiding but said nothing. Come Wednesday of every week the same ceremony took place. The old man would regale me with legends of the village and glimpses into his past. This day there was a strange excitement about him, an eagerness I never saw before. I continued on with my work as if no one were in the room. Twenty minutes of silence. Suddenly he opened his mouth and said:

"Bille Keed."

I looked up.

"Quien?" I asked.

"Usted sabes. Usted escribe mucho y leye mucho. Bille Keed. Todos saben del Bille Keed."

"Si, Poncho. I write a lot and read a good deal but it's not all Billy the Kid. And it is true that everybody knows about Billy the Kid."

"But not what I know."

"And what would an old man hidden away from civilization know?"

"Mucho, mi amigo, mucho."

"Are you sure it's not some village gossip?"

"Bille was my amigo."

This was not impossible. Pancho (as he preferred to be called, a nickname for Francisco) was twenty-five when Garrett killed the Kid. I leaned back against the gypsum wall, put down my pencil and asked the old man to tell me about the "Keed" as he knew him. He reached into his shirt which was clean that day out of respect for the padre, and pulled out a photograph about five inches long and three inches wide. He walked over to the desk and placed it in front of me. Near the bottom of the photo I read: William Antrim. Age 16. Las Vegas (Old Town), 1875. It showed the complete left side of the face and part of the right of a round-faced cherub. Whiskerless, blonde, pink complexioned, healthy looking, two front teeth slightly protruding that quickly put me in mind of a gopher, the face was otherwise handsome if not slightly feminine looking. It was authentic. The old man had cherished that picture as a patron saint.

"Pancho, where in the world did you get this?"

He was pleased at my reaction. There was laughter in his eyes.

"This Keed herself gave me." Spanish-Americans in the hill country always say him for her and visa versa. I have as yet been unable to find the explanation for this. "I carried letters sometime for Jacobo (Jim Greathouse) to Keed hiding in bosque down the river. (The village was along the Pecos) San Miguel, Anton Chico, La Questa (present Villanueva) I know where Keed is always. This Keed herself she gave me."

"It has value."

"Si, amigo, it has value."

"What do you plan to do with it?"

"It is not mine any more. The padre at Ojo Caliente. I promised it to her. I keep promise. You give it. You write. You give it."

And so I did. Why I never took it to a photographer for a re-production to add to my own collection I shall never know. When I did ask for a loan of the picture for that purpose it was already in Indianapolis and there I lost trace of it. The old man told me tales of his experiences with the "Keed," some of which I incorporate here for he was one of the many who believed that the outlaw was a Robin Hood and loved the natives of New Mexico.

Brooklyn is given as the place of birth of the Southwest's most notorious outlaw. The date of birth is supposed to be November 23, 1859. Some authors base this on an announcement said to have appeared in a New York paper. Brooklyn was a separate city at the time. Why it should appear in a New York paper and not a Brooklyn paper is a mystery. One possible explanation is that possibly the mother was better known in New York, where her parents settled when they came from Ireland. William H. Bonney, the father of the child, seems to have been an actor with roving tendencies, for he left his wife Kathleen, with two children—William H., Jr., and Edward, two years younger—when the older child was about five years of age. The mother never referred to the father before strangers nor did the children. It seemed to be a case of abandonment although some authors say he died. Of what, when or where no one bothers to say. When asked about her first husband one time in New Mexico, Kathleen changed the subject and made no further reference to him except to give the impression that he was a "stinker." Edward also disappears from the scene at Santa Fe. Did he live? Or is he the man from El Paso who in recent years before his death claimed to be Billy the Kid? If the Kid did not become what he did no one would have bothered about all this. Some maintain that the family was a complete unit when the Bonneys moved to Coffeyville, Kansas, where William senior hoped to escape the poverty that dogged him possibly because of his illness. T. B. seems to have been his ailment which he sought to cure by excessive drink. No doubt the young widow (or abandoned wife) took the two bags of bones she called her children, to Colorado because she heard that high altitudes helped such affliction as well as that fact that she could make out very well in the mining camps in her line of work as a cook, waitress and general helper in a boarding house. It was while she was manager of a boarding house in Colorado that a prospector named William Antrim courted her and won her hand in marriage. Due to her strict bringing-up and early training, she would not have re-married had her first husband been alive so it must be presumed that he was dead.

It has been said that William Antrim did not love his step-children. This is not true. When Billy the Kid was killed by Sheriff Pat Garrett, many people in the vicinity of Fort Sumner were of the opinion that he would go gunning for the lanky marshall and avenge the death of his stepson. There were even bets that when the two met a gun battle would ensue. It chanced that when they did meet the results was a friendship until Garrett's violent death but not at the hands of the prospector. Antrim was not a go-getter. This marriage did nothing to increase the family fortunes of the Bonneys but did a great deal in making them quasi-qypsies.

Unlucky in Colorado the Antrims followed the pot of

gold at the end of the rainbow into New Mexico. Gold had been discovered on Willow Creek on the Maxwell Land Grant. Antrim prospected in Baldy; the Mrs. opened a boarding house. No luck. Boarding house closed. Family moved to Elizabethtown. Antrim prospected; the Mrs. opened a boarding house; no luck. Boarding house closed. Family moved to Santa Fe where the Mrs. opened a boarding house while Antrim worked as a teamster along the Santa Fe Trail.

In Santa Fe William, or Billy, as he is called, learned to speak Spanish like a native. Left to himself more often as not he and his younger brother roamed about the plaza of the historic old city, Fort Marcy, the governor's palace, gambling dens, cantinas. It has been said that his mother cooked at the old Exchange where the La Fonda now stands. She sent Billy to the San Miguel school where the Christian Brothers taught him to read and write. He preferred to meander about the town. His hand writing was not very neat. It shows the hand of one who labors at it rather than familiarity with a pen. Besides, the family was on the move again.

Antrim decided to try his luck in southwestern New Mexico at a place once known as San Vicente but now called Silver City. Here he hoped to strike it rich. Again a boarding house was opened as the prospector dug around the country side for rich minerals that seemed to be there. But not for him. No further mention is made of Edward. Whether he died at this time or because no one was interested in him because he lived the life of a respectable citizen is hard to say. Old man Antrim never made reference to him.

There is a story that has made the rounds that when Billy was twelve years old his mother took him shopping. Passing a blacksmith shop, the smithy said something that Billy from his rounds to cantinas and gambling houses, knew to be very uncomplimentary to say the least. He was quick tempered. This his step-father vouched for. He bent down, picked up a stone and hurled it at the blacksmith. He missed. He made a better member of a gun club than a ball team. The Smithy rushed out to chastise Billy but was prevented by Harvey Moulton, a prospector who was witness to the action. This

Moulton later showed up in the railroad town of Raton. We shall meet him again in the Gus Mentzer story.

Several weeks after this Moulton had cause to defend himself in a tavern brawl, not an uncommon thing in a mining town, Billy happened to be in the cantina at the time and remembered how Moulton befriended him. The affair was rather one-sided; Three against Moulton. Billy pulled out a knife and stabbed one of the attackers who very conveniently, according to tradition, happened to be the smithy who insulted his mother. How touching. As the victim was a man of ill repute nothing was done by the vigilantes, the law nor the citizens. Nobody seemed concerned that a twelve year old boy would stab someone to death and not be questioned by the authorities. After this Billy is supposed to have run away. But he did see his mother time and again and walked the streets of Silver City openly. This killing is unknown to the public until Garrett's life of the Kid appeared in 1882, about a year after the outlaw's death. This would place it in the year 1863. Garrett was no where near New Mexico that year and for several years to come.

Be that as it may, Mrs. Antrim again folds up her apron, closes her boarding house and comes to the village fast growing about old Fort Barclay near Fort Union. This was on the site of present day Watrous. There was plenty of activity here because Fort Union was the largest military post, the supply depot of a number of posts in the Southwest, and a melting pot. Close by also was Tiptonville, Loma Parda, Las Vegas, Cimarron, Rayado and Mora. It was a crossroads and a likely place for a woman interested in making a living especially if she were married to a not too dependent bread winner. Here she ran an eating place and boarding house. Here rustlers were busily engaged in robbing stock from Fort Union. If at any time in his life Billy Antrim was exposed to the rustling business it must have been during these days near Fort Union. It has been said that Billy spent some time in the jail at the garrison but this has never been definitely proven.

His roving nature soon cut him away from his mother's apron strings, and if there were any other insults thrown at her he was never around to avenge them. Cowboy life appealed to him. No doubt he began as a cook's helper and by the time he was sixteen was an experienced wrangler. He knew how to shoot, ride, rope, brand and gamble. He did not plan his way into things nor out of them. He took them as they came. Most of his spare time was spent at the faro table. This love of the gaming table made a rustler of him. He cowboyed near Tucson, Benson, Nogoles and the Gila country. Always on the go; always that nervous restlessness for new places, new exploits. He was a neat dresser and clean about his person. He loved guns and practised for hours the use of them.

When Billy and a friend ambushed three Indians near Fort Bowie in the Arizona Territory, it was not because he believed that there was no Indian like a dead Indian as many a frontiersman said, but because he was broke and they had pelts, ponies, blankets and guns. The sale of these articles across the border made it possible for the youth to return to Tucson and monte. At this town a card game ended in the death of a player who called Billy a cheat. It is said that Billy killed a Negro soldier at Fort Union shortly afterwards but there is nothing in the government records to substantiate this. If he killed a soldier it must have been outside the garrison as he would hardly have escaped trial for a killing in a government post. Billy was supposed to have said that he killed twenty-one men—one for each year of his life. And everybody is intent on placing those twenty-one men not to make a liar out of him. They would rather have him a killer. As Billy was in Mexico shortly after this supposed killing, no doubt he may have killed someone and escaped across the border. If this someone were a soldier it may have been one from Fort Cummings or a fort close to the border rather than Fort Union.

In Sonora Billy cultivated the friendship of Melquiades Segura, the pair often placing the town in a state of excitement with their pranks and escapades. They opened a monte den in Agua Prieta and before long Billy had difficulty with a fellow about his own age by the name of Jose M. Martinez who was a little too concerned with the way Billy dealt cards. Billy up and killed him. Next he rode to Chihuahua. There he and Segura had no difficulty robbing at will. Here he marked up another killing to his credit and found himself one jump ahead of the law as he pulled rein in El Paso where he stayed long enough to replenish his purse before going up to Mesilla. There he dropped Segura to take up with Jesse Evans, the first desperado we have any definite knowledge of Billy's associating with. Little is known of their life together except that it was not on the side of law and order. Cattle rustling was their major occupation. One time they saved an immigrant train from Apache attack. Billy killed several Indians which no doubt he counted among his twenty-one.

Evans and Antrim were joined by Billy Morton, Frank Baker, McCloskey and Jim McDaniels. It was McDaniels who referred to him constantly as "The Kid" not because he was childish in any way but because in contrast to the others his features were rather delicate and boyish. For as many hours he spent in the sun his features never became leathery nor weather beaten but roseate. McCloskey, Morton and Baker went up the Pecos valley to work for Chisum and later for Murphy, Fritz, Dolan and Riley.

While still engaged in the seemy trade of appropriating stock, word came to Billy that Segura was under arrest at the village of San Elizario near the placita of El Paso, Texas. He rode from Mesilla with McDaniels and Evans released his one time pal in a jail break that was as thrilling as it was daring. Segura hurried over the border and out of the life of Billy the Kid. This brings to light one of his redeeming characteristics. His sense of loyalty to a friend and to a cause even if that cause be wrong if he reasoned that he should abide by it he stuck it out to the end. This he proved in his loyalty to Brewer, McSween and Tunstall when the Lincoln County War brought him into prominence as a desperado.

One day when Billy and a companion by the name of Tom O'Keefe were riding the range they were beset by a number of Apaches. After Billy killed five of them they called off the attack agreeing that the marksmanship of the young fellow made his capture rather hazardous and hardly worth the loss of so many warriors. They spread his fame among the tribe and hereafter were cautious about attacking any band he traveled with. After this Antrim made his way to Cow ranch on the Rio Ruidoso where he stayed that winter and in the spring went up to Chisum's where he worked a while before being hired by Dick Brewer to work for Tunstall. Here he became acquainted with Tom O'Folliard whom he considered his buddy and Charles Bowdre who had his own little adobe shack to which he brought his Spanish-American bride from Anton Chico. Charlie was quite attached to her as she was to him and she never forgave Garrett his death. The sheriff often felt that if she were ever given the opportunity she would put a bullet through him for the loss of her husband.

Governor Axtell removed Copeland from office and placed George W. Peppin in his stead. President Hayes removed Axtell from office and replaced him with a military man, Lew Wallace, who had been a general during the Civil War. Although he had now become an author of note, it was his job to break up cattle rustling and promiscuous killing in New Mexico. Some authors believe that the President had in mind the Lincoln County War but actually he was fed up by the entire state of affairs in New Mexico. Rustlers, bandits, killers, gamblers, land sharks were out on a merry holiday. Wells Fargo, Santa Fe Trail trains, Cattle Trailers—nobody and nothing was safe. It was bad enough chasing Cochise, Victorio, Coloradas Mangas, Nana and Colorow all over the Territory but these desperadoes were fast becoming a major problem. Coe, Crockett, Allison, Baker, Brewer, Griego, Montoya, and a band of cutthroats near Algodones, to say nothing of Lincoln and Dona Ana counties. It was a sorry state of affairs indeed. The President wanted it stopped. And if Wallace couldn't do it he would put in a man who could. Specific orders for Lincoln County were to come out of Washington later.

Now that Brewer was dead, Billy the Kid was looked upon as the logical candidate to succeed him. Sheriff Peppin decided to bring him to justice. Antrim was fighting the Lincoln County War now not so much out of sympathy for McSween as out of loyalty for Tunstall, his employer, whose tragic end was brought about by former friends of his. He could not quite fathom that these men whom he knew to be rustlers were now acting as deputies. It was as if worlds crumbled around him. If these were the type of men Murphy hired, then there must be something wrong about Murphy's cause even if his own was not entirely right and just. He was riding one day, shortly after the events related in the last chapter, on his way to the Fritz ranch. With him were Frank McNab, Frank Coe and Jim Saunders. He stopped at the spring close by for water. The sheriff's posse happened to be at the Fritz ranch on this particular day and it was quite interested in McNab who was wanted for participation in the death of Brady, McCloskey, Morton and Baker. Antrim had not as yet come into his own.

The war entered its second phase. The sheriff saw the men at the watering place and opened fire. In this battle Saunders was wounded and Coe taken prisoner. McNab was killed. Another fight took place at the Ellis home near the far end of Lincoln town. Shots were exchanged on both sides but nobody was hurt.

The major battle of the Lincoln County affair took place in July. A lucky July for the Kid. He was to have one brief year of blood and thunder. Next July he would be dead. Dolan's men were at the store and hotel at the west end of town as you entered it from the foothills that now make up Lincoln National Forest. Almost directly facing, on the opposite side of the street, was the Tunstall & McSween store. Along the hills that stretched beyond like an over-sized prairie dog village, stalked the Dolan and Riley partisans. Bodies pressed close against the flat top adobe roofs stretched the proned bodies of the hired hands. Some McSween partisans captained by Martiniano Chavez awaited expectantly at the east end of the village which guarded the approach from Fort Stanton. They took up their battle stations in the homes of El Señor Don Montaño and El Señor Don Patron. Watching from the lawyer's store were Charlie Bowdre, George Coe (cousin to Frank Coe) and Henry Brown. Across the street in the McSween residence were Billy Antrim, Tom O'Folliard, Jim

French, Doc Skurlock, Harvey Morris, Francisco Zamora, Ignacio Gonzolez, Vicente Romero, Jose M. Chavez y Chavez, Eugenio Salazar, Mrs. McSween, Mrs. Elizabeth Shield, her sister, and Mrs. Ealy, wife of the minister Rev. Ealy who left his Presbyterian congregation in Atchison at the instigation of McSween who felt the need of a minister of his denomination in Lincoln as there were a number of others of that faith besides McSween in town. In addition to this there was the spiritual care of the soldiers at Fort Stanton considered members of his congregation. As there was no church of the donomination in Lincoln, services were conducted every Sunday in the Tunstall & McSween store.

Sheriff Peppin fired the first shot. The McSween household had just settled down to breakfast. At the first shot all ducked under the table hunger forgotten. In a moment the battle was on. All day long the siege continued. From the Patròn house. With Crawford was Lucio Montoya who was also shot by Herrera but not killed. On the third day of the fighting Mrs. Juanita Mills walked the whole distance to Fort Stanton for Col. Dudley's soldiers. Two squadrons of troops and a train of four-mule wagons rushed to the scene of the fight. The contingent took along two gatling guns. Evidently Governor Wallace's orders were determined. The colonel himself led his men. If the president wanted desperadoes wiped out he would do it for glory if not for promotion. He halted at the McSween home for a parley. All this was observed by Dolan who selected Andy Boyle, Jake Pearce and Charlie Hall to follow him behind the adobe homes to the McSween yard while his enemies were occupied with Colonel Dudley. They took advantage of the opportunity to start a fire. And what a fire that was!

Various interpretations have been given regarding the conversation conducted at the front door between McSween and Dudley. The majority of authors are agreed that the commander placed the responsibility for the whole affair on the shoulders of McSween. He had known Murphy, Brady, Dolan and Riley for a long time. Coal oil helped the fire spread.

"Smoke them out," yelled Dolan. "Then pepper them with lead as they come out."

It was useless to fight the flames. Mrs. McSween watched the fire lap up her home. Her piano. So much effort it cost to bring it over the Santa Fe Trail to this! She asked the men to move it into the next room in the hopes that the fire would burn itself out before touching it. She sat down. Softly her fingers fondled the keys. Suddenly the opening bars of Home Sweet Home harmonized with the cracking flames. Over and above this she sang the words—the swan song for the home, the piano but not her courage. Tears, as hot as the fire coursed down her cheeks, but were not plentiful enough to quench the roaring holocaust. She was clothed in the tragedy that engulfed her. To come from Kansas for this! To establish a law practise for this! To have built an empire out of dreams only to have it evaporate in smoke! She arose from the piano and without a word from her lips, opened the door and went out to face the bullets.

Silence.

This was not a war against women. She walked to where the colonel had pitched his tent. Her faithful Colored servant went with her. She begged the officer to call off his men as well as Dolan's. The sheriff, he told her, was only performing his duty. Dolan was not the transgressor. He was ordered to break up lawlessness. She walked back. The colonel sent for Martiniano Chavez and induced him to call off his men as this was not his fight. To continue would be to classify him as an outlaw. The men left town. He told Patròn and Montaño that he would train his gatlings on their homes if they persisted in aiding McSween. Again Mrs. McSween sought the colonel's aid. When he had her bodily forced out of his tent she yelled that she would leave no stone unturned to bring the colonel to justice.

Of the many rooms in her home three now remained untouched by the hungry flames. Again she sat down to the piano and the Star Spangled Banner was the last music to issue from the McSween home. The other two women were sent to neighbors for safety. At the urgent request of her husband

Mrs. McSween went to join them. The sheriff and his men waited patiently. The fire reached the last room of the house. He was safely hidden by the blanket of darkness that made the night. Anyone coming from the McSween house would be exposed to the light of the fire. It was death in either case —the choice of a bullet or consummation by flames. Lead or cremation. McSween was the first to attempt a break. Bible in hand he struck for the open only to be cut down by the sheriff's men. Tom O'Folliard tried it next. That night at least his life was charmed. Not a bullet hit him. Next in order came James French, Doc Skurlock, Jose M. Chavez y Chavez, Ignacio Gonzolez, Eugenio Salazar, Billy Antrim.

From the store across the street emerged Charlie Bowdre, George Coe and Henry Brown. Salazar and Gonzolez were wounded. The others lived to fight some more. McSween and four others who fell with him became burnt offerings at the altar of loyalty or stubbornness, depending on how you look at it. Of the Dolan faction those shot in the cross-fire of escape were Bob Beckworth (killed), John McKinney (wounded) and Dan Pearce (wounded). Mrs. McSween, as promised, filed suit against Colonel Dudley. Her witness was the faithful servant.

"The case of General (he was promoted since the conflagration) Dudley indicted for the burning of the McSween house in Lincoln, is set by the court for today (at Mesilla). The general had been compelled to undertake a journey of over eight hundred miles to meet the charges against him, and on his arrival here with his witnesses there are none to appear against him. Mrs. McSween, the leading witness for the prosecution, cooly informs the Court that she employed counsel to prospecute the case and on account of failure of that counsel to appear in Lincoln and escort her here, she had been unable to attend. General Dudley is thus put out on an expense of over fifty dollars a day upon a most grave charge and is entirely without redress. Judge Bristol has stated that the case must be disposed of at this present term of court and unless witnesses for the prosecution appear it will be doubtlessly dismissed." (Santa Fe New Mexican Dec. 6, 1879)

U. S. District Attorney Barnes was ordered by Attorney General Devers to defend General Dudley, assisted by Judge Newcomb. The jury deliberated two minutes and returned the verdict "not guilty." Mrs. McSween never went to see her husband's charred body, nor did she attend his funeral. Beckworth was buried with honors at the Fort Stanton cemetery. Mrs. McSween later re-married and lived happily for many years at White Oaks as one of the great cattle women of New Mexico. A reference to William Antrim as the Kid appeared in print was a restraining order posted at Fort Stanton by command of General Dudley as we gather from the Santa Fe New Mexican for January 4, 1879:

General Dudley has issued a general order establishing a kind of non-intercourse wall between the soldiers of the garrison and the outside world, especially Lincoln, under certain restrictions but positively prohibiting The Kid, Scurlock, H. B. Chapman, Jim French, the Coe Brothers, ex-sheriff Copeland, and other notorious characters, including all parties who are recognized as the murderers of Roberts, Brady, Tunstall and Beckworth. This is owing to the return within the last month to the county of Lincoln of many of the notorious murderers, horse thieves, cattle thieves, escaped convicts and desperadoes who have figures prominently in the late anarchy, lawlessness and crime of that county."

The Kid, as he was now called, Charlie Bowdre, Tom O'Folliard, Jim French, John Middleton, Henry Brown, Fred Wayte and Doc Skurlock banded together as rustlers and outlaws preying mostly on Dolan and Riley stock. Governor Wallace arranged a meeting with Antrim in the hopes of converting him into a law-abiding citizen. He was more successful with his book: *Ben Hur*.

On August 5, 1879, the Kid killed Indian Agency Clerk Joe Bernstein, of the Apache Mescalero Reservation simply because he prevented him from taking some horses. George Chapman, a Las Vegas attorney, in Lincoln on same business with Mrs. McSween, was killed by a Dolan partisan by the name of Campbell as he was walking to visit his client in her new quarters. For this deed he was jailed at Fort Stanton but contrived his escape and was never seen in Lincoln again. The Kid continued the profitable business of rustling. Legends now began to take shape concerning him. Tascosa, Mesilla, Dona Ana, Fort Sumner, Trinidad, Las Vegas, Anton-Chico, Denver, Lincoln deeds of the young outlaw were making the rounds, some true more false, but good stories nevertheless.

As new members of the gang rode Dave Rudabaugh, Billy Wilson, Tom Pickett and for a short time Webb. Old-timers who knew Billy the Kid have stated that the only man he was ever afraid of was Dave Rudabaugh. The Kid came to know Lucien B. Maxwell at Silver City. When that place became a mining center in 1870, his mother operated a boarding house there which Maxwell, one of the founders of Silver City, frequented. The owner of the tremendous Grant had sampled her cooking at Elizabethown and later on at the place near Fort Barclay. Pete his son and Billy became quite friendly and when the Maxwells moved to the vacated military post of Fort Sumner, the friendship endured following the death of Lucien in 1875. Billy was as much at home with Pete as he was with O'Folliard, Bowdre and French. It is possible that he assisted at the elder Maxwell's funeral although I have found no verification of this. Billy was never interested in Pablita Maxwell other than counting her among his friends. Romance did not enter the picture.

Pat Garrett worked at Pete Maxwell's as a cow poke when the Kid first met him Billy was nineteen at the time; Garrett not quite twenty-eight Most of the horses Billy appropriated came from the Karl Fritz ranch. Karl had settled at Bonito Canyon following the death of his wife in childbirth and now took to wife Dolan's daughter. Brown, Middleton and Wayte drifted to other fields Brown eventually had himself hung in Kansas for bank robbery. Garrett did not seek the sheriff's office simply because he wished to track down The Kid. He had a record in Kansas as an outlaw but decided that he would be better off as a law abiding citizen.

A sheriff's office in those days was a lucrative position. While frought with danger, it had its financial compensations, especially if a good deal of reward money were posted by railroads and express companies for some outlaw wanted dead or alive. In addition to this he collected various taxes, fines and other public monies, out of which he received his commission. The office was not too well sought after because many preferred less money and a longer life. Everybody wore guns in that eventful era and any time the sheriff showed his face on the street might mean his death. There have been instances when marshalls lasted but a day. Garrett was young. He had come to the area seeking employment. At Anton-Chico he met a beautiful Spanish-American who consented to be his wife only to lose her and his child in her effort to bring him into the world. He married a second time, a girl whose father worked for Pete Maxwell at Fort Sumner. A sheriff fast on the draw and ability as a detective could retire from the job, if he lasted that long, fairly well off. Several died wealthy ranchers and bankers. To run for sheriff would stabilize Garrett and change him from a vacillating cowboy to a man of position commanding respect. His friendship for the Kid as a man never diminished; his duty as an officer became even the more urgent with the shooting of Deputy Jim Carlyle by the Kid at the Jim Greathouse ranch (related in detail in the chapter on Jim Greathouse).

Garrett's hunt for the desperado led to the death of Tom O'Folliard and the capture of the Kid at Stinking Spring (which involved also the capture of Dave Rudabaugh and consequently related in that chapter). It was about this time that the Kid began using his name of William, whether out of deference for his step father who was also William Antrim, or because becoming of age he now had the right to his former name by some agreement with either his step-father or his mother has not been adequately explained. Suffice to say that now he becomes William Bonney, the Kid. When taken to Messila by Pat Garrett to stand trial before Judge Warren H. Bristol for the murder of Sheriff Brady, the name William H. Bonney appears on the records.

Why just Brady? Perhaps because he was better known as a citizen than most of Billy's victims. He certainly was known to Judge Bristol who was a member of the same Masonic Lodge with him, as were Tom Catron, Murphy, Dolan and several other prominent citizens of Santa Fe. Bristol was not one for forgetting the violent death of a fellow member of the Lodge. With the exception of Clark Bernstein, all of Billy's victims were drifters and cow-pokes unsteady in their occupation as in their aim. Brady was the most widely known of the lot. Bonney was never tried for the killing of Jim Carlyle any more than for the death of Roberts. The only charge of murder ever brought against him was for the death of Major Brady. Why he alone was singled out for the death of the sheriff has never been explained. Perhaps because Brewer was dead, many of the others gone, and someone had to be victimized.

Deputy Sheriff Robert Ollinger and Deputy Sheriff John W. Bell were selected as custodians of the Kid over and against the day he would be hung. Of all places to imprison him! The Dolan store used on occasion as the County Courthouse! There in a corner of the upper story of the large adobe building the Kid made his plans for escape. Ollinger had a past a bit on the shady side but like Garrett thought better of it and converted his ways. Bell had come to White Oaks in quest of gold. Ollinger was a poor choice. There was bad blood between him and Billy. Perhaps this was why he was selected. He took his job seriously and devoted much time to making the Kid as miserable as possible. At first Bell was rather resentful because of the death of his friend at the hands of the outlaw but in time this wore off and prisoner and guard became quite friendly. Ollinger taunted the outlaw in the hopes that he would do something drastic and have to be killed which of course would mean that much fame and glory would accrue to his slayer.

The Kid was kept in chains. Perhaps Dolan tired of all the bloodshed on the premises and turned the immense building over to the county for a courthouse and jail. Two-storied —unusual for adobe—it was by far the largest building in Lincoln. Upstairs, on the side facing the former McSween home, or the far end of the building, several cots were brought in to accomodate Billy and his guards. The west end of the building housed the arsenal used by the sheriff and his deputies.

This Billy knew. That room and its precious contents were as much on his mind as his lady love in Fort Sumner. She was sister to Pat Garrett's wife. The weeks drifted into months. The Kid never gave up hoping.

Opportunity knocked that day in April when Pat Garrett went over to White Oaks, some say for the purchase of the lumber to make the scaffold from which the Kid was to hang. Whatever the reason he was to be gone quite some time. Not that he had not been away before especially to track down an outlaw with a price on his head. Ollinger was dining at the Worthley Hotel across the street. Bonney and Bell settled down to a poker game to while away the time. Ollinger could have had his dinner downstairs where meals for the prisoners were prepared, but he enjoyed visiting with some pals across the way. A card flitted to the floor. Bell reached down to pick it up placing the butt of his six-shooter exactly where Bonney expected to be if a card dropped. Panic seized Bell. Bonney claimed later that he tried to keep Bell from running down that flight of stairs but the guard refused to listen. As he bolted for the door and down the stairs, just before he made the elbow turn, a bullet stopped him.

Bonney hobbled over for Ollinger's shotgun. The chains clanked with as much noise as a second apparition of Marley's Ghost to Scrooge. The Kid was on the porch outside the room, facing the hotel. As he had expected Ollinger ran out at the sound of the shot. Instead of jerking out his six-shooter, he made for the back entrance to the courthouse. He looked up and saw the Kid there on the veranda, shotgun in hand and calling out to him. Not another soul in Lincoln was on the street. By instinct they knew what that one shot was. A second shot was heard shortly afterwards. Ollinger never digested his dinner. Lincoln gave the Kid wide berth. He had time to hobble down the stairs and empty the second barrel of the shotgun into Ollinger. He then collared Goss, the jail cook, and told him to bring an axe to cut his leg chains. Billy Burt, the county clerk's horse was close by. Goss was dispatched to round him up. It took longer than it would have ordinarily and Goss was afraid that Bonney would shoot him for being so slow about it. But he succeeded in bringing the animal to the outlaw. He would not have minded one bit putting a bullet through the steed for of all days for the normally gentle animal to act unruly and spirited he selected this. The Kid rode out of Lincoln town unhindered.

However uncertain the number of men he killed, there was no doubt about the two he put away at this jail break. He knew now that he would be shot on sight but rather that than the march to the hangman's rope. I sometimes think that he was rather tired of life but did not want to commit suicide. He had all the opportunity in the world to flee to Mexico or parts unknown. But he chose to remain in the area where he was quite well known. This has been explained away by authors that a sweetheart in Fort Sumner kept him from leaving New Mexico. The sweetheart in Fort Sumner was not his first, nor did he expect it to be his last. He was not the marrying kind. He had a sweetheart in Las Vegas, Anton Chico, La Questa, Mesilla, Tucson, El Paso, San Miguel del Bado. In Mexico he did not bother to count them. He had a sailor's attitude of love them and leave them and was not particularly concerned about any one regular girl. First of all because his was a roving spirit. If he married anyone he knew that soon she would be a widow. Again, he preferred gambling and rustling to a settled down married life. Nor could he ever bring himself to trust any one woman enough to marry her. Billy spoke Spanish fluently. He had no difficulty with Spanish belles. No, it was not a girl that kept him at Fort Sumner. He knew that no matter where he ran to whether it be Colorado or Mexico he would depend on his gun and rustling to see him through and the end would be the same. He believed he was destined to stop a bullet. Had he stopped one anywhere but at Fort Sumner his fame would have been interred with his bones.

Then came the night of July 14, 1881. Of the three who went to Pete Maxwell's house, on a tip-off, to look for the Kid, only Garret knew him well; McKinney slightly; Poe not at all. Garrett was lying down in Maxwell's bed when the Kid entered, carving knife in hand to cut himself a chunk of meat for a midnight snack. He had seen McKinney and

Poe outside but passed them off as Pete's friends rather than deputies. He didn't bother to ask Pete's friends what they were doing outside his door at midnight. He saw nothing unusual in it. But he did see something unusual in the tall form prone on the bed. Garrett has heard the short brisk conversation between the two men outside and the Kid. They evidently mistook him for a sheepherder coming in to tell Pete some important news. Why he should do it with a knife in his hand did not strike them at the moment.

The Kid never dressed as a sheepherder nor did he look like one. He was neat about his appearance whenever in town for he gave himself over to dancing, gambling and women all of which a neat appearance would add to his advantage. They mistook him for a sheepherder because he had a shy, hesitant approach in coming up to the two men, which they mistook for the deference some sheepherders about gave Americans as they stood in awe of them, very much like a servant before his master. Actually Billy was just being cautious. He could not place McKinney in the dark. Poe he never met. He decided to go into Pete's bed room before cutting himself some beef hanging from a viga in the patio of the house and feel at ease in finding out for himself whether they were friends of Pete's or members of a posse. It just wouldn't do to shoot them then tell Pete that he thought they were the law. Pete was quite a stockman and ranchers came and went all hours of the day at his place. While the night was not particularly bright that night, yet enough light streamed in through the window for the Kid to be aware that there were two in Pete's bed. Pete was short and round. His stomach rounded off the blankets as if they covered a barrel. The other form was long, still and thin. He bent over this form to shake Pete and ask:

"Quien es?"

Pete's mother was a native of Taos. Her family was half French; half Spanish but she spoke only Spanish. Maxwell remarked more than once that his son was more of a native than a businessman. He preferred the Spanish-American way of life to all others. He spoke better Spanish than English. The Kid always spoke to him in Spanish. Seeing a second person in the room made Bonney forget the two men outside. Now he concentrated on the man in the room with Pete Maxwell. Again it was the question of whether he would be shooting a friend of Pete's if he shot first and asked questions afterwards. Garrett says he was sitting down when the outlaw came in the room. Garrett was tall enough to make a nice center on a modern college basketball team. He was six foot six inches. Sitting down, with boots on and a sombrero, with a faint glimmer of moonlight streaking in, the Kid would never have asked "Quien es?" It would have been Garrett's funeral. His size would have marked him. Garret had his hand on his gun under the pillow. If the Kid had not opened his mouth, nor sought the midnight snack, he might have lived to see another day.

Garrett fired twice. The first bullet got him. The second missed. One at close range was enough. He was dead before he hit the floor. It has been said that after that Pete became a drinking man. Did he feel guilty? Was he trying to forget the memory of that night when he heard the outlaw enter his room but could give him no que as to who the other man was? Did Garrett ever bother to thank him or share the reward money? Poor Pete. This was the price for trying to be friends with everybody.

The amazing thing about Billy the Kid is not his life as a desperado, for there were many far more vicious than he, but rather his life as a legend. Up to the time of the Lincoln County War he was known only to his partners in crime, a few Spanish-American families, and a few cowboys in Mesilla, Socorro, Seven Rivers, Anton Chico, Las Vegas and Fort Sumner. When he finally breaks into print he is known as William Antrim, then the Kid, then William Bonney. As far as being news when he is alive, his exploits are limited. Naturally, following his jail break from Lincoln posters splurge his name all over the Southwest. Following his death it is amazing the number of people that knew him. It is like reading the list of places advertising: Washington Slept Here, which of course if he did would place him in bed a sight more often than at the head of the Continental Army.

Mrs. William Kelihor over in Castro County, Texas, was

alone with her little children. She had been reading the horrors of the Lincoln County War. That evening a knock at the door startled her. She locked the children in the bedroom. With bravado that deceived no one she approached the door. A slim, dapper medium-sized fellow, well dressed, tipped his hat, smiled and asked for lodging for the night.

"Young man, if I put you up for the night there will be no shinnanagins."

"Yes, mam."

So he slept there. The next morning he ate breakfast and was ready to leave.

"You seem like a well-mannered young man. What is your name?"

"William Antrim, mam."

The woman fainted as the Kid made his exit.

Over at Cavallo near Las Cruces an old man sat looking into his beer.

"This is Billy the Kid country, isn't it?" I asked the bartender.

"Shore is. Shore is. That old gent over there. He knew the Kid."

"Well, what do you know!"

I walked over to the old man. He was ninety years old. A likeable old chap who drank beer like most people drink water on a summer's day.

"Yep. I knew the Kid. Attended his funeral. Worked at Fort Sumner at the time. They say one bullet stopped Billy. 'Twerent a hole I saw when I lifted his shirt to see the wound. Buckshot. Yes, sir. Buckshot. Garrett pumped him plumb full of buckshot. I know."

"Was it the Kid you saw?"

"Sure 'nough was. None other. Garrett got the kid. No doubt 'bout that. But with buckshot. Knew the Kid nigh on three years. Dead as a doornail. Never escaped to Mexico. Buckshot, I say, belly full of buckshot."

Old man Teats had the mail contract between Fort Bascom and Las Vegas. He took a trip to Tascosa, on the Canadian in the Texas Panhandle. There he met Dr. Hoyt, an old friend of his. As they were preparing to leave the town in rode a youth leading a fine Arabian horse.

"Beautiful horse," said the doctor.

"Sure is."

"I'd like to have him."

"He's for sale."

"What's his name?"

"Dandy Dick."

"Let me ride him a few days and I'll let you know what I decide. Can't see why a young fellow like you would want to get rid of such a beautiful horse."

"I have my reasons."

The doctor who was destined to be General McArthur's chief surgeon in the Philippines during the Spanish-American War, thought it over. He suspected that the steed was not really the property of Billy the Kid. He knew this young man. When the Kid was wounded as one of the Twelve Regulars under Brewer, Dick called in the doctor to dress the wound. Loyal to anyone who befriended him in any way, the Kid, who had actually come to Tascosa to sell the horse, in a sudden burst of generosity, offered it to the doctor. When the medical cowboy told him of his suspicions, the Kid wrote out a bill of sale still to be seen at the museum in Canyon, Texas. While the doctor made his rounds at Tascosa from the back of this Arabian, the people of Tascosa held him under suspicion for a long time even though they did not doubt that he came by the animal honestly.

Whose horse was it?

L. G. Murphy had presented it to Sheriff Brady when he took over that office. When Brady was killed, the Kid took the horse for two reasons: First in payment for the blood the Murphy faction caused him to spill, even though it was a light flesh wound in the leg. Secondly, the sheriff would have no further need for it.

It was at Black Springs Draw near the site of the present city of Portales that the Kid's gang usually butchered the cattle it rustled and sold through a third party to the commissary at Fort Stanton. Pat Garrett had often hoped to trap the out law here but failed miserably. When the Kid realized how intently the place was watched he moved his camp to other quarters.

While the majority of authors describe the Kid as fair-complexioned and blonde, Nath Horde, for many years wagon boss on the T. H. Ranch in Eastern New Mexico, said he met Billy often and described him as of slight build, dark complexion, with a small hatchet face. He had protruding teeth, which gave him the expression of always smiling, hence the tradition that the Kid always went into battle grinning. When the outlaw was on the "dodge" he often stopped to eat with wagon crews, according to Horde. He was generally liked, or disliked, not according to personality, but to the attitude toward his enemies. "I did not consider the Kid any worse than the people he fought. In fact, the best man in the Lincoln County War was the Englishman, Tunstall, the outlaw's friend and boss. The Kid was loyal to the end, and that is more than can be said for some of his enemies." Frank Collison, old-time buffalo hunter and cowboy living in El Paso who was at Tunstall's funeral, said that the Kid remarked over the grave: "You were the only man that treated me like I was free-born and white," and swore to avenge the death of his friend. It helps to prove that a persecution complex was a motivating force that spurred on many of the deeds of the desperado and kept him like a moth to a flame around an area where his presence would ultimately mean death. He wanted to die with his boots on and thought it a disgrace to dangle from a hangman's noose.

Of all the influences in the life of the desperado the one taken under least consideration is that of William Antrim, his step-father. He was not an educated man, nor a very well read man. He lived, ate and slept gold. He was forever looking for the pot at the other end of the rainbow. Short, spare-ribbed, a little stooped, he was originally from Missouri. He had his say-so in the Civil War, after which he concluded that farming was too much like work. He would rather look into the idea of prospecting. Colorado offered golden opportunities. Everyone else seemed to strike it rich save William Antrim.

He was of Irish descent, quite a wit and a dandy with the fiddle. Leadville, Golden, Georgetown, Cripple Creek, Aspen—wherever there was a gold rush. But he always ended up fiddling away for a living. There were other jobs such as hauling freight, shoeing horses, but he was a drifter at heart, and declined to stay put. In one of the mining towns he boarded at the home of a young widow, whose two little youngsters clung to her as if in fear of being lost. He liked her cooking, her looks, her cleanliness, her children. She liked his wit, his devotion, his Irish charm and his dreams. So they were married.

Antrim packed his newly acquired family, his mules, his buckboard and headed south for New Mexico, where newly opened mines would make them rich. How much Mrs. Antrim staked in the move she kept a secret. Bland, Baldy, Elizabethtown, Willow Creek, Fort Barclay, the Oscuras, Alma, Golden, Cerillos, Georgetown. Antrim found that the gold dust always eluded him. Fortunately he knew the blacksmith business and was able to keep his family from starving. The Mrs. helped with her boarding house routine. This sort of existence tired Mrs. Antrim and stormy scenes often resulted which probably accounts for the fact that Billy was never interested in marriage although he was interested in girls. No children came of this marriage. Billy grew up, if you could call it that, in a confused state of mind. It hurt him to see his mother suffering so, and he could not quite make out the shiftlessness and gaiety of his step-father. He usually weathered the storm by meandering about town, acquiring Spanish, slang, saucy speech and a view of the seemy side of life in taverns, dance halls and gambling dens. The Children's Aid Society was not around to place restrictions on the owners of such establishments.

There were whole days when he hung around the plaza in Santa Fe watching the Santa Fe Trail caravans as they rolled into the city with their goods from the East. Often he watched the French stone masons as they slowly piled stone on stone around the old Parroquia Church to place the foundation of the cathedral that would not be completed until some years after Billy lay in his grave. There was always something exciting going on in Santa Fe for the little urchin to occupy his time. His short experience with school was enough to make him shudder. As far as school was concerned he had claustrophobia. The short time he did spend there to learn the fundamentals was for his mother's sake. A truant officer would have washed his hands of him. Often the Sisters of Loretto at Our Lady of Light Academy took him in and fed him to put some flesh on his bones. He was always partial to Sisters. Later on Sister Blandina was to be aware of that when he was willing to spare the lives of some doctors for her sake. His short experience with the Christian Brothers taught him to respect things religious. He never in his brief career ever passed a derogatory remark against any man's religious beliefs. He may not have agreed with McSween about carrying a Bible into battle but he did not, as some authors would have us believe, ridicule him for it.

William Antrim was a human grasshopper. He lived for the present for the future would take care of itself. While he had no education himself he was interested in Billy's acquiring one, but the lad stubbornly resisted. He often took the boy with him to the smithy, on hunting trips and on freight rides. He taught his step-son what little he knew of shooting but it was enough to keep the lad occupied in constant practice. Billy had seen enough tavern brawls to know that a quick trigger finger was necessary as well as a quick draw if you were to get the drop on your enemy. Antrim spent as freely as he earned which meant that Mrs. Antrim had to keep her boarding house open if she and Billy were to survive. More and more he took to eating and sleeping at a friend's house. The marriage gave no promise of happiness for all concerned. He drank coffee by the pot full.

Mrs. Antrim spent much time at the parroquia. William Antrim said years later that his wife spent hours in church ever praying for her husband Bonney who was not around and who was never quite out of her thoughts. She was always telling the boys about "their father who did this—their father who did that" and he would storm out of the house to seek refuge in a glass of forgetfulness or consolation at playing the fiddle in some cantina, or home of a friend. To her Bonney was the model husband. Antrim was just a consort. He related that as a boy Billy was stubborn and if there was anything he wanted he would sulk, rage, sit down and kick the floor until his step-father promised to get it for him. He had a violent temper, which did not often show itself but when it did the little lad was a holy terror. Antrim seems to have been associated with no religious denomination.

At Alma he entered partnership with David Russell and ran a successful blacksmith shop, but Mrs. Antrim continued to run her boarding house just in case. Billy was a neat dresser whenever he had decent enough clothes to wear. Russell and Antrim played the fiddle at all social gatherings in Alma. It was at Alma that Billy played his first game of cards and liked it. He decided to become a professional gambler because they always wore good clothes and had plenty of spending money. Billy seems to have been eleven years old when his step-father and mother went their separate ways.

Business slowed up in Alma not because horses did not need shoeing but because Antrim and Russell were birds of a feather. Alma, unsuccessful as a mining town, settled back into becoming a cow town, which would have proved a boost to the partners had they so relished it. Instead, they decided to trade the shop for a pair of mules and headed for the copper camps of Arizona. Antrim, who mellowed into a nice old man with a merry twinkle in his eye, lived until 1932. He could have told tales about the boyhood of his step-son that would have given us a proper slant on his early days but he preferred to remain silent. He did say upon occasion that the boy was "bull-headed" and that they quarreled often.

Who was the real power behind the throne in the Lincoln County War? Were Murphy, Dolan, Fritz, Riley but tools in the hands of a friend of many years standing? W. L. Rynerson (some spell it Ryerson) had come in with the California Column. He served under Fritz and introduced Murphy to Catron. When the Column disbanded in 1866 and the friends decided on the sutler's trade at Fort Stanton and later at Lincoln, they never lost contact with the lawyer—Brady, Fritz,

Rynerson, Dolan, Murphy, Martin, Riley—did they have any connection with Tom Catron's Santa Fe Ring building up as a political machine at the time? Rynerson was the brainiest of the outfit. All seemed to drift their way until Tunstall and McSween entered the scene. When McSween refused to testify against Chisum in favor of Murphy, Rynerson said some pretty trenchant things that did not cement matters any. Rynerson watched with a tinge of envy the gravy flowing towards Tunstall and McSween. The thought that he did not have Lincoln "all sewed up" rattled him. The death of Fritz, as far as he was concerned, played right into his hands. Now he would be able to retain control of Lincoln, and the voting would go the way the Ring desired. On February 14, 1878, he sent this note, written in Lincoln, to his buddies:

Friends Riley and Dolan:

I have received letters from you mailed the 10th inst. (from their ranch). I am glad to know that you (Dolan) got home o. k. If Mr. Wilderman interfered with or resisted the sheriff in the discharge of his duty, Brady did right in arresting him, and anyone else who does so must receive the same attention.

Brady goes into the store and takes his interest (reference to McSween). Tunstall will have the same right then that he had before, but he neither must not obstruct the sheriff, nor resist him in the discharge of his duties. If he tries to make trouble the sheriff must meet the occasion firmly and legally. I believe that Tunstall is in with the swindlers of the rogue McSween. They have the money belonging to the Fritz estate, and they know it. It must be made hot for them all; the hotter the better. Especially is this necessary now that it has been discovered that there is no hell (reference is to the Atheist Ingasoll).

It may be that the villain Green 'Juan Bautiste Wilson' will play in their hands as Alcalde. Shake that McSween outfit up till it shells out and squares up, and then shake it out of Lincoln. Get the people with you. Control Juan Patròn, if possible. You know how to do it. Have good men about to aid Brady, and be assured I will help you all I can, for I believe there was never found a more scoundelry set than that outfit." (Letter quoted in the Las Vegas Daily Chronicle in an article on Rynerson October 24, 1884)

Rynerson is better known as the killer of Slough, the man who led the Colorado Volunteers to Fort Union to save New Mexico for the Union. It was put in the books as self-defense. He lived until 1893 and could have told much about the Lincoln County War had he so chosen. It is an astonishing fact that no one who took part in the Lincoln County War ever wrote about it. Not even Garrett who wrote, or caused to be written, a book on Billy the Kid, shortly after his death, was in the Lincoln County War. All our authorities are foreigners as far as the disturbance in Lincoln County is concerned. But they are all we have to go by and it becomes increasingly hard as the years go by to separate the "tall-tales" from the facts.

When Garrett killed the Kid it was said that William Antrim went gunning for him. "William Antrim denied the report started by some smart aleck that he intended to kill the sheriff for killing Billy the Kid. They met at Albuquerque, had a quiet talk and parted friendly" (Messilla News August 19, 1882). Antrim and Garrett were well known to each other. They first met when Garrett was a buffalo hunter and Antrim hauling freight. They met often at White Oaks and in Mesilla. When they crossed paths at Albuquerque, they went into an eating place, ordered dinner and Antrim asked Garrett to tell him about the Kid's end, his funeral and burial. They lingered over the meal quite some time, each closeted with his own thoughts of this tameless youth they both had cause to remember. Garrett had been going about for material on a book about the desperado.

"Sheriff Pat Garrett has written a Life of Billy the Kid which will soon be published. Every citizen should purchase at least ten copies of the work, to assist the writer. Mr. Garrett, as sheriff, took the life of a noted desperado and people have rewarded him. This would have satisfied some men. We can see no pressing necessity for the work he is to have printed, and can only look upon it as a means of reaping further harvest from a lucky shot. By all means let the people buy the book and thus encourage literature and the performance of duties by public officers." (Mora Pioneer October 27, 1881)

Necessity brought Pat Garrett to New Mexico. He was a cowpoke out of a job. Born in Alabama on June 5, 1850, he wasn't too much older than the outlaw he killed and whose death brought him fame. Garrett was no Wild Bill nor Wyatt Earp. He was in his teens when he wandered into Haynesville, Louisiana, and in his late teens when he settled at Lancaster, Texas. When Goodnight, Pierce, Chisum and others began shaking up dust to open up cattle trails Garrett cowboyed with them. Shortly before the Santa Fe railroad made its appearance over the Raton Pass, the area about Anton Chico boomed as a good grazing center for the moving herds. Several large mercantile establishments and warehouses made Anton Chico a boom-town. Garrett came up from the Texas Panhandle where he had been working as a buffalo hunter and applied for employment at Anton Chico. Here he married for the first time. In short order he lost his job mostly because Anton Chico stopped booming, and went to work for Pete Maxwell at Fort Sumner.

It was at Anton Chico where he went for a conference with Jim Greathouse, that the Kid first met Garret but friendship did not spring up until they met again at Pete Maxwell's. About this time mining camps sprung up at Mal Pais, White Oaks and Bonito. Billy obtained a job at Pete Galligar's ranch as buck-board driver carrying supplies to White Oaks. Garrett and Billy became such good friends that the outlaw on one occasion gave Garrett his horse, saddle and bedding. Leaving the employ of Maxwell, Garrett became the partner of George Fulton in a grocery and saloon business at Fort Sumner. Here he married a second time—Apolonia Gutierrez whose father worked for Pete Maxwell. It was her younger sister who aroused the love interest of William Bonney.

Garrett was a tall man. Several inches over six feet. Lincoln County was out to elect a new sheriff. It has been said that the Kid went electioneering against Garrett in favor of his own candidate, distributing much hard liquor to get votes for his candidate. While he won in his own district, his candidate lost the election to Garrett. As Billy was hardly of the age to be interested in politics from the viewpoint of being anyone's campaign manager, he may chalk this up as another legend, of which there are many, about the desperado.

Whatever Garrett's faults and antecedents, he was as kind a sheriff and frontier marshall as ever held office. When he found out that Bonney, Rudabaugh, Wilson and Pickett were not fed at the Las Vegas jail, having gone sixteen hours without food, he hunted up Sheriff Romero and told him in no uncertain terms what he thought of him. They were fed at once. From the time his book on Billy the Kid appeared to the present day the legend about the outlaw grew to fantastic proportions. The Las Vegas Optic for Saturday evening, September 10, 1881, says:

Scarcely has the news of the killing of William Bonney, alias McCarthy (?), but known the world over as Billy the Kid, faded from the public mind before we again are startled by the second chapter in the bloody romance of his eventful life—the disposal of his body. Billy was killed on July 14 and was buried on the 16th in an almost abandoned cemetery at Fort Sumner—a long neglected military burial ground, we believe it was. When the rude and comely funeral services were completed and the last cold clod had been heaped upon the rough sand mound, then should have ended the thrilling romance. But it did not.

The fifth day after the burial of the notorious young desperado, a fearless skelologist of this county (San Miguel) whose name, for substantial reasons, cannot be divulged (eventually said to have been Dr. Tipton by some, Dr. DesMarias by others) proceeded to Fort Sumner and in the silent watches of the night, with the assistance of a compadre (a reporter from the Las Vegas paper) dug up the remains of the once mighty youth and carried them off in a wagon.

The stiff was brought to Las Vegas, arrivng there about 2 A.M. in the morning, and was tipped quietly into the private office of a practitioner, who by dint of diligent labor and careful watching to prevent detection, boiled and scraped the skin off the 'pate' so as to secure the skull which was seen by a reporter last evening. The body, or remains proper, was covered in the dirt in a corral, where it will remain until decomposition shall have robbed the frame of its meat, when the body will be dug up again and the skeletons fixed up—hung together. by wires and varnished with shellac to make it presentable. Then the physicians will feel that their labors have been rewarded, for the skeleton of a crack frontiersman does not grow on every bush and the bones of such men as Billy the Kid are hard to find. The skull is already 'dressed' and is considered quite a relic in itself. The index finger of the right hand, it will be remembered, was presented to the Optic at the time the exhumation was made. As this member has been sent East (to Boston), the skeleton now in process of consummation will not be complete in its fingers, but the loss is so trivial that it will hardly be noticeable."

Whether this was a hoax or the truth depends on what you would find if you dug the grave at Fort Sumner. The above item fell into the hands of a young lady in California who wrote to the newspaper saying that she was the Kid's sweetheart and wanted the finger. Said the editor: "Billy the Kid had a sweetheart, so we have just learned. The young lady's name is Kate X and she lives in California. She read in the newspaper that the Optic had the index finger of the Kid in pickle and she has written for it with a request also to send a photograph of the young killer. We have written Miss X a sorrowful epistle full of touching condolences and broke the news gently that we had just sold the relic of her lover for $150 and that Billy was such a contrary fellow that he would not sit still long enough for a photographer to get his camera turned loose on him, hence the photograph she craved must ever be forthcoming." (Las Vegas Optic September 19, 1881)

Said John Milton Scanlon, who wrote the life of Pat Garrett the same year that Garrett was killed (1908) about Billy the Kid:

"William H. Bonney, better known as Billy the Kid, was not the typical character depicted by the yellow-kid magazine and newspaper writers. He was about the last person one would select for a 'gunman.' He was never 'attired' as a brigand or guerilla. He usually wore a black frock coat, dark pantaloons and vest, a neat boot, and a wide hat to protect his face from the sun. He swore, naturally, but his oaths were not of the obscene kind—he expressed them in better phraseology, bordering on the picturesque—if swearing can be picturesque. He was not beastly in his demeanor, not so much as some of the 'society' men of today. He was polite and cordial, inviting confidence. It was one of his traits, and a very rare one, to never betray a friend. He was about five feet eight inches in statue, stood straight and weighed about one hundred and thirty-five pounds. His form was well knit, and he was very muscular, tough and active. His hair was of dark brown, glossy and luxuriant, and not worn long as depicted by 'fake' magazinists. His eyes were deep blue, dotted with spots of hazel hue, and were bright and expressive. His face was oval, the most noticeable feature being two projecting front teeth, which was not a disfigurement but sufficiently prominent to attract attention. Newspaper fakers have described these as 'fangs' and depicted him as an ogre. He was more handsome than most men."

There was an old poem, author unknown, that made the rounds shortly after the death of the Kid that gives the general impression people had of him following the publicity that made a legend of him:

> There wasn't a man in Santa Fe
> Who'd go the mat with Shag Bronte.
> He could ride a horse and shoot a gun
> Like the devil himself. The deeds he's done
> Would put him in jail for a thousand years.
> He was ever changing brands and rustling steers.
> He'd kill a man on the least pretext,
> Whenever his one-tracked mind seemed vexed.
> His lineage ran in a tangled strain
> To English, French and a tinge of Spain,
> Wtih a trace of Scotch. Indian tones
> Were manifest in his high cheek bones.
> The rest was pure hell unrefined.

A non descript with a mongrel mind,
He was hated and feared in every place
That men knew his voice or evil face.
And even the ones that formed his clan
Cursed and despised him to a man.
But the curses never were voiced or heard
By so much as the sign of a whispered word.
But there came a night when Shag Bronte
Made a mistake in Santa Fe.
A stranger leaped on the long horn bar
And slowly puffed a mild cigar.
A tenderfoot you would say at least,
Who ought to be back in the quiet East.
A man not meant for the turbulent way
Of frontier times in Santa Fe.
He dressed the West, but his clothes betrayed
To a normal mind they were tailor made.
And the guns that hung to the belt he wore
Were nickel-plate of a minor bore.
He paid no mind to the jibes and jeers
So plainly meant to reach his ears.
Then Shag walked in. He quickly saw
The tenderfoot. A loud guffaw
Boomed from his chest. He neatly drew,
Shooting the stranger's cigar in two.
The stranger neither moved nor spoke.
He merely ordered another smoke.
Shag stood watching. The play begun,
His right hand holding the smoking gun.
The stranger placed the cigar with care
In his mouth, and with a careless air
Made a motion as if to scratch
In a masculine way, a ready match.
All looked on. Not a soul divined
The move the stranger had in mind
As his hand came up. A nickeled gun
Crashed its shot, and the game was done.
Deadly Shag Bronte was dead before

His body even reached the floor.
Now he would never live to know that he matched
   his brains
With the man most feared on western plains.
Billy the Kid quietly rode away
To the Texas line from Santa Fe.

So, the Kid in brief time made his memory lasting. Frank, sociable, generous among his friends, he insists that his plight is such because he is tempted to the commission of guilt by open opportunities, by the strange concantinations of circumstance and by prophetic visions of things to come. Fate and the metaphysical seem to conspire against his ever being virtuous. Never wholly destitute of feeling of sympathy from the natives he befriends and who in turn befriend him, he is accessible to pity as he ranks the loss of a friend above all, and secondly the love of his followers. He has a zest for life but recognizes no zest if there are no friends, no loyalty and the loss of such becomes tantamount to weariness. O'Folliard gone, Bowdie gone, Wilson imprisoned, Rudabaugh wanted for participation in the killing of a jailor and under sentence of death, Pickett denying he ever rode with Billy the Kid, Greathouse saying: "I know not the man." Only a girl in Fort Sumner dares uphold him but only at night. He must hide his face by day. And he must hunt his food at night like a depredator, and with the stealth of a coyote. Butcher knife in hand he seeks food and and finds a bullet and Garrett runs about like a mad man: "I have killed the Kid, I have killed the Kid."

Said to be Tom Pickett about the time he rode with Billy the Kid.

The stone, fortress-like jail at Cimarron. It once housed Clay Allison, Davy Crockett, Porter Stogden, Dick Rogers, Dave Rudabaugh, and a number of other desperadoes famous for their exploits as rustlers, bandits and producers of gunsmoke.

BOOK FIVE

HEADLESS IN PARRAL

(Dave Rudabaugh)

In the State of Chihuahua, south of the border, close to where the lower extremity flirts with the State of Durango, the terrain is rugged, hilly and desolate, fit more for lizards than the haunts of men. Naked vines abounding with shoots for want of dressing choke the scene to give it a barren, desertlike, forlorn, shrub-laden barrage of desolation to which the natives have rightly bestowed the name parral. Here in this wasteland the Spaniards settled the village they called Parral after this type of vine growing there. Barren as it was on the surface, the sub-surface was found to contain silver and this brought life to the desert. In the 80's it became quite a mining center, all the more so since that was the decade that prospecting was a fever not a hobby. Here Apaches and Navajos brought their spoils of raids for barter; here American outlaws sought refuge from justice; here gambling dens, brothels, cantinas placed it on a par with Tombstone, Dodge, Las Vegas, Raton and other frontier "end of track" towns controlled by the tameless until the rise of the vigilantes and the influx of law and order. False front towns that never obstructed justice during those days of weening, simply because there was no justice to obstruct. Parral numbered about five thousand inhabitants when Dave Rudabaugh (often spelt Radabaugh) drifted in, as unkempt as ever, just a jump ahead of the law that halted on the other side of the Mexican border in Arizona.

Go to Parral and visit the cemetery. The old one. In a corner, on unconsecrated ground, where repose the remains of cheats, suicides, undesirables, foreigners, desperadoes—in any one of those unmarked, cursed and forgotten graves, repose the bones of Dave Rudabaugh, one of the toughest hombres ever to tote a six-shooter. In daring deeds, he reached above the heights of Billy the Kid, victimized by pulp writers, and perhaps outshines Clay Allison. As far as New Mexico desperadoes are concerned, for my money they rank in this order: Rudabaugh, Bonney, Stodgen, Allison, Crockett and Fowler.

Frank Collison was cowboying for the Wyle & Coggin outfit in Eastern New Mexico. Into his camp, looking for supper, rode some cowboys from the Chisum outfit. With them were the men who had just returned from the fight at Blazer's Mill. Collison and Antrim got to talking about the battle. Their friendship endured. Looking back through the years and the many times he met the Kid on the range, he remarked sixty years later: "If ever there was a living man the Kid was afraid of, it was Rudabaugh."

What brought Dave Rudabaugh to his grave was not the fact that he was not quick on the draw. It would be better to say that he was too quick. He made the mistake so many Americans make in Mexico. He treated the natives with disdain, contempt, kicking them about when they got in his way or failed to understand him, mocked and mimicked them, even shot a few for no particular reason, cussing them out as foreigners and greasers. And in their own country! It reminds me of a number of our boys during the Italian Campaign looking over the beauty of Rome and exclaiming: "Say, these foreigners sure are artistic." Gathering together in a cantina at Parral, a few of the boys decided that they had enough of the insolence of "the unkempt gringo," as they referred to one not in particularly good standing with them.

It was the night of February 18, 1886. Rudabaugh entered his favorite cantina, ordered a drink and sat down to a game of cards as was his custom. He did not quite understand their language but he saw enough and heard enough to know that on this particular evening they were going out of their way, becoming very insulting to say the least. If anyone was ever given the "freeze play" it was Dave Rudabaugh that night in the saloon. He had worked around Mexicans long enough to know that remarks they passed to one another concerning him were not complimentary but rather acrimonious. They were actually going out of their way to be obnoxious. He accused one of cheating. The accused arose indignantly and pulled out his pistol. Rudabaugh, an old hand with the six-shooter, had the bead on him before he could quite focus the gun. He shot the fellow right between the eyes. Another player, seeking to avenge his fallen comrade, drew and shot at Rudabaugh, but missed him. Rudabaugh turned to him and shot him through the heart. The others in the cantina went about their business as if nothing unusual had taken place. Rudabaugh turned his back on them and went outside for his horse. The street was deserted. His horse was nowhere in sight. He walked up the street. Barricaded. Then he knew. He was marked for death. A million times he escaped bullets, posses, jails, capture. Here he stood, the leader of the toughest gang of bandits ever to ride the plains of Kansas, the hills of New Mexico.

Cautiously he moved back to the cantina. What he expected to do there he hardly knew. At least there was some light there. Here was darkness. One step. Two. This was the end of the line. No one knows what passed through his mind as he backed towards the cantina that awful February night. Despite the fact that he was a leader of outlaws, that he had ridden with Billy the Kid, he was always a lone wolf. His thoughts were very much his own. Chains he could slip out of; jails had no bars for him; more than one posse believed him a devil to appear and disappear at will. But this? This was a prison such as he had never seen in Kansas, Texas, Colorado, Arizona or New Mexico. Chained to walls, handcuffed, shackled, he always managed to escape. Now, with six-shooter in hand, ankles free of shackles, waist free of iron bands, wrists not cuffed together by ribbons of steel, stars overhead and music and frolic issuing from the cantina behind him, he felt trapped, suffocated, jailed. Where would death strike? From a tavern window? From somewhere along the rows of houses that engulfed the street? He was a shadow in the night. A target.

"Come on out and fight like men," he yelled to the houses. Silence.

"Afraid to die?" he jeered.

A rifle cracked. Another.

"Cowards."

That was the last word he ever uttered.

Out of the houses poured the people. One brandished a sword. Rudabaugh's head was severed from its body and stuck onto a pole. Torches were lit and a procession formed. There was light now, light and life. Up and down the frenzied citizens marched in their orgy of blood and triumph. They mocked and laughed. They threw sticks and stones. For two hours they paraded the trophy. Then they went to the cemetery, dug a hole, dragged the body in and threw the head after it. They went home. Lights out. Silence. The street was as empty and dark as Rudabaugh saw it for the last time. Commented The Las Vegas Optic for February 23rd, 1886:

"Dave Rudabaugh, who was recently killed at Parral, in the State of Chihuahua, Mexico, was what might be called an 'all-around desperado.' He was equally proficient in holding up a railroad train or stage coach, or, as occasion offered, robbed a bank, 'shooting up' a frontier settlement, or running off stock. He indulged in these little peculiarities for a year or two in Arizona, and inasmuch as many of our old-timers doubtless remember him, some of them to their cost, the following sketch of the antecedents of Rudabaugh, communicated to the Tombstone, Arizona, Democrat, by one who knows, will prove of interest.

"Ten years ago, just after the Santa Fe railroad had invaded western Kansas, a train was held up near Kinsley, and robbed of everything of value that it contained. Detective Hudgens got after the gang and soon had them all in the Leavenworth penitentiary, with the exeption of Dave Rudabaugh, who turned state's evidence. After that David became a desperado, and was finally outlawed at Las Vegas for numerous other crimes. In 1880 he became a member of the famous Billy the Kid gang which eventually got him into jail. He escaped the jail at Las Vegas and fled to Arizona where he rustled with varying success for nearly two years when he was driven out of the Apache country and struck for Old Mexico, where he became manager of the cattle interests in Chihuahua of the governor thereof. Dave continued to be a desperado, however, and became engaged in his final difficulty in the ancient town of Parral. He fatally shot up two persons before the buzzing ball caught him in a fatal shot and ended his life. The natives of Parral got up a procession in honor of the event, and Dave's head, which had been severed from his body, was carried on a pole and exhibited about the streets . . ."

Headless in Parral. Buried without benefit of clergy, blanket, or shroud. Forever to rest in foreign soil. O'Folliard, Bowdre, Pickett, Billy the Kid—tourists drive hundreds of miles to see their graves and stand in awe. I have never seen anyone at the graves in Fort Sumner (Pickett is buried in Arizona) with a look of amusement on their faces. Whatever they remember of Rudabaugh, it is not his death.

Born in Missouri, the family became interested in the Free Soil Party and moved to Kansas. Shortly before the Civil War the Rudabaughs moved to Texas. Dave's father fought for a time with Sibley's Brigade, sustained a wound and returned home to die. He was eighteen when his father died. Beaten by the poverty that surrounded him, he struck out for a job as a cow-hand, he trailed cattle north where he came to know New Mexico, Colorado and Kansas. Uneducated, he saw no particular advantage in being neat and clean. He forever went about with that "five o'clock shadow" and more than likely wore the same unwashed shirt for Easter that he wore on Christmas. If he was aware of soap and water, he had no applicative knowledge of it and shunned it as totally unnecessary to his existence. Sanitation was beyond his comprehension. As he spent money as fast as he got his hands on it he was soon in with a gang of cattle rustlers.

Rudabaugh worked for George Peshaur, the cowboy leader of the Texans, who so vainly tried to unseat Wyatt Earp as marshall of Wichita in 1874. While there was a thousand dollar reward coming to the man who would kill the marshall Rudabaugh was cunning enough to realize that this was hearsay. He wanted positive proof. He never got any. Besides, if he sent Earp to Boot-hill it would mean that some gunfighter would come along for the honor of shooting it out with the man who shot it out with the marshall. It was like a boxer of today always aiming for the title bout. He was also one of the cowboys who served under Mannen Clements in an attempt to take over Wichita that same year.

With the discovery of gold in the Black Hills of the Dakotas, a few of the cowboys abandoned their outfits and turned prospectors. Disillusioned, they banded together to form the Texas Gang, took to holding up stages, selecting Deadwood as their headquarters. Later they were known as the Dunc Blackburn outfit. In the spring of 1877, they set up camp in the nearby hills and soon had Wells Fargo so worried that it almost decided to fold up. Every attempt to capture the outlaws failed. A number of stage drivers and shotgun messengers (i. e. armed guardians riding with the driver) were killed or wounded. Dave was a part of all this. When Scott Davis finally caught up with Blackburn and killed him, the gang broke up. Rudabaugh then took up with Billy Wilson, Mike Roake, Ed West, Charles Bowdre, King Fisher, Tom Emory and a host of others who guarded the herds around Dodge City in 1877. Emory eventually took a job in the Texas Panhandle and became one of the men to hunt down the Kid.

Some of Earp's biographers have made him out to be a superman, a sort of indestructable god who lived a charmed life. No bullet could touch him. They say that he was the man that went after Rudabaugh for the Kinsley robbery. As U. S. Deputy Marshall he tailed Rudabaugh for robbing the mails, not for the train hold-up. Fifty years after the event Earp said of Rudabaugh:

"Rudabaugh was about the most notorious outlaw in the range country. He was a rustler and robber by trade with the added specialty of killing jailors in the breaks for liberty at which he was invariably successful whenever he was arrested. After a series of hold-ups, word came that Rudabaugh and

Roake were in Texas and as I was a Deputy U. S. Marshall, I was offered ten dollars a day and expenses to get them."

Rudabaugh did break out of every jail that confined him, but there is no record in Kansas, Arizona, Texas or New Mexico, much less Colorado, of his ever having killed a jailor. Actually the jailor, Antonio Lino Valdez, at Las Vegas, was killed by John Allen with Rudabaugh accessory after the fact. The only time that he actually made an attempt to kill a jailor was on the night of September 23, 1881, when he sought to make a break from the Las Vegas jail by shooting at Florencio Mares, the jailor. The gun jammed and Rudabaugh was overpowered and placed in chains. Earp was in Tombstone, Arizona, at the time. When the news reached him it came in the version such happenings do, that Mares was added to the list with Valdez.

Rudabaugh and Mike Roake worked along very nicely together. They were not too interested in adding too many members to their crew as it tended to make capture simpler for one thing, and meant less of a cut on the take for another. After an unusually successful hold-up they back-tracked to Texas on a spending spree before an attempt to rustle mules and horses belonging to the soldiers stationed at Fort Griffin. This post was in the present Shackleford county under the shadow of the Antelope Hills. Built in 1867 as a protection for the north settlements against Comanche raids, it soon became the focal point for trade and gatherings. Here mule skinners, buffalo hunters, cowboys, gamblers, dance-hall girls, frontier lawyers, Cyprians and other sundry characters had their rendezvous in the valley below the fort. This town outside the limits of the military reservation assumed such proportions that by the time Rudabaugh and Roake came there to spend their ill-gotten gains, it was considered the principal supply station on the Dodge Trail. Here Rudabaugh met Doc Holiday and was to know him better later when the dentist-desperado opened a saloon in Las Vegas. Had Rudabaugh any inkling that Holliday was the one who informed Earp of his whereabouts, he would have killed him in Las Vegas. Holliday appointed himself Earp's guardian angel and was with him a long time in Tombstone following the sale of his cantina in Las

Vegas. Holliday thought he was too much of a gambler to join Billy the Kid's gang. He looked down on rustlers.

The trail from Dodge to Fort Griffin was almost a straight line north and south between these two points. When Marshal Earp found out that Rudabaugh was at Fort Griffin, he hurried there with all possible speed only to find out that he was too late. Uncertain as to where to look next he searched out Shanassey, an old friend of his who ran a saloon there, and asked him if he knew of anybody who could put him on Rudabaugh's trail. The tavern-keeper told him that the only person who might know of Rudabaugh's whereabouts was Doc Holliday. It was while in search of Dave Rudabaugh that one of the strangest friendships of frontier history was struck up.

For a week the dentist-killer listened as he dealt out cards until he overhead talk that Rudabaugh and Roake were at Fort Davis. This was rather a disappointment to Earp as it meant several hundred more miles travel, west and south, to the foothills of the Davis Mountains southeast of Pecos, Texas. This fort was built when Jefferson Davis was Secretary of War and named for him. Established in October, 1854, by Colonel Washington Seawell as a protection against predatory tribes, it encouraged settlers to move in until soon ranchers, heartened by the presence of the soldiers, made a thriving community of the place. Frontier posts were also the best pickings for rustlers who wished to replenish their supply of horses and pack mules. It was easier for the government to make up the loss than ranchers. Besides, stealing from ranchers more often as not meant a neck-tie party.

The sutler at Fort Davis told Earp that Rudabaugh had been seen around the garrison, but evidently his actions were under close observation as he made off with no stock from the post. He hinted that the marshall should try Fort Clark as these rustlers usually made the rounds from post to post. Fort Clark was then situated in Kinney County near the site of the county seat, Brackettville. Established in 1852, it became a military reservation for the Seminole Indians. The post survived until comparatively recent date (1946). As was the lot of frontier garrisons, it rapidly became a trade center. Almost under the noses of the guardians of the plains, Rudabaugh ran off some non-government cattle, mules and horses. He took them into Mexico by way of Candelaria, back tracked up the Rio Grande east to Fort Clark, where he succeeded in picking up some more government beef.

At ten dollars a day and expenses, Earp probably didn't mind the merry chase. At Fort Clark it was the same story: Rudabaugh had been around long enough to obtain fresh horses. Northeast of Fort Clark was Fort Concho on the Rio Concho, forgotten now in the growth of the modern city of San Angelo on the site. This fort was established in 1867 as a safeguard for cattlemen settling in the area. Here Rudabaugh and Roake managed to run off some stock, change brands and palm them off on new homesteaders who asked no questions. Disposing of their loot, the outlaws headed for Fort McKavett in Menard County about twenty miles west of the ruins of the old San Saba mission. There in the stealth of the night, with the silent cunning he learned from Arapahoes with whom he was on extremely friendly terms, often spending days at a time with them, he cut out some horses and mules, retaining the best mounts for himself and selling the remainder to migratory teamsters. It was easy to dispose of stock as the country had not quite recovered from the devastation of the Civil War, drought and insect plagues. The coming of the railroad that killed the Santa Fe Trail, cattle trails and freight trails also helped to kill the cattle rustling industry. This explains the rise of the train bandits.

At the invitation of Webb, Rudabaugh went to Las Vegas, now booming into a New Town because of the Santa Fe railroad. Las Vegas from the day the first train tooted into it to this has been, and perhaps always will be, two towns in one: Old Town settled in 1835 and New Town in 1879. Here Rudabaugh again met up with old cronies and often stayed with Doc Holliday (often spelt Holiday) at the cantina he opened on Center Street. The Las Vegas Optic makes reference to this following the famous fight at Tombstone: "Doc Holiday, the man who shot Mike Gordon on Center Street two years ago last August, is now on trial for murder at Tombstone,

Arizona. The prospects are that he will be convicted." He wasn't. (See Las Vegas Optic for December 3, 1881.) The exploit for which Dave Rudabaugh was most noted was the train robbery near Kinsley, Kansas.

Kinsley, the seat of Edwards county, was founded in 1873 by a group of homesteaders from Massachusetts. Disappointed as they were that the windy, treeless prairie was quite unlike the green wooded hills of New England, they nevertheless dug in with zest to combat wind, crop failure and pestilence. The railroad and the Kinsley Mercury weekly newspaper saved the town. Here the Santa Fe took on freight, cattle and grain. It was a sparsely settled area, the nearest settlement being Lewis, about ten miles to the west, and the watering place at Offerle, about ten miles to the east. In between was the prairie—rolling plains—God's billiard table—someone called it. Just within sight of Kinsley the train was blocked and every person from the engineer to the porter was asked to contribute to the kitty. Not a passenger was spared. One look at the leader of the bandits was enough. This fellow played for keeps. He was polite to the women, but they had to cough up just the same. He went on a spending spree which included drinks, women and gambling but not a suit.

The railroad officials demanded action. They stormed at Detective Hudgens and told him to produce results or else. Rudabaugh they wanted dead or alive. It was getting so that people would rather ride in a buckboard and take their chances with the Indians than ride a train to be stripped of their money and trinkets. Hudgens had better get busy. And he did. He visited gambling dens, interviewed Cyprians, questioned bartenders, haunted dance halls. Certain that Rudabaugh was the man he wanted, he asked Sheriff Bat Masterson for help. Masterson told him that he was sheriff of Ford county and had no jurisdiction over Edward's county. By some ruse they got Rudabaugh into Ford county where Bat promptly arrested the bandit. They demanded to know where he got his money and who were his accomplices.

"Lots of people spend freely nowadays," said Rudabaugh. "They don't give away watches with certain tell-tale inscriptions." The detective held one up. "This came from a certain train robbery at Kinsley.

Rudabaugh looked at Masterson.

"If these men surrender, what's in it for me?"

"Be our star witness. Turn State's Evidence and you are free."

The gang was turned over to the law, three of them convicted and sentenced to Fort Leavenworth prison.

"Thanks, Dave," said one of the men as he was being led away.

"Don't mention it."

Dave went out to rob the Wells Fargo express.

Whatever glory is given Masterson and Hudgens for rounding up the Rudabaugh gang during a violent snow-storm as it huddled around a fire at Lowell's cattle camp, it was Rudabaugh who made the capture possible. These were not the type of men to be taken by surprise even in a snow-storm. Not a shot was exchanged. Rudabaugh was quite diplomatic about it. The men were trapped before they realized that their own leader had betrayed them. Had they suspected it at the moment, Rudabaugh would never have left the camp alive.

When not engaged in stage hold-ups, Rudabaugh hired himself out as bar tender in the saloons at "the end of track" in Kansas, Colorado and New Mexico, always taking time out to stage another hold-up, always broke the day after as the day before. Easy come, easy go. While dance halls were not too excited at the sight of him, they welcomed his free spending. Most of the girls would have avoided him had it not been for their bosses. Money was money, said the boss. Dirt was dirt, said the girls. Put them together, laughed the proprietor and you get pay-dirt.

"On August 30, 1879, the stage was robbed. The stage robbery took place on one of the mountain passes on the old stage road between Las Vegas and Tecolote. The robbers halted the stage, ordered the passengers out and proceeded to rob them and the mail sacks as well as whatever money was deposited with the stage company strong box. The robbers then unhitched the horses, mounted them and rode off. The robbers were identified two years later as Joe Martin, Dave Rudabaugh and Joe Carson. Strange as it seems, other men were tried and convicted for their crime." (Las Vegas Daily Gazette February 27, 1881)

Rudabaugh was connected with the police force in Las Vegas and knew every shipment going out and coming in. His other companions were also connected with the sheriff's office. In hiring desperadoes on the side of Law and Order, Las Vegas was doing no more than Abilene, Caldwell, Tombstone and other frontier towns of the day. Then men were quick on the draw and frequently drew sometimes at each other thus saving the taxpayer much expense. In reality there was no such thing as a "peace officer" in those days because there was no peace nor was the sheriff left in peace. Often as not he was left in pieces. Some frontier marshalls lasted a day, luckier ones lived to tell the tale. But these were very few. Many citizens would have relished the job if it didn't also mean sudden death. Many outlaws became very proficient marshalls and once in office went on the straight and narrow for life. Many are surprised to learn that some of the West's greatest marshalls were once wanted outlaws.

It was Webb who induced the city fathers that Rudabaugh should be a law enforcement officer. Hoodoo Brown (Justice of the Peace), Webb, and Rudabaugh overplayed their hand in the murder of one Michael Keliher, but the people of Las Vegas managed to have Webb indicted for the crime. Hoodoo they never caught; Rudabaugh would be tried for his participation in the murder of jailor Antonio Lino Valdez. It was agreed that Rudabaugh would come out of hiding on a certain night and aid Webb in a jail break. Taking into his confidence another desperado by the name of John Allen, they approached the jail on the night of April 2, 1880.

Antonio Lino Valdez, keeper of the outside door of the jail, saw them trying to by-pass him and stopped them. He asked what they wanted. Rudabaugh told Valdez that he had something important to tell his friend Webb that could not wait till morning. It would only take a moment. Approaching the cell in which Webb and the Stakes brothers were confined,

Rudabaugh demanded of the jailor the key to the cell. He further told the jailor that he had come to liberate Webb and nothing was to stand in his way. At this point, Allen, without further ado, drew out his pistol and fatally shot Valdez. The key was thrown to Webb who refused to make use of it hoping that by doing so he would prove his innocence in the slaying of Keliher. The desperadoes seeing that they availed nothing, fled before the alarm was raised. Rudabaugh had a hack waiting. It was the property of J. M. Talbot, who was beginning to wonder about it as he had rented it out to a driver for taxi purposes.

Carl Caldwell had rented the hack. As he was driving along Center Street in the hopes of picking up a fare, just as he reached Houghton's hardware store he saw two men flaging him down. Allen caught the reins as Rudabaugh went up to the driver's seat and literally kicked him out of his place and told him to keep going without stopping to talk to anyone if he knew what was good for him. The new proprietors of the hack promptly went into Houghton's hardware store and boldly helped themselves to three carbines and rifles, throwing them in the back as further assurance should they have to battle their way out of town. Rudabaugh, armed with a brace of six and sixteen shooters, did the driving.

As Webb refused to avail himself of the opportunity, Rudabaugh made haste to skip town for he reasoned correctly that Caldwell sought out the sheriff. The pair sped away pursued by four Spanish-Americans who came to the scene aroused at the sound of the shot. They took one look at the prone body of Valdez and dashed after the fast disappearing hack. As they were armed with revolvers and a round of shells these proved ineffectual against the moving target. They jumped on their horses and gave chase. By five o'clock in the evening, both New Town and Old Town had assembled at the jail to organize a posse under the leadership of Colonel Lockhart and headed in the general direction taken by the fugitives.

About twenty-five miles from Las Vegas they came upon the abandoned hack as well as the returning natives who told them that the traveling arsenal proved too much for them. Talbot's horses were found in the hands of a sheepherder who had traded fresh horses for them. One horse was so completely exhausted that the posse decided against bringing it back. A Spencer carbine was found in the hack. This was the one that Rudabaugh took from Bennet's shop prior to his encounter with Caldwell. Lockhart's men gave up the chase as the evening was far spent and darkness closed in. Rudabaugh and Allen parted at Anton Chico; the former joining Billy the Kid while Allen went on to Dodge City. With Billy, Rudabaugh found Tom Pickett another companion of Kansas and Las Vegas days.

While at Las Vegas, Rudabaugh also found time to occupy himself as bar tender. A cantina was a listening post. Here Rudabaugh could keep his ears open and hear things not meant for his ears. Often a hold-up resulted from what he gleaned. Said the Las Vegas Optic for December 18, 1879: "Dave Rudabaugh (the paper insisted on spelling it Radabaugh) has joined the white apron brigade. He is now a silver-tongued persuader who spins glasses to perfection on Brahm's counter in the Baca building."

"Yesterday afternoon, about 3 o'clock, one of the boldest and most desperate deeds ever committed in this community was perpetrated at the jail by Dave Rudabaugh and Jack Allen. Th facts, as elicited by a Gazette reporter, from eye witnesses are as follows:

It seems that the two men got into a hack in East Las Vegas (New Town) and drove over to this side. The hack belonged to J. M. Talbot and at the time was driven by Mr. Carl Caldwell. On arriving at the jail Rudabaugh and Allen got out of the hack and asked to be admitted into the placita of the jail; they were permitted to enter and when on the inside they asked the jailor to show them Webb's cell. The jailor showed them the cell occupied by Webb and the Stokes boys. One of the men then handed a common newspaper through the cell door to the men on the inside. They then demanded the keys of the cell from the jailor, but Mr. Valdez said: 'I have no right to give them to you.' Whereupon Allen said: 'You must give them up or we will kill you . Then Valdez said: 'You may kill me but I won't give up the keys.' Allen told him that it was an easy matter to do that, and at once drew his pistol and fired the fatal shot. The keys were then taken from the pocket of the fallen man by one of the men, who threw them down at the door of Webb's cell and said:

" 'Here are the keys. I must go.' "

Allen and Rudabaugh then went out, got into the hack and ordered the driver to drive to New Town as quickly as possible. They covered the driver with their revolvers and ordered him not to flinch at his peril. They also covered everyone they met on the road until they were safely past them. On driving in the New Town they drove to Houghton's Hardware Store, and one of them boldly entered the store and threw two or three rifles into the hack, ordered the driver to get out, when Rudabaugh took the hack and drove east at a rapid rate.

"The men drove directly east and went up on the mesa. By this time the deputy sheriff and a posse of men who were in hot pursuit had closed up within shooting range. Allen and Rudabaugh, in order to keep this party at bay, got out of the hack and kneeled down and fired a volley, which was returned by the pursuers. Several more then exchanged by both parties, when the sheriffs posse gave back and the two men entered the hack and drove on.

"The excitement in the city was intense. Crowds of men could be seen during the entire evening standing on every little eminence surveying the western slope of the Nine Mile Hill with field glasses in order to get a view of the exciting chase. The sheriff's posse was continually being increased by armed recruits from the city and at last accounts the fleeing men had been overtaken and the fighting renewed. It was reported about dark that one of the horses driven by Allen and Rudabaugh had been shot. The fighting was still going on at dark." The editors (Beecher and Mills) of the Las Vegas Eureka were forced to confess:

"Dave Rudabaugh and Jack Allen made good their escape Friday night. The second party that started after made a good effort but never overtook the fugitives or got in sight. They took the La Cinta road and after getting out two or three miles Ignacio Sena who was after them on horseback caught up near enough to shoot. He fired several shots at the hack, one ball going through the upper part. The hack was stopped and one of the men got out and returned the fire. Sena not having much ammunition then returned for a new supply. The fugitives after this encounter continued their journey with increased speed. About eighteen miles out they came upon some herders with saddle-horses. These they immediately appropriated to their own use taking the pistols from the boys and also meat and other provisions. Thus freshly mounted, they distanced all pursuers. The herders we understand were in the employ of Don Antonio Montoya. They reside at San Geronimo and one of their names is Antonio Gonzolez. The sheriff was not in town and the deputy appeared to be totally unprepared to do anything effectually and promptly. In this emergency a number of citizens saddled their horses, hunted up their guns and started in pursuit. Among these were Hilario Romero, Col. Lockhart, Peter Simpson and several other good men whose names we did not learn. They pressed forward as rapidly as possible, riding some thirty-five miles before night closed down and rendered further pursuit hopeless. Their horses by this time were tired out and the night being so dark that nothing could be seen they were forced to turn back and arrived home yesterday morning. They brought back the hack which had been left with the sheepherders. Allen and Rudabaugh left two of the guns in the hack, likely considering that with fresh horses they would have no use for long range arms.

"It was a bold and desperate attempt to liberate Webb which failed on account of the lack of nerve and courage on the part of the projectors. When they had shot the jailor and obtained the keys they threw them into Webb's cell, telling him that there were the keys and they must go. How did they imagine that he should get out without arms? It was an ill advised plan for their object and nervelessly executed. They made a good escape, however, and luckily for them they met the mounted herders, otherwise the chances are that the Romero and Lockhart party would have overhauled them, in which case it would have been a dead sure thing they would have been captured. (Las Vegas Eureka March 7, 1880)

Such carryings on worried the respectful citizens of Las Vegas who were trying to promote the city and the hot springs several miles above the town. It was the proprietor of the Las Vegas Hot Springs Hotel who wrote:

"Under the impression that Las Vegas is a bad and dangerous place, many health and pleasure seekers, who would like to come here and take advantage of the climate and springs stay away. During my travels through Colorado during the past few months, I have noticed that the feeling prevails among invalids and tourists, scores of whom I have met and conversed with, that it is not safe to come here; I would say to such of these as may read this article, that the place has been very generally misrepresented and the accidents and crimes that have occurred here have been greatly exaggerated. True, there have been several atrocious murders committed but they have been committed by and upon habitues of dance halls and gambling halls, and the victims, who are better out of the world than in it, have, with but one or two exceptions, all been roughs. Men of this sort always congregate in frontier towns and will continue to do so for all time, and crime must follow. Let any man come here and avoid low places, keep sober and mind his own business and he will be as safe on the streets of Las Vegas as any city in the United States. The majority of the low characters who thronged here when the town was the railroad terminus have taken flight. Lynching is something they very much fear, and as that sort of thing was indulged in pretty extensively, they became alarmed and sought new regions wherein to play their nefarious schemes and work of crime, and their places have been filled by a more respectable class of men.

"It is not to be denied that there is plenty of bad whiskey in town, but where will you find a town in the West that is not more or less afflicted in the same way? The climate here is unequaled on the continent and consumptives should know it. The hot sulphur springs are, it is said, superior to those in Arkansas, and are the rheumatic's boom, but they have not yet been properly advertised. The ride to and from them over a good road and through a charming country is pleasant and interesting in the extreme. The hotel and bathing house at the springs are substantial structures of stone and wood, and may justly be classed among the first in the land . . ." (Las Vegas Gazette March 15, 1880)

Rudabaugh may have succeeded in escaping but Las Vegans were patient. There would be a time when he and Allen would want to return to town and they would be vigilant. Ropes were prepared. At Anton Chico Rudabaugh hunted up Jim Greathouse who introduced him to Billy the Kid. As a freighter Greathouse was aware that Rudabaugh was wanted by the authorities, but he chose to have the two desperadoes meet in the hopes that some day the favor would be returned. The Lincoln County War was over when Rudabaugh joined The Kid, but not rustling days. And Greathouse knew this. He was an outlet for a good cut.

Stinking Spring near Fort Sumner was also known as Arroyo Tiván. Here Pat Garrett was to break into the limelight with his capture of the Kid and his men. The capture was timely. Close to Christmas when the reward money would come in handy.

"Posses of men have been in hot pursuit of them for some time, but they succeeded in evading their pursuers every time. However, the right boys started out well mounted and heavily armed and were successful in bagging their game. Yesterday (Sunday) afternoon the town was thrown into a fever of excitement by an announcement that the Kid and other members of his gang of outlaws had been captured, and were nearing the city. The rumor was soon verified by the appearance in town of a squad of men led by Pat Garrett, deputy-marshall of Lincoln county, having in custody the Kid, Dave Rudabaugh, Billy Wilson and Tom Pickett. They were taken at once to the jail, and locked up and arrangements made to guard the jail against any attempt to take the prisoners out and hang them. Feeling was particularly strong against Rudabaugh, who was an accessory to the murder of the Mexican jailor, in an attempt to release Webb some months ago.

"It will be remembered that Frank Stewart, with a party of picked men, left Las Vegas on December 14 to join Pat Garrett and his squad who were waiting at Fort Sumner. The boys made a quick trip of it, arriving at the designated place of meeting on the night of the 17th instant. Nothing unusual transpired until the following night, when the Kid's party approached the place for the purpose of clearing out Garrett's squad, not knowing that re-enforcements had come. Precaution had been taken to place a guard on the outside of the house, and upon hearing the clatter of horses hoofs in a distance, he warned his companions of the danger and they at once prepared to give the outlaws a warm reception. The night was very dark and foggy, and even moving objects could be seen but at a very short distance. The first rider who came in range of the trusty Winchesters was Tom O'Folliard, who fell dead from his horse under the unerring aim of half a dozen frontiersman."

Tom O'Folliard was a young Texan who came up to cowboy on the Chisum ranch. He was a great talker and well liked. One might call him the practical joker of the gang. He was six foot three inches tall, weighed one hundred and seventy-nine pounds, sandy haired, had blue eyes with grey glints. He was several months older than Billy Bonney. While he could "talk the ear off you" as some old timer said, he was one of the deadliest shots ever to come to New Mexico. Like his leader, in town he was a snappy dresser, a good dancer and the heart throb of many a muchacha. His friendship for Billy was tantamount to hero worship. If the Kid feared Rudabaugh, he loved O'Folliard. Tom Pickett was following immediately behind, but, after the first volley, he turned his horse and fled for his life.

"Pursuit was out of the question, owing to the intense darkness that prevailed and the additional fact that a heavy snowstorm had set in. Dave Rudabaugh's horse was shot, but succeeded in carrying its rider a distance of twelve miles before dropping dead. The party of plucky pursuers now laid over two days starting forward on the evening of the third day, which was the 23rd of December. Promptly at the hour of twelve, they mounted their horses and rode twelve miles to Wilcox's ranch. Here it was obtained that the Kid and his followers had taken supper just the night before, and were at their rendezvous, a vacant store house, about three miles further on. After a few moments halt the brave pursuers, for such they proved themselves to be, put spurs to their horses and rode quietly to the house designated as the hiding place of the Kid's men. Upon approaching the premises at two o'clock in the morning, three horses were seen hitched to the front door ready to be mounted at a second's notice.

"Garrett and Stewart at once surrounded the house, giving their men further instructions to lie in the snow and await further orders. Just at daybreak of the morning of the 24th, a man supposed to be the Kid, but afterwards proving to be Charles Bowdre, appeared at the door. His body was pierced by two balls almost in an instant. Bowdre was the son of a Texas father and a native New Mexican mother. Swathy in appearance, he spoke his mother's tongue with as easy facility as English. He had black, wavy hair, brown eyes, square jaw and a perfect set of teeth. He worked for a time in the stock yards in Kansas before turning to cattle rustling. As a ranch foreman he had his own home which often served as a hideout for the Bonney gang. He was obligated to Tunstall and McSween and took on their fight in payment for their kindness to him. He was five foot six inches tall, weighed one hundred and fifty pounds, a good dancer, gambler, drinker. He was the most taciturn of the gang. He only spoke when spoken to. He married a native girl from Anton Chico who was so broken over his death that she had to be forcibly detained from shooting Garrett.)

"The signal for shooting was given immediately upon the appearance of Bowdre, as the Kid, who is a sure shot, had often boasted he would never be taken alive. The only way to capture him was to shoot him on sight. The killing of Bowdre alarmed those upon the inside of the house and they endeavored to ascertain what party was in pursuit of them. Their calling out, however, elicited no response. Two of the three horses standing near the door were shot down in their tracks and the third was shot in the doorway while the Kid was in the act of getting the animal on the inside out of reach of the deadly bullets. The carcass of the dead horse across the threshold prevented the Kid from leaping upon his horse, which was in the room with him, and attempting to escape.

"About 4 P.M. the surrounded party displayed a flag and Rudabaugh walked out boldly and said they were willing to surrender provided they were guaranteed protection. This was promised them, and in turn, the Kid, Billy Wilson and Tom Pickett joined Rudabaugh and gave themselves up to their captors, who put their prisoners on horses, doubling up on occasion as was necessary, and rode back to Wilcox's ranch, from which place a wagon was sent back to collect the young arsenal left at the robbers' rendezvous. The captors and their prisoners remained at the ranch all night, starting for Las Vegas on Christmas morning. They arrived before supper last night, riding very rapidly.

"The party of men who risked their lives in an attempt to rid the country of this blood-thirsty gang of murderers is deserving of unbounded praise and should be rewarded handsomely for its efforts. The men will undoubtedly obtain the reward of $500 offered by the governor for the capture of the Kid and it remains for interested citizens to raise a purse of money and present it to these sixteen men as they have paid out money and endured hardships in an endeavor to hunt down and bring to justice one of the most desperate gangs of outlaws that ever terrorized the Southwest.

"Billy the Kid is about twenty-four years of age (actually 21) and has a bold, yet pleasant countenance. When interviewed between the bars at the jail this morning, he was in a talkative mood, and said that anything he might say would not be believed by the people. He laughed heartily when told that the newspapers of the Territory of New Mexico had built him up a reputation second only to that of Victorio (one of the great Apache chieftains at war against the Whites at the time).

"Dave Rudabaugh looks and dresses about the same as when in Las Vegas, apparently not having made any raid on clothing stores. His face is weather-beaten from long exposure. This seems to be the only noticeable difference. He inquired somewhat anxiously in regard to the feeling in the community and was told that it was very strong against him. He remembered that the newspapers had all published exaggerated reports of the depredations of the Kid's party in the lower country. According to Rudabaugh, it was not half as bad as had been reported. . . . "

Then follows an interview with Tom Pickett which we reserve for the chapter on that amazing character.

"The Kid, Wilson, Rudabaugh, under the escort of Garrett, Frank Stewart, Cosgrove and one or two others, were taken to Santa Fe this afternoon. As the train was ready to leave the depot, an unsuccessful attempt was made by Sheriff Romero to secure Rudabaugh and turn him to the county jail. The engineer of the outgoing train was covered by guns and told not to move his engine. If the sheriff had been as plucky as some of the citizens who had urged him on, the matter would have been settled without any excitement whatsoever. The prisoner, Rudabaugh, the only one wanted, was in the hands of a U. S. Marshall. As they were arrested by men in the name of the Federal Government, the prisoners were to be turned over to the authorities in Santa Fe. The sheriff and a few picked, trusted men might have gone over to Santa Fe with the party and after settling regarding the status of Rudahaugh, might have convinced the court in Santa Fe that Las Vegas had the first choice because of the killing of Antonio Lino Valdez. Rudabaugh is badly wanted in Las Vegas, not only by the Mexicans but also by all the Americans who desire to see the law vindicated." (Las Vegas Daily Optic Monday, December 27, 1880)

Rudabaugh was five foot nine inches tall. He possessed an endurance and patience that baffled Billy the Kid. Fair complexioned, brown haired, his eyes were grey with glints of green. He weighed one hundred and fifty-nine pounds and would have been called handsome if he had any regard for his personal appearance. He was uncouth in dress and language. He had no religion and lived for quick and ready cash, killing if necessary, to obtain it. He drank hard liquor like water yet no one ever saw him drunk. He was loyal to a friend and willing to risk his life in the name of friendship. He loved all women but trusted none. He had no particular choice. He was just as at home with an Indian squaw as with a dance hall girl. He might have made a successful conquest and reformed if he bothered a little with soap and water and some clean clothes. Whenever he did buy clothes he bought them to wear them not to fit into them. At times he was mistaken for a walking scarecrow hidden in his clothes.

If Billy the Kid had Ollinger to remind him of the rope, Rudabaugh had George Parker whom he knew from Dodge City days. Awaiting trial in Santa Fe, Rudabaugh spent his time joking, playing cards and sneering at Parker, the jailor, who told him that he would not sneer much longer as the rope was ready.

"Dave Rudabaugh's trial came up at Santa Fe yesterday (February 16, 1881). He pleaded guilty to two charges brought against him: robbing a train and a stage coach. He will probably be given the full extent of the law. Twenty years for each crime. Although heavily shackled and handcuffed, on leaving the courtroom Rudabaugh managed to strike George Parker a severe blow in the face in payment of an old grudge." (Optic)

All the time authorities in Las Vegas worked to have Rudabaugh brought to Las Vegas, knowing that he would be given just a jail sentence if he remained in Santa Fe while they were prepared to give him the hangman's rope. They insisted that Rudabaugh must be brought to Las Vegas to stand trial for murder which was a more pressing charge than robbing a train or stage. They won out. Said Judge Prince as Rudabaugh boarded a wagon at Santa Fe: "That man will never hang." Upon leaving the Santa Fe cell, Rudabaugh turned to the other inmates and said:

"I will tell you all good-bye for good. I leave for Las Vegas. They will murder me just as soon as I get there." But the vigilantes did not seem to care anymore. Rudabaugh languished in jail from February 27th to December 3rd, 1881. The only comment the editor of the Optic had when

Rudabaugh arrived was: "The prisoner retained a stolid hangdog look, and showed no disposition to remember any of his friends."

Rudabaugh was not without friends. A case knife and a pick without a handle were smuggled in to him. Ten men were in the cell with him and all were in favor of escape, this time including Webb. Those not chained took turns in picking at the cement, the debris dropping noiselessly on the soft mattresses, which was more than most prisons could boast of. Never once were the four guards who slept across the plaza from the cells aware that a break was contemplated. So well organized was the escape that it was not discovered until feeding time at 7 A.M. in the morning.

The prisoners crawled through a hole in the wall, seven by nineteen inches. They stripped themselves of their clothes, then crawled through on their stomachs, replacing their apparel on the free side of the carcel. Four refused to avail themselves of the opportunity of liberty. Those remaining were: Griffin, Rogers, Fogerty (the Cutter) and Jack McManus. Rogers we will meet in another chapter. Those escaping were: Dave Rudabaugh, J. J. Webb, Tex Quinlan (wanted in Texas; with a price on his head he was captured by Pat Garrett and Franklin of Las Vegas. He was brought to Vegas from Santa Fe to await requisition papers from the governer of Texas. Garrett and Franklin split a $1000 reward for his capture), Goodman, Kelly, Schroeder and Kearney. Quinlan, Webb and Rudabaugh went to the St. Nicholas Hotel where Mrs. Quinlan had a room. As Rudabaugh was chained he had a little difficulty getting about. Pistols were waiting in Mrs. Quilan's room, They ate something then made for the railroad tracks. One of Charles Blanchard's mercantile workers heard the noise of Rudabaugh's chains as they hit the railroad ties. He saw Dave hobbling along alone. Rudabaugh pointed his gun. The worker valued his life. He said nothing. The other two were far in advance of Rudabaugh. At Naranjo, six miles above Las Vegas, he found someone to cut his chains.

In Arizona Rudabaugh took up where he left off before his capture and continued to rustle, hold up stages and annoy posses. He spent much of his time in Mexico where he lived like a king on the fruits of his raids until broke, then he would go back to Arizona to work again. Caught and imprisoned in Tombstone, he managed to escape to Chihuahua. He returned to Arizona to work for the Hash Knife outfit with Tim Pickett. Next he acted as foreman at the ranch of the governor of the State of Chihuahua. He maintained this position for quite some time before it was discovered that he was not adverse to rustling a few head now and then. He drifted to Parral where he held up the payroll several times and enjoyed his haunts as usual. Rudabaugh lived too soon. Alcatraz or Sing Sing would have tested his metal. He was forty-five years old when killed.

Pancho Grico, a terror in Santa Fe, he would not rest until he met Clay Allison. Clay attended his funeral.

Book Six

ANTON CHICO EXPRESS

(Jim Greathouse))

It was raining. A street urchin, nose running in concert with the downpour, watched the three men who had just returned from the wars. He leaned back on his haunches, taking in the rain like a Texas blue-bonnet. He was hungry, cold and miserable. He had run away from home, hitching himself to a chuckwagon cook in the wake of a moving herd. But the cook proved to be a slave driver and the lad decided to strike out on his own. All this great world beyond his Texas home fascinated him. As yet it was but a dream. He couldn't get beyond Fort Worth. Here were wagon trains, mule skinners, scouts, soldiers, Indians, teamsters, cowboys, gamblers, freighters.

"New Mexico is closer to the markets. Better chance for the cattle." The boy hoped. These boys in grey were planning on moving a herd. "Looks like the West will be the beef market of the East," said another.

"Wish those longhorns were not so d—m skinney."

The boy approached the men as they turned into the hotel:

"Please, sirs. Any messages. Any errands. A meal is all I ask in payment."

They looked at him a moment. The shortest one laughed:

"No need to work on a night like this. Come on in. We'll see what can be done about feeding you."

Supper over, the boy told them he had no place to sleep. That, too, was arranged. Slade, that seemed to be the name of the generous one, was changing to civilian clothes. He was headed Santa Fe way with a freight wagon to do some hauling along the Santa Fe Trail. Jim Greathouse, the boy, was invited along to help with grooming the horses, carrying water, chopping wood. Freighting was to be the work of his life.

In Santa Fe he learned to read and write betweeen trips as well as pick up Spanish. During these years he came to know Elkins, Maxwell, Catron, Seligman, Ortiz, Otero and others whose names are star-dust in the firmament of New Mexico history. Had he taken advantage of his opportunities he might have been one of the Territory's Greats. At times he would join a band of returning cowboys south down to Brice's Crossing in San Saba county in Texas to visit his folks. They decided not to stand in the way of what he wanted. Besides, he seemed to be pretty capable of taking care of himself. He loved the freighting business in preference to ranching. That they would not take away from him. A body might do worse. Greathouse was offered a job by Lucien B. Maxwell but declined it, for he was engulfed and wrapped in his own vision of greatness. He dreamed dreams of the largest freighting business along the Santa Fe Trail. These dreams might have become a reality had it not been for the progress of the railroad.

As the Iron Horse puffed its way westward there was less and less need of his services as a teamster. If he wanted an express company it would not be along the fast dying trail. Pushed by progress and crowded by ambition, he fell in with a group of cattle rustlers that operated in the area between Las Vegas and Fort Sumner.

Jim Greathouse was short of stature, slight of build, dark complexioned and wore a long mustache. He was often mistaken for a native New Mexican and often disguised himself as one when he entered the bosque at Anton Chico to visit Billy the Kid in hiding and when he rustled cattle which baffled the posse as to his identity. He developed a cleverness in arousing public sympathy in his favor so that he was stamped as a victim of circumstances and a tool used by outlaws who eventually brought about his destruction. Greathouse was not the innocent lamb led to the slaughter that the newspapers of the day portrayed him to be. Every deal he manipulated he worked to his advantage. Let others suffer in poverty; he would live in greatness.

When working as a teamster he freighted to Fort Stanton, where he made the acquaintance of Emil Fritz, Dolan, Brady and Murphy. Giving up his job with the freighting house in Santa Fe he drove for a time for the Moore Mercantile Company that managed sutler stores at Fort Union, Fort Craig, Fort Bascom, Fort Stanton and Franklin (present El Paso). All the time he picked up a tremendous knowledge of the country. If ever a man could select a hideout Jim Greathouse was that man. He was not a spendthrift. He saved his take and soon had himself mules and wagons of his own. He opened his freight yard at Anton Chico, then a boom town and in good cattle country. Here he met and married a native girl and while he made her work like a slave he treated her with tokens of affection, buying her the best dresses on the market, building her a nice home and otherwise treating her with all the respect a wife is entitled to. Dick Brewer, Tom O'Folliard, Bowdre, Bonney and others were often guests at her home. While this was not to her liking, there was nothing she could do about it. Greathouse was often away for weeks at a time but she attributed this to his freighting business rather than to rustling. He had himself made deputy sheriff for Anton Chico often bringing prisoners to Las Vegas who opposed his will or were beginning to suspect some of his activities. He always managed to find a pretext for their arrest. If they said anything to the authorities in Las Vegas he always came back with the reply of defamation of character because he had the nerve enough to arrest them.

"John H. Mink, James Greathouse and a Mexican came in last night (to Las Vegas) from Anton Chico with two thieves who had stolen the mules advertised by Mr. Mink in the Las Vegas Gazette yesterday morning. He also brought the mules in with him. The men confessed that they had stolen the mules at some point near Santa Fe. The mules are in town and the thieves in jail" (Santa Fe New Mexican, October 18, 1879)

The Socorro gold stampede in the late 70's led prospectors

to the Rio Bonito area. Jack Winters and Harry Baxter decided to give up the idea of cowboying for Chisum and branch out on their own as placer miners. They were fairly successful but did not strike it rich until Johnny Wilson, a desperado from Texas, accidently hit upon the North Homestake and the South Homestake claims for them. When Wilson was asked to join as a third partner he said that he had no use for gold nor did he intend to be tied down to any one place by a mere gold mine. When he left his friends he had nine silver dollars to his name. His discovery produced $3,000,000 in gold. But Wilson went on his way as a cattle rustler, seeking out gunfighters, gamblers and fellow desperadoes. Baxter and Winters could not long hide their secret. Soon the whole Jicarilla range was spotted with mining camps here, out of which the most notable to fashion itself into a beautiful town was the camp of White Oaks.

Twelve miles from Carrizozo that was to replace Lincoln as the county seat, White Oaks by 1880 was quite a bustling place. Brick and stone buildings soon replaced the tent city and for all practical purposes it looked like the town not only arrived but was here to stay. Mrs. George L. Barber, formerly Mrs. McSween, was later to make it her home and here at White Oaks she was to emerge as Cattle Queen of New Mexico. Here during World War I Albert B. Fall, United States Senator and Secretary of the Interior during the Harding administration, made his home and was happy until the Teapot Dome bubble burst him into a decidedly unhappy frame of mind. White Oaks also boasted the law firm of W. C. McDonald, who became first governor of the State of New Mexico. Emerson Hough, reporter for the White Oaks Golden Era, called the town "Heart's Desire," which indeed it was. Now a ghost town it once boasted a population of 2,000. And it gave Jim Greathouse his golden opportunity.

Las Vegas, capitol of the wool industry at the time, worked a rigid program to bolster commerce and income for the merchants of the city by catering to the needs of Socorro, Park City, Magdalena and White Oaks. A stage ran on regular schedule to these places and mail contracts were drawn up.

Greathouse, impressed by the influx of miners in the White Oaks area, decided to expand. He purchased a ranch forty miles from White Oaks on the Anton Chico road and here he put up a stage station, warehouse and residence. This would be the place where his freighters would change horses, rest and feed as they hauled between Las Vegas and White Oaks. A minor station was built twenty miles closer to the mining community. He was beginning to see the fructification of his dreams. He continued his friendship with Bonney, Rudabaugh, Bowdre and others.

The United States Government tired of the killings in Lincoln county, sent Secret Service Operative Azariah F. Wild to investigate the lawlessness and to work with deputy marshall Pat Garrett and future Sheriff John W. Poe, an investigator in the services of the cattleman's association, formed with the purpose of protecting their stock against the inroads of rustlers. They united in an effort to break the stream of desperadoes and other unwanted characters flowing into Lincoln and White Oaks. Wild became suspicious of Greathouse. He reasoned that any man so companionable with such outlaws as Bonney, Rudabaugh, Pickett, Wilson and numerous others was certainly not on the side of law and order. Garrett agreed with him and a man was appointed to shadow Greathouse by falling in with him and, if possible, to work as one of his drivers. The Kid had been so close to capture so many times yet always managed to make his escape. He knew every move the posse made. He was getting this information from some one. Wild claimed that this someone was Greathouse.

One day his man who seemed to have worked himself into the good graces of the freighter, brought Wild a letter written by Greathouse. In it were mapped Poe's and Garrett's movements. The evidence was conclusive. Wild came to the conclusion that Greathouse was no better than the rest despite the legitimate business he operated. In time five more letters were intercepted and it was decided to arrest Greathouse in order to trap William Bonney, who was known to go to great lengths for a friend. But other events took place to prevent their carrying the plan into operation and brought Greathouse before the public attention as a very disabused and misunderstood man. The last thing Garrett, Poe and Wild wanted to do was to make a martyr of Jim Greathouse.

Under cover of darkness one night, Billy the Kid, Dave Rudabaugh, Billy Wilson, Charles Bowdre and Tom O'Folliard slipped into White Oaks to replenish their supplies, and pick up a few drinks. Billy himself was not a drinking man to any extent although he did polish off a dram now and then. They dared not come in the daytime for there was a price on their heads and White Oaks was full of men who would shoot first and ask questions afterwards. The reward money would help grubstake them. According to Greathouse, the road seemed clear of the posse and they could make it very nicely if they left town before sunrise. It was after the Lincoln County War. McSween and Murphy were both dead but the gang continued to operate strictly as rustlers with a killing thrown in now and then.

They had supper at the home of a person they trusted, and gave him a list of supplies needed. Some authors maintain that the purpose of the visit to White Oaks was to celebrate Bonney's birthday. Men like the Kid didn't wait for their birthdays to celebrate. Nor did they risk their lives to celebrate it where they would be shot on sight. Bonney was not the type to make much of a birthday. From the way he was brought up he would rather curse the day. Pat Garrett says that Billy told him his date of birth but as yet no one has come forth with any certificate of proof. While the announcement was supposed to be in a New York paper, I have never seen any photostatic copy of it. Neither do I believe has anyone else.

At dawn the next day the gang decided to skip before the town came to life. As they rode out, O'Folliard spied Deputy Sheriff James Woodland standing near the Pioneer Saloon, just in the process of completing his survey of the place to make sure that all was well before retiring for the day as he was the night officer. Deputy Sheriff Will Hudgens would take over the day shift. Hearing the sound of many riders, Woodland stood where he was without drawing a gun until certain. O'Folliard and Woodland grew up together in Texas and although they were on opposite sides of the fence, the tall outlaw would no more think of shooting his friend as he would his leader. Billy, more as a joke to watch O'Folliard's reaction, pulled out his six-shooter and fired at the feet of the officer. Even Woodland knew that the desperado could have killed him had he chosen. William Bonney was one of the most accurate shots ever to see the light of day.

At the sound of the shot deputies Jim Carlyle and James N. Bell rushed out from the Pioneer cantina and sent a volley after the rapidly disappearing riders. When safe from the firing, O'Folliard rode up to the side of the leader and asked:

"Why the shot?"

"The way I figure it, a friend of yours should be on our side. That was a sign of protest."

"I don't like that kind of protest on my friends." O'Folliard scowled and his usually jovial expression gave way to one of anger. The remainder of the trip was made in silence. That was the closest the two ever came to a rift.

Nor did White Oaks like that kind of protest. It was to have far reaching results. Above all it brought about the fall of the house of Greathouse. The citizens took exception to anybody's taking a pop shot at a deputy even in jest and when the culprit happened to be Billy the Kid something had to be done about it. Woodland reasoned correctly that the next time the Kid met him the aim would be higher up. Indeed, as the Kid rode along, his thought to himself, he had just that in mind since O'Folliard seemed to place such store by the deputy, then the officer had to go. Fortunately these thoughts were never given a chance to materialize. That shot was a tocsin that united a posse under Deputy Hudgens in a mad dash to overtake the gang. With the deputy were Jim Carlyle, Bell, Jim Watts, John Mosby, James Brent, Joe P. Longston, Ed Bonnell, Walter G. Dorsey, J. P. Baker, Charles Kelly and John Hudgens, brother of the deputy.

It was a raw day in November. The sky was overcast and there was the taste of snow in the air. There had been a storm several days before and travel was difficult with this additional threat. The deputy hoped that it would not come down to wipe out the fresh tracks of the desperadoes. The trail led to Coyote Springs, where Greathouse maintained a sub-station for his freight wagons. It was a small place stocked for feed for the horses and mules and fresh water. Here the outlaws drew rein. The Kid, suspecting that Woodland would not take the shot lightly and that a posse would tail him, would not permit a fire. The men had to content themselves with a cold breakfast which none of them relished on that dismal morn. Bonney's humor was about as glum as the weather. Cautiously the posse approached the adobe hamlet. Carlyle had spotted the horses lowering in the strong wind. He knew about as much of the habits of the gang as Billy the Kid himself.

Carlyle had a reputation as a gunman. Texas born, he had worked as a cowboy in Ellsworth, Abilene and Dodge City. His boon companions were Bob and Tom Emory, noted gunfighters for a time before giving themselves over to peace and order. In Kansas he became acquainted with Dick Brewer, Dave Rudabaugh, Tom Pickett and Jimmy Oglesby. He was one of the cowboys working for Shanghai Pierce the cattle baron, when the latter was thrown into jail for disorderly conduct by Marshall Wyatt Earp, and in the group attempting the liberation of the cattleman. Following an altercation with Bat Masterson over a killing in Ford county, Kansas, Carlyle headed for the southwest to work on the Murphy & Dolan ranch. He worked for a time with Emil Fritz and then for Chisum. With the gold rush to White Oaks he struck out for himself in the hopes of hitting pay dirt. He just plainly struck out. He worked for a time in a cantina as well as taking on the obligations of a deputy sheriff. He had known Pat Garrett when the tall marshall was broke in Kansas looking for a job in the stockyards and not adverse to a little rustling. Fortunately the lad took to buffalo hunting and did not stray too far afield as he steered his career into tracking down the Kid for which he has been canonized ever since. Pat swore Jimmy in as deputy because he knew him to be quick on the draw and fearless in a fight. Like Garrett, his wild days were over and he was convinced that nothing was to be gained in fighting law and order and a lot to be lost if he pursued that course. It has been said that he fought for Murphy during the Lincoln County War. This could be possible since he had been connected with the firm as a cow puncher. So much research has been done on who worked for Tunstall & McSween because of Billy the Kid that no one has bothered to find out who worked for Murphy in his store, his hide business and on his ranch. It would be nice to have a book on the Murphy side of the situation.

The noise of horses crumping the hardened snow was not lost on Bonney. He warned his men and they broke camp making for their mounts. They ran through a fusillade of bullets. Carlyle killed the Kid's horse. In the wild scramble that followed Billy left his heavy coat and gloves behind and Carlyle claimed them as the spoils of war. Dodging bullets and returning shots, the Kid managed to escape through the brush and stunted cedars without being hit. This proves the haste with which they hoped to wipe out the outlaws. All were excellent shots, but not a man was wounded in the heavy exchange of fire. Perhaps they were not trying hard enough, for the pursued were even deadlier shots. After a half-hearted attempt at pursuit, the posse gave up the chase. The outlaws fanned out in different directions, making it hard for Hudgens to decide which one to go after. The Kid they left to his own course. With him behind a bush every one was a target for his gun and how many he would take with him before being hit was a question they didn't care to answer. After a time they went back over the trail in the hopes he would be too tired, but the wiley outlaw had hidden himself so completely they gave up.

Back in White Oaks they poured life into their benumbed bodies as they talked over their mis-adventure of the morning. They had a sympathetic audience in the other men playing cards at the Pioneer cantina. Carlyle said that he thought he had an idea where the gang could be found. Just as soon as he rested up he was going to make another try. Rudabaugh, Wilson, O'Folliard and Pickett knew him to be friendly. They had been too busy trying to escape to note who the members of the posse were. Carlyle was on fairly good terms with William Bonney. The deputy headed for Anton Chico. There he watched Jim Greathouse buy supplies and ammunition. More than was needed for the few hands that worked for him.

"Quite a load of ammunition you got there, Jim."

"Sure need it with all the rustlers on the loose. Got to protect my freight."

"Yes, guess you have."

Back in White Oaks he told the deputy Will Hudgens that if they were to capture the Kid and his gang they'd better get to Greathouse's ranch but fast. All night long like so many silent, moving shadows, they pushed on certain of their quarry. The sun just peeped over the horizon as they saw the Greathouse before them. Sequesting themselves in the shrubbery about the house, Winchesters drawn, they waited. The door opened. Out walked Johnny Steck, the freighting outfit cook, axe in hand to cut the firewood in preparation for the morning meal. Cautiously and soundlessly Dorsey and Baker approached him as he chopped. They grasped him from behind, Baker clapping a hand tightly over his mouth. They dragged him to the brush to be questioned by Hudgens.

"We don't aim to harm you any," whispered the deputy, "Jest you tell us if the Kid and his gang are inside."

"They be. They be," squirmed the frightened cook.

"Fine. Fine. Pick up an armful of wood. Take this note inside."

Wrote the deputy: You are surrounded. You haven't a chance. Come out without your guns and with your hands up.

Steck was rather reluctant to bring in the note. Hudgens pointed a gun at his back. "Get going." He motioned the cook to the house. The posse waited a few minutes. The door opened. Jim Greathouse carried the answer. Written below the deputy's note were three words in Billy's childlike scribbling: Go to hell.

It was to be a fight. Greathouse knew this as well as the deputy. He would be safer here out in the open than in his own house. Carlyle realized that a fight would also mean the death of many of the posse. Rather than have blood spilt unnecessarily, he offered to go in and talk to the Kid.

"I've known some of these men in there for years. I am sure they will listen to me."

"He is right," said Greathouse hopefully. "The Kid and O'Folliard have praised him often. It is worth the try. I am sure the Kid will do nothing to hurt him. If the Kid holds him, you've got me as a hostage." It sounded reasonable enough to Hudgens.

"If the Kid harms a hair of Carlyle's head, I'll stand up before your guns," offered Greathouse.

Hudgens was not satisfied, but decided that it was worth a try under the circumstances.

"Tell the Kid," he said to Carlyle, "If you are not here by two o'clock it means war and Greathouse will receive the first shot. Induce him to surrender if possible since he cannot escape, for we plan to wait right here from now to doomsday."

Carlyle stood up in full view of the house so that all within could see he was unarmed and he tossed aside his Winchester and unbuckled his gun belt. He approached the house. The door was opened to let him in. The station boasted a small cafe where travelers were served meals, and a small bar. The Kid took down a bottle and offered Carlyle a drink, pouring one out for himself. Carlyle reached into his pocket to pull out some tobacco in order to roll a cigarette. In doing so a glove slipped out and fell to the floor. Billy reached down and picked it up. He looked from the glove to Carlyle. Then it dawned on him. This man was no longer a friend. Loyalty was a sort of religion with William Bonney. To him Carlyle was a Judas.

"Did you get my coat, also?"

"No, Baker got that."

Billy reached down and pulled out his revolver. He looked at it for a moment and said:

"Jim, you haven't finished your drink." Pickett lived for over fifty years after this event, but as long as he lived he never forgot this cat and mouse scene. "Drink up. You won't be able to later. Your type are not permitted the opportunity of drawing even if you had a gun." Carlyle lifted the glass and began to drink. The Kid put his gun away.

"So, you want me to surrender. To go to jail. Me, Bowdre, O'Folliard, Rudabaugh, Pickett—all with prices on our heads. Who profits by our capture? Not us. So, we don't surrender."

"If you don't plan to surrender let me go and tell those waiting outside."

"We have time. It's not two o'clock yet."

Two minutes after two one of the posse shot his gun in warning. The battle was on. All the time Carlyle was figuring how to get out of the place. There was a window close by. The warning shot was not pre-arranged consequently Carlyle figured that Greathouse was killed. He went through the window with a crash but before he quite hit the ground the Kid put a bullet through him. The shot merely wounded him. Instead of lying still he began to crawl towards the posse. A second bullet made it unnecessary. All afternoon until eight o'clock that evening the firing continued.

When the battle commenced Greathouse was with Deputy Hudgens. As the officer concentrated more and more on the battle he paid less and less attention to his prisoner. Inch by inch Greathouse worked away until he had enough distance to get up and run to the horses. He jumped on one and was off to Anton Chico. Meantime the chill of the night made the posse uncomfortable. It was decided to ride back to White Oaks. They were permitted to take the body of Carlyle with them. Believing this to be a ruse, about midnight the Kid kicked the door open and guns blazing away the gang made for the corral and their horses. It was a waste of ammunition. Cold and hungry, the posse actually rode on to the mining town.

All of White Oaks turned out for Carlyle's funeral. Resentment was at white heat against Greathouse. This proved conclusively that he was in with the gang.

"If the gang didn't have the Greathouse place to go to, it might help," said a miner. All agreed that this was correct. "Let's burn it down." Back to the freight station they went. There was no sign of life stirring. The place was abandoned. Coal oil was poured over the rough floors, the adobe walls, the vigas, the corrals, the out-houses. Torches lit the blaze that crushed Jim Greathouse. Several days later Greathouse viewed the ruins. He used this vandalism to his advantage. Said the Las Vegas Optic May 19, 1881:

"Jim Greathouse will arrive today from Anton Chico with a freighting outfit. Jim has had hard luck, and was the victim of bad associations. Last November his house on the road to White Oaks was burned, the result of a 'siege' against Billy the Kid and party. Greathouse has been hard at work at Anton Chico and has inspired a confidence in many who were inclined to believe that he has been in standing with lawless characters. He has purchased four yoke of oxen and two teams and comes here to solicit freight for White Oaks. He is regarded as an honest, faithful fellow, and any who have freight to be taken to the Oaks should make terms with him. He will run a freight train regularly from here to the big camp."

Over in the Oscuras was the little mountain village of Guadalajara. A ghost town now, at one time it gave promise of becoming a cattle center for San Antonio, Carthage, San Pedro, San Antonito and Mal Pais. In the hills about the village rustlers hid cattle and changed their brands. Here Greathouse had his headquarters when not engaged in freighting. One of the rustlers he dealt with was Joel Fowler who had a ranch close by. They were quite friendly for a time until Fowler began to suspect him of tricking him. They became bitter enemies. Greathouse told Fowler he was mistaken in believing that he did not receive his share of the take. One thing led to another and each vowed to kill the other on sight. Cowboys in the vicinity heard of the possible gunfight and took up bets on the victor. Fowler kept an eye on Greathouse from a distance. He studied his habits until he had a pretty good idea of the freighter's schedule. He knew when, where and how he could trap him.

Greathouse did not seem particularly concerned about Fowler's threats. He had confidence in his own skill and knew he was quicker on the draw than his enemy. Fowler knew so too. To show his contempt for Fowler, Greathouse began to rustle his cattle. The day that Fowler selected for killing Greathouse everything went wrong. In the first place Greathouse changed his schedule. And to top it all, instead of being alone he had two other men with him. Trailing the trio into the mountains, he waited until they pitched camp and began cooking supper. He had a better chance against them if they were out of reach of their rifles.

He had no difficulty picking them off. Cowboys discovering the bodies two days later claimed that all three were shot in the back. Here by the side of his camp fire died the dreamer of dreams, the man who envisioned great freight lines all over New Mexico, Texas, Colorado and Kansas. Perhaps it was better that way. He might have died in jail.

The marriage of Emma Silba (to Victor Rodriguez). From the day she was adopted by Vicente Silba to the day she burned to death at Las Colonias, N.M., her's was a hard lot.

BOOK SEVEN

THE LAST OF BILLY THE KID'S GANG

(Tom Pickett)

Standing there at the grave of Tom Pickett in Winslow, Arizona, looking northeast to the San Francisco Mountains and southeast to the Painted Desert, I guess it doesn't make too much difference now in the light of our present generation whether he rode with Billy the Kid or not. As evening shadows fall each night buries the past. Looking at the grave and thinking of how many people had to be born to make just this one life interesting the ghosts of his past ride into the horizon of the Arizona sky along the path of memory lane defying us to forget. I guess it doesn't matter now what Pat Garrett was before he killed Billy the Kid, or after; why Brazil killed Garrett; why names like O'Folliard, Bowdre, Rudabaugh, Wilson, Pickett will ever live in legend as long as these tales are told simply because the Kid has become a legend and dying becomes as immortal as Shakespeare, Napoleon, Lincoln. I guess the deeds of men ride on forever; only the men die. For every schoolboy that knows General U. S. Grant five know Billy the Kid. For every schoolboy who learns to play a fiddle, a hundred have learned to shoot a gun even if it's only a toy. That's the way of the world, my friend. That's the way of the world. Perhaps men like Pickett, who reposes here, have made some sort of contribution to our history. Who knows? He is not so far away from the Hash Knife Ranch where he blazed away in glory in the Graham-Tewksbury War similar to the Lincoln County War only in that men died a-shooting and with their boots on. The grave is the rallying point.

Pickett lived by the six-shooter but strangely enough he died a peaceful death. Over beyond the Hash Knife is Holbrook where he met his lady love and mourned her many years as she preceded him in death. His was the way of a transgressor; his was also the way of the Penitent Thief. His life might have been more thrilling perhaps if he made his exit as did Bowdre, O'Folliard and the Kid himself but he lived to fight another day and to enjoy the comforts of life made possible to Everyman following the first World War. He lived in one great era to overlap another.

1857. The eyes of Texas are focused on something unique and novel in the history of our country—camels. On May 14 of that year thirty-four camels were landed at Powder Horn. The Federal Government was interested in the experiment of a Camel Brigade for the Southwest. Once on tierra firma the animals kicked, jumped and made funny noises strange to the pickets and raced around their enclosure with the greatest display of energy they showed before or since. They rated headlines as they moved from Indianola (Port Lavaca) to San Antonio.

Up in Decatur, north of Fort Worth, in Wise county, the Pickett family, the most important in town, was not concerned for the moment with camels. A new addition had come to the family and his name was written in the family Bible as Thomas and his relatives foretold great things concerning him. The father was well known in Texas political circles and is remembered for his acts as a member of the legislature. The boy would be remembered for other reasons. This was also the same year that saw the Buffalo Bayou, Brazos and Colorado Railroad complete thirty-one miles of track from Harrisburg to Richmond as forerunner of the death of the romantic cattle drive that was to introduce Tom Pickett to Kansas and New Mexico.

George B. Pickett, father of Tom Pickett, moved to Texas in 1842. He was a native of Kentucky. Pickett's mother was Cordelia Scarborough. George Pickett was one of the few settlers able to get along with Indians until the Civil War when the Comanches suddenly turned against him and cleaned him out. George was an officer in the war serving the Confederacy and had command of the military post at Decatur. After the war he served as district judge and was elected several times to the state legislature.

The boy grew up on the ranch much as other boys. A little bit of schooling, chores, hunting, milking cows, feeding chickens, mending fences, then a horse and saddle of his own to ride the range. These were difficult years. Drought, Indians, rustlers, the aftermath of war, the rise of the cattle industry, frontier forts, buffalo hunters, the cattle drives. Tom grew tall and straight as a poplar tree. He was over six feet. Most of his free time was spent in target practice for he had already made up his mind to become a cowboy and trail herds to the Kansas stock yards. He often joined cowboys as they rounded up the longhorns around Decatur and the freedom of the open range fascinated him. His mother never had a harsh word for him nor would she permit her husband to be severe with the lad in any way. This Tom took advantage of and before long he found himself involved with cattle rustlers. It was exciting and it brought ready cash which he enjoyed spending. He was seventeen by the time that the sheriff caught up with the thieves and the terrible news was carried to the Picketts that their boy was in some way involved. Tom's father went to see the Justice of the Peace. If it were possible in some way to keep the boy out of jail he would appreciate it.

"Cattle rustling is a serious charge," said the Justice. "Men have dangled at the end of a rope because of it."

"Isn't there some way to keep him out of jail? Tom isn't a bad boy, just got himself mixed up with the wrong crowd." Parents are parents the world over and have been since the dawn of time.

A heavy fine was imposed. So heavy that the Pickett home ranch was mortgaged to pay it. No one could convince the mother that the lad was mixed up in the affair. She pampered him and refused to believe that it was anything but a trick of political enemies. Things went along smoothly for a time and the young man joined the Texas Rangers. For a year and four months he rode on the side of the law, chasing rustlers, killing

Indians, making the name of Texas Ranger feared by the enemies of law and order. Then, as suddenly as he entered he gave it up.

Back to Decatur he drifted into listlessness, hunting up old friends, and living a life of ease. He took to riding the range, again fell in with rustlers and made raids into Cooke county. Gainsville, Muenster, Marysville and Sivell Bend were being colonized by hard working settlers from Europe who had come to America to make a living. Many of them were handicapped by the lack of English, struggling to adjust themselves to a frontier so new and so different from Old World ways. They were an easy prey for Indians, land sharks, outlaws and rustlers. But they had the fighting spirit that characterized them as Texans and refused to give up.

The steady loss of stock around Myra, Lindsay, Muenster Valley View and Woodbine became alarming. Try as the sheriff from Gainesville might, he always ended in a stalemate. Pickett he had seen around often but knowing of his fine record as a Texas Ranger he never bothered to question him. Not until Tom began spending freely and frequently at Gainesville. He was eventually hailed before the court and tried on five charges of cattle rustling. He escaped, joining an outfit trailing a herd to Kansas. There he became acquainted with Rudabaugh and others he was to know in Lincoln county. The Santa Fe railroad moved on to "end of track" at Las Vegas and Pickett joined the Dodge City gang there under Hoodoo Brown. The city officials, hearing that he had served as a Texas Ranger, made a constable of him. At times his conduct was not very becoming an officer as we gather from the Las Vegas Optic for January 30, 1880:

"Tom Pickett, policeman in the Old Town, took off his star last night and went to bed. Dr. Shout is waiting on him and thinks he can bring him around in two or three days." Tom enjoyed his drinks and as he made the rounds the bar tenders in Las Vegas. After a time this life bored him and he went to offered them freely and they were freely accepted. Despite these drinking bouts, Pickett was soon chief of merchant police White Oaks where he hoped to strike it rich, but ended up as a bar tender. This also proved not to his liking and he hired out as a cowboy at the Yerby ranch where he became acquainted with Billy the Kid and joined his gang. This was after the Lincoln County War. Pickett never knew McSween nor Tunstall.

"Tom Pickett, who was arrested with the Kid's party at Stinking Spring, was in New Town today accompanied by officers. He was trying to secure bondsmen. No charge has been brought against him, and Major Morrison has concluded to release him without an examination provided he can give bond for his appearance at the next term of court in the sum of $300. After leaving Las Vegas some months ago, Pickett went to White Oaks and was employed in H. J. Patterson's saloon as bar tender. From there he went to Fort Sumner and hired out to work on Yerby's ranch which was in charge of Charles Bowdre. He first saw Billy the Kid in Fort Sumner and met him again on the road and at the ranch. His calling as a cowboy required him to ride over certain ranges in order to prevent the cattle from straying away, and it was while on a ride of this type that he met The Kid on that fatal day. They rode together to Bowdre's place where they were overtaken and captured in a bunch by Garrett's party. Pickett claims no connection with Billy the Kid's gang."

On December 31st. Pickett was arraigned before Judge Morrison. He waived an examination so the judge fixed the price of his liberty at three hundred dollars, plus fifty dollars court costs, with the injunction that he was to make his appearance at the next term of court. From the comment of the Las Vegas Optic reporter we gather that Pickett made a fiasco of his prison term: "Tom Pickett, who was once a policeman in West Las Vegas, greeted everybody with a hearty grip of the hand and seemed reasonably anxious to undergo an examination. Pickett is well connected but he has led a rather wild career. His father lives in Decatur, Wise county, Texas, and has served as a member of the legislature. All the home property was once mortgaged to keep Pickett out of prison, but he unfeelingly skipped the country, betraying the confidence of his own mother." (Daily Optic Monday, December 27, 1880)

Pickett was no more interested in the next term of court than he was in paying the fine. With Billy Wilson, Rattlesnake Sam and several others he established headquarters in the region of Seven Rivers in Lincoln county and went back to cattle rustling. This was good grazing country and natives often brought their cattle and sheep here to feed. Others bought ranches in the region and went back into the stock business. Juan Lerna had a ranch at Seven Rivers and hired Melquiades Flores, Sisto Gutierrez and Teodoro Ulibarri to cowboy for him. His cattle were well attended and the market prospects good. Pickett often eyed this stock and planned to appropriate them. But the natives were too cagey for him. He decided that the only way to run off the cattle was to kill Flores, Gutierrez and Ulibarri. The others agreed. Riding up to the two preparing dinner they demanded the cattle. When refused, they were shot and the cattle run off. The sheriff eventually rounded up Pickett but he was released for lack of evidence.

Discovering that Judge Morrison dropped the charges concerning his position with Billy the Kid, he returned to Las Vegas, dressed up in hunting togs, permitted his hair to grow in imitation of the famous poet-scout Captain Jack Crawford, and strutted about the streets of the city with a brace of revolvers and bragged that he was the last of Billy the Kid's outlaws. He walked about with a sneer and a devil-may-care look. Children feared him. People crossed the street to avoid him. He defied anyone to draw on him. One day Bat Masterson came town.

"I hear it said that you are plenty tough and quick on the draw, Tom." Pickett stood there for a moment, dazed.

"Well, draw, Mr. Pickett, draw. I'm waiting."

"I'm no gunman. I just wear these to impress people."

After this children came up to him: "How is Billy the Kid's sidekick today? Why did you let Masterson go?"

Pickett left town.

He next associated himself with the Hash Knife outfit in Arizona, a short distance south of the Little Colorado River, southeast of Holbrook, in an area called Pleasant Valley and the Tonto Basin. It was cattle country until the Tewksbury's decided to drive a herd of sheep over the rim of the Mogollon Mountains to graze on the lush, rich grass so useful to cattle ranchers. Cattlemen didn't mind sheep if they just ate the grass but they pulled it out by the roots. With enough sheep in the valley the place would eventually become a dust bowl. It was bad enough fighting Apaches but now the very existence of their stock was at stake.

The Aztec Land and Cattle Company was more popularly known as the Hash Knife outfit from the shape of its brand. It originally organized in 1883. It boasted about sixty thousand head of cattle ranging from Pleasant Valley far south into the Tonto Basin. John Jones was the first foreman. Rudabaugh worked for him a short time prior to his job for the Governor of Chihuahua. Actually this outfit had no connection with the Tewksbury-Graham War, but many of the cowboys took up the fight for Graham partly because they wished to preserve the grass for cattle and partly because they were ever on the side of excitement. Pickett, Billy Wilson, Lancaster, George Smith, Paine, Gilespie (called Glasspie by some), McNeal, Peck and several others decided to enter the battle.

The feud started in 1882 when George and William Graham were charged by the Tewksburys with larceny. A second charge was brought the following year but witnesses failed to appear and the Grahams were acquitted. Not to be outdone, the Grahams charged the Tewksburys with cattle rustling. Knowing that the Grahams would disapprove of sheep in Pleasant Valley, the Tewksburys signed a contract with the Daggs Brothers of Flagstaff who were sheep men. Night riders rode among the sheep, cutting them out and shooting them down. Killing sheep was not as bad as killing men. The sheep were eventually driven out of Pleasant Valley in 1887.

Ed Rogers, the Hash Knife wagon boss, was in agreement with other ranchers that sheep should be kept out. This is one reason why he hired so many cowboys with a reputation for being quick on the draw. When Martin Blevins disappeared from the valley, Pickett among others, decided that he had been killed. John Paine, Tom Tucker, Bob Gillespie, Robert Carrington, Tom Pickett, Buck Lancaster, George Smith and

H. Blevins went in search of the body under the leadership of Tom Tucker. It was a hot day in August. They rode until they came to the Middleton ranch near the eastern border of present Coconino county. Stopping for dinner there as was customary in those days, they encountered Jim Tewksbury who told them that he was not running a hotel. Tucker told him that they would try Vosberg's, the next ranch. All were rather taken aback at the lack of hospitality and at the affrontery of Tewksbury, who was not the owner of the Middleton place. As they turned to go, they were fired upon from the house. This sudden outburst unnerved them for a moment and they scattered for cover. Hamton Blevins had been shot through the head. Paine drew and shot at Tewksbury but was too hasty to take any aim. Tewksbury shot his horse.

Jumping so as not to be pinned under his horse, another shot fired from the house took off Paine's left ear. Holding his hand to the wound to staunch the flow of blood, and running for cover, Tewksbury took deliberate aim and shot him down. Tom Tucker received a bullet through the lungs. Carrington was wounded in the arm; Gillespie in the shoulder; Pickett in the leg. Pickett fired at the ranch house as he sped away, but as no target was in view this shooting proved uneffectual. The Middleton home was later reduced to ashes, no doubt in retaliation by some of the Hash Knife outfit. John Tewksbury, William Jacobs, Ed Tewksbury and Joe Bayer were charged with the murder of Paine and Blevins but they were eventually released for lack of evidence.

Seven days later Billy Graham was killed by Jim Houck, a Tewksbury partisan. Tom Graham decided to wipe out the Tewksburys after this and gathered a group of men under the leadership of Andy Cooper, a well-known desperado. Pickett felt that his leg was well enough for him to go along. Actually the wound never healed properly and years later he had to have the leg severed. Within sight of the Tewksbury ranch they came upon John Tewksbury and William Jacobs and shot them down.

Surrounded and outnumbered the Tewksburys had no choice but to fight it out. Outside the little ranch house a few were cut down. As the battle raged and the hogs got the scent of blood they began to feast on the prone bodies. Those within could do nothing but gaze at the scene in horror. Mrs. John Tewksbury decided to bury them, come what may. Shovel in hand she walked to where her husband lay and dug a grave deeep enough to prevent the swine from molesting the dead. Jacobs, lying next to her husband, received the same consideration. Not a shot was fired until the brave woman was through. After she returned to the cabin the battle was renewed. News of the affair was sent to Payson and Justice of the Peace John Meadows arrived with some men to save the Tewksburys from annihilation.

Sheriff Mulvenon came in from Prescott and took possession of the Perkins' General Store, a building built of stone as a protection against Indian attacks, during Apache war-path days. This building was within sight of the Graham ranch house. He secreted his posse within, drove the horses out of sight, and sent several men to ride by the Graham place so as to be seen by the Grahams who would suspect that the few remaining Tewksburys had hired more gunmen to carry on the fight. Opposite the store was a stone wall, part of a building abandoned before quite completed. John Graham and Charles Blevins eventually rode over to the store. Sheriff Mulvenon ordered them to put up their hands. This they refused to do. Rather they reached for their guns. From both hideouts came a cross-fire. Their guns were never used.

Shortly after this on October 8, 1887, Tom Graham, who somehow managed to escape the sheriff's trap, married Anne Melton and it looked like the range war was over. During the lull, Pickett took time out to court and win a bride. He was now thirty years old and decided that he was the marrying kind. Over in Holbrook Mrs. Kelly ran a boarding house. Many of the section hands from the Santa Fe railroad were her boarders. Her pride and joy was a daughter by the name of Catherine. She was a tall girl with sparkling Irish eyes, pink skin and rather wide mouth. She and Pickett hit it off very nicely and the Hash Knife boys gave them a wedding to remember. She was a good influence on Pickett. A year later she died in childbirth. Nor did the child survive. Something died that day in Pickett too, for he was no longer interested in Graham, the Hash Knife nor Arizona. He wandered from pillar to post as a monte dealer, a gambler, a prospector, a lost soul. His huge frame took on more and more weight and his leg bothered him to no end. He followed the gold rush into Nevada but had no luck. During the Wilson administration he served as a deputy U. S. marshall in Nevada. At the turn of the century he had petitioned for and received a full pardon from Texas on the five charges of cattle rustling still hanging over him. His leg got no better so he had it amputated. Possibly because he wished to end his days near the place where he first met Kate, possibly to re-live the Hash Knife days, he returned to Arizona and died at Pinetop on May 14, 1934, and was buried at Winslow. He was one of the very few to ride with Billy the Kid to live a full life, although not a very lengthy one. He was seventy-six when he died.

Book Eight

BLOOD MONEY

(J. Joshua Webb)

The snow fell silently, evenly, without spinning or whirling, as if tired and glad to rest on the ground. The doctor from up Webster way was drying his hands and pondering the advisability of riding in that snow. An elderly man bent with the weight of cares rather than age stood behind him.

"Another mouth to feed, Job," said the doctor without turning.

"Yes. Makes eleven."

From the corner of the cabin the new-born baby wailed. His mother fondled him a moment.

"Guess I'll get up tomorrow to milk the cows."

"Yes. Moab can chop the wood. Samuel can take care of the corn crib. Penny is big enough to help in the kitchen. Time Jonathan shifted for himself. Fifteen. He's a man now. David must quit hunting about the Delta river and mooning. Goes about like a rich 'un."

"What name for the new born, Job?" asked his wife.

"Joshua."

"I fancy John."

"Then John Joshua shall it be."

Job Webb had pioneered in Iowa. He had moved in with the Great Free State movement traveling from New England by way of Albany and the Erie Canal. Buffalo, the Great Lakes, Ohio, Illinois—increasing his tribe as he increased his wandering. Job was a restless soul looking for an Utopia the way some people look for gold. He was forever searching the Law and the Prophets for an answer to his problems.

Job was in sympathy with the Friends of Universal Reform. To him the world was cold, unfeeling, bred by commercial interests and isolation. To exist, expand, feel, possess himself in his own uniqueness was a force that compelled and impelled him from place to place like a wanderer seeking peace and happiness that always seemed to elude him. They were never without their daily bread, the Webbs, and for this he was thankful enough. In Iowa, on the banks of the Delta he built his cabin free at last from an ever spreading world that always crowded him. Here on February 13, 1847, John Joshua came to add to his burden and his grief.

But even Iowa seemed beyond him, for he hitched up the schooner one day, packed his goods and his family and headed for Weeping Water, Nebraska. The years passed eventfully enough but the urge to move would never lie quiet with him and again the family was off this time for Oskaloosa, Kansas. The seat of present Jefferson county, it was once the scene of Samuel Peppard's "sailing wagon" that started out for Pike's Peak as a prairie vessel. It never got there. Oscaloosa was also known for its Lazy Club in the 60's and a Barlow knife was awarded each year to the best loafer. Here the Webbs seemed to rest, for after Oskaloosa there is no more moving. Here Joshua apprenticed himself to some buffalo hunters and in time became quite a hunter himself. He took a contract to supply rail workers with meat.

In 1867 Willow Creek in northeastern New Mexico became the scene of feverish activity and excitement over the discovery of gold despite the fact that this was private property belonging to Lucian B. Maxwell. However effectual he was about other things he was very ineffective in keeping the gold hungry horses off his property and soon there were thriving mining camps at Elizabethtown, Bland, Baldy, Willow Creek and Virginia City. Joshua staked out a claim at Willow Creek, where he had no luck, giving it up to work as a bar tender at Elizabethtown. He became involved in gambling and drinking and the spilling of blood. He made a hasty retreat from the camp and joined a government surveying party as a teamster and assistant buffalo hunter. The party left Baxter Springs, Kansas, in January, 1870, working south along the Neosho to the Creek Indian Agency, across the Arkansas from Fort Gibson, south again to the Red River into Choctaw territory, west and north through the Chickasaw, the Seminole, the Creek, the Cherokee. Paid off at Arkansas City in June 1871, Webb decided to try the mining camps in Colorado. It was while working for the surveying outfit that he became acquainted with Wyatt Earp, the boss buffalo hunter of the expedition, and with whom he was to work for a time as deputy in Dodge and Abilene. The Colorado venture proved as luckless as the New Mexico. He gave up the idea of prospecting for wood. He was a hunter, a gambler and a freighter. He was connected for a time with Wild Bill Hickok, Jack Martin, Billy Ogg and Andy Johnson, noted scouts of their day.

Like Coe, Webb was a striking figure of a man whether in his buffalo hunter's outfit or in store clothes. On the hunt he wore a heavy woolen shirt, a buckskin jacket made by a Creek Indian friend of his, trousers to match leather leggings. On his feet he wore moccasins. In town he wore black calfskin boots, white linen shirt open at the collar, a long-tailed frock coat of black broadcloth with dainty velvet collar attached covering a vest of fancy bead work that he obtained in a trade with a Chickasaw Indian, giving him a revolver for it. Beneath the turn-down shirt collar was worn a black, thin string tie. As a head covering he wore a wide-brimmed flat black sombrero.

Then came the profitable years. Up to this time buffalo hunters supplied railway construction gangs and army posts, Santa Fe caravans and some freighters with bison steaks, little caring about the hide. Following 1870, merchants began to interest themselves in the hides for Eastern markets. Wholesale slaughter commenced, the primary object being the hide rather than the beef of the animal. The extinction of the buffalo even for ulterior motives helped the progress of the West in several ways. It gave the army a better opportunity to corral Indians on the rampage, thus making the plains safer for travel. It helped agriculture, for wheat fields and corn fields sprang up where once the buffalo roamed. It decidedly advanced the cattle industry.

But Webb, the buffalo hunter, was not interested in the march of civilization. That he and a host of other hunters made the extinction of the buffalo a definite contribution to the forward progress of America was of little or no concern. The East was paying plenty for hides and he was out for all the money he could get. Buffalo hunting was commercialized. Webb hired several drivers, stock tenders, a camp guard, skinners and other hunters under contract to him. He supplied the horses, wagons, groceries, all of which he received on consignment. These were to be paid for at the end of the hunting season. When the hides were brought in, usually to the fast-growing settlement of Dodge, he was paid off in full. He kept one-half, out of which he paid all expenses; the other half was divided among the help. While he made a handsome profit he lost it at faro, in cantinas and painted harridans.

Over in the southeastern part of Sumner county, Kansas, old man Stone put up his trading post and general store which became a gathering place for buffalo hunters. Overnight the place blossomed out into a village, as lawless, wild, unruly and dangerous as any frontier town of the day, and the more so since it was near the border of the Nations Territory that was to become part of Oklahoma. The place was called Caldwell. The railroad had not as yet reached the place and the collected hides loaded into bull-wains were carted to the railroad by the thousands. During a major part of the hunting season, climatic conditions made it possible to keep buffalo meat in good condition until the buyers could ready it for shipment. Hindquarters and tongues were in as much demand as the hides. Webb decided to try another season, this time holding on to his money.

He averaged about eighty-five bison a day which was good shooting, since the top experts got a hundred a day at best. With a Sharp's rifle and his knowledge of the habits of buffalo he made out better than many. He invested his profits in a cantina and gambling hall. He was well respected and liked in Caldwell where he was made deputy sheriff and marshall. As marshall he gave a good account of himself and ranks with Earp, Masterson, Tilghman, Mather and Hickok as among the best in Kansas frontier history. He was quick on the draw, cool in a crisis and fair in his dealings with desperadoes and rustlers. Stern and unflinching in his work, he never used his office to take advantage of anyone nor to increase the patronage of his drinking establishment. With the downfall of the hide industry he sold out in Caldwell and took up hunting once more. Like his dad he was a roving spirit at ease only when away from the haunts of men.

He had no particular use for the railroad for it encroached on his life of freedom and brought in conventional living, education and dudes. It cropped close the long flying hair of free roaming, rugged individualism and the "Rugged Christianity" of Charles Kinsley. Back in Dodge he worked for a while as a bar tender. At a bar a man had an opportunity if he kept his ears and eyes open and his mouth shut. Here merchants, railroaders, cowboys, stockmen and freighters would come for drinks and seek out wagon bosses, skinners and hunters. Into the saloon one day walked one of the biggest merchants of them all—Andrew Charles Myers—builder of the trading post at Adobe Walls in the Panhandle of Texas. Webb gave up his job to become a teamster for Myers. Adobe Walls was an interesting place. Situated near the conflux of Adobe Creek and the Canadian river in Hutchinson county, it had good prospects for a future as tremendous as Dodge where Myers had his main store. Years before one of the Bent brothers attempted a post on the site, building it of adobe. A cattle trail passed on the site of the abandoned post and it was called Adobe Walls because of the ruins still standing. Here Kit Carson had his famous battle against the Comanches and this was the site of other famous battles involving buffalo hunters and wild tribes. Before long Myers realized his mistake and gave up the post, thus throwing Webb out of a job.

Webb next went to work at Fort Lyon in Colorado as a teamster driving a six-mule train. He worked the Fort Lyon-Fort Dodge route. As the railroad closed in his services were no longer required. At this time Dave Rudabaugh and his gang were the scourge of the country. Webb was deputy under Masterson in the arrest of this gang for the Kinsley train robbery. Dave turned State's Evidence and roamed around Dodge freely. He and Webb became friends. Another to join them was H. G. Neill, better known as Hoodoo Brown. Mysterious Dave Mather, Joe Carson and a character known as Dutchy joined the group. All of them served as marshalls or deputies at one time or another. Whatever Webb's connection with the group it soon enabled him to put up one of the more elegant saloons at Dodge which he called The Gay Lady. Owning a saloon was not held in ill repute. James H. Kelly, half owner of the Alhambra, was elected first mayor of Dodge.

Webb's Gay Lady was south of the railroad tracks which meant of course that it would not be frequented by polite society. For two blocks east and west from Second Avenue, First Street was the main street of town and housed the business establishments of the city. The depot, water-tank and freight house were at the east end of the plaza, and just south of the railroad tracks was the jail built in the form of a square, one room, the floor, walls and ceiling of which was composed of two by six timbers, spiked flatsides-to to one side of which the city judge and clerk perched a light board shack they used as an office. The Dodge House hostel was two blocks east of Second Avenue on the northeast corner of the plaza facing First Street and siding Railroad Avenue. Here Webb roomed. The postoffice, Wright & Beverly Mercantile Company, Delmonico eating establishment, the Long Branch, the Alhambra, the Dodge City Opera House, a gun store, two barber shops, the Wright House Hotel made up the respectable part of town. South of this and the tracks were hotels, corrals, dance halls, bagnios, gambling houses and forty saloons. Charlie Bassett, Bill Tilghman and Bat Masterson asked Webb to act as sort of deputy on this side of town, for they knew him to be a handy man with a gun. They had been buffalo hunters with him. Earp had several fights with cowboys in the Gay Lady.

As much as Webb hated railroads his next job was as chief of guards in the railroad battle for the Royal Gorge. He felt that the Gay Lady was too confining. He sold it and drifted into Colorado. As sorely as he wanted money he refused a bribe of eight thousand dollars if he would sell out to the rival railroad. He said his job was chief of guards and no amount of money could buy him. Whether General Palmer rewarded his faithfulness or not he never said. Heads were broken, men were killed, as the fight for the Gorge made railroad history and through it all he led his men like a veteran. He had qualities of leadership but itching feet kept him on the move.

In 1879 the Santa Fe railroad reached Las Vegas in New Mexico. The lawless element from Dodge that had taken over Otero at the "end of track" now moved into Las Vegas with the railroad. The Adams Express Company, impressed with Webb's work at the Royal Gorge, hired him as its agent in Las Vegas. Here he met Dave Rudabaugh, Hoodoo Brown, Mysterious Dave Mather, Joe Carson, Tom Pickett, Joe Martin and others he had known in Kansas. Carson, Webb, Rudabaugh, Mather and Martin became policemen and marshalls.

Mysterious Dave Mather, a distant relative of the great Divines of New England — for what student of literature is not acquainted with Increase Mather, Cotton Mather, Richard Mather and Samuel Mather?—and came into Kansas from New England because of the Free Soil Party movement. As a marshall he ranked with Wyatt Earp; as a shooter he was equal to Bill Hickok. But he loved gambling, dancing, drinking and brothels. All of which meant money which he didn't have to spend. Eventually he got it the easy way by joining Dave Rudabaugh as a bandit and rustler. He loved a fight and became one of the most popular gunfighters along the Texas cattle trails. He was pretty serious about his job as marshall in Las Vegas despite his association with the Dodge City gang. Said the Optic (January 8, 1880):

"Mysterious Dave, Webb and Combs left here a few days ago for the vicinity of Fort Sumner for some one that the law was reaching out for with its strong right arm. When the boys arrived within some ten miles of Fort Sumner, they were met by a crowd of big, burly fellows, each armed with a Winchester rifle and a couple of six-shooters, and informed the men that they were well known and that no minions of the law were wanted in that country; that they had better about face and tale the trail back to Las Vegas. They need not stand on the order of going but go at once. The boys held a short council and considering discretion the better part of valor turned their horses heads toward the setting sun and soon found themselves at home. Dave says that he lost no one either in that part of the country or in Lincoln county. Don't go to Lincoln county to make arrests. 'Taint safe, they say." Later we find: "Mysterious Dave, Charles Kirkland and several other Las Vegas boys (Webb among them) are in Santa Fe to give testimony on the late stage robbery." (Ibid February 24, 1880). Dave was twenty-two years old when killed in an argument with Joseph Costello in front of McKay's resrant in Las Vegas. He is buried at Las Vegas.

The Las Vegas Optic liked poking fun at the Justice of the Peace, Hoodoo Brown: "Squire Neill spliced his first couple Christmas Eve. He stood Joe Carson and Dutchy up on the floor and practiced on them before starting for the house where the bride and groom awaited him. Passers-by thought he was reading the riot act to Joe and Dutchy. He hoo-dooed them for life, though. . . ." December 26, 1879)

Miguel Otero, who became governor of the Territory of New Mexico, recorded these days at Las Vegas in a book, *My Life on the Frontier*. He said: "When the New Town section of Las Vegas organized as Precinct No. 29, and held an election of officers, the Justice of the Peace chosen was a 'mystery man' named H. G. Neill, who afterward became more generally known as 'Hoodoo Brown.' This very appropriate name was given him by one of the dance hall girls in Close & Patterson's in commemoration of one of her old lovers, the word Hoodoo meaning one who brings bad luck to anyone having anything to do with him. Associated with Brown as constable was a criminal known only as 'Dutchy.' The two succeeded in assembling in East Las Vegas a group of notorious confidence men, gamblers and killers who went locally by the designation of Dodge City Gang." It was because of this gang that the vigilantes organized and published this warning:

A TIMELY WARNING TO MURDERERS, CONFIDENCE MEN AND THIEVES:

"The citizens of Las Vegas have tired of robbery, murder and other crimes that have made this town a byword in every civilized community. They have resolved to put a stop to crime even if in attaining that end they have to forget the law, and resort to a speedier justice than it will afford. All such characters are therefore, notified that they must either leave this town or conform themselves to the requirement of law, or they will be summarily dealt with. The flow of blood must and shall be stopped in this community, and the good citizens of both Old and New Towns have determined to stop it, if they have to HANG by the strong arm of the law in this country.

(Signed) VIGILANTES"

Listed as undesirables, yet permitted to run the city as well as the police department were: Caribou Brown, Dirty Face Mike, Hoodoo Brown, Scar-face Jack, Pawnee Bill, Kickapoo George, Jack Knife Jack, Flyspeck Sam, Mysterious Dave, Hatchet-face Kit, Durango Kid, Pancake Billy, Cockeyed Frank, Rattlesnake Sam, Split-Nose Mike, Wet-fingered Billy, Wink the Barber, Double-out Sam, Jimmie the Duck, Flapjack Bill, Buckskin Joe, Cold-duck George, Pegleg Dick, Red River Tom, Hag Jones, Long Lon, Scrappy Smith, Stuttering Tom and Tommy the Poet.

Closely associated with Webb was City Marshall Joe Carson. Tom Henry (alias for Thomas Jefferson House), John Dorsey, James West and William Randall went about the streets of Las Vegas armed to the teeth. James West was better known as James Lowe. Webb, Carson, Mysterious Dave and Rudabaugh told them to take off their guns if they wished to have the freedom of the town. Instead of complying with the order, they marched up and down the streets of Las Vegas calling the constables all the dirty names they knew and more they made up. To bolster up their courage they went from saloon to saloon, dance halls, bagnios, gambling dens; all of which were quite plentiful at the time. The four carried two pistols each with an extra one tucked away in their belts. At the rate they were going something was bound to pop and Webb was rather alarmed. For four days nothing the constable and his associates could do would stop them. They could try to clamp them in jail but they knew that to do so would mean a massacre one way or the other.

On the night of January 22 (1880) they entered Close & Patterson's saloon in New Town (opposite the present Castenada Hotel now a vacant lot) very much saturated and extremely bellicose. They dared and defied everybody in the place. As Joe Carson was the constable on duty at the time he went over to them and asked them to turn their firearms over to the bartender. They laughed in his face and began to abuse him. The constable told them that they were under arrest. But they refused to be arrested. The lid was off.

Forty shots were exchanged. Carson had nine bullets in him, Randell four, Dorsey three in one leg. House and Dorsey and Lowe made their escape. House was for high tailing it to Texas but the wounded Dorsey pleaded with him not to forsake him. It was decided to hide out in the home of Antonio Dominguez, a friend living at Buena Vista near Mora. Webb and Rudabaugh were quite broken up over the shooting of their friend Carson. They questioned a few natives and one of them said that he suspected that the fugitives sought sanctuary at the Dominguez home. For a price he would find out. When certain that they were at Buena Vista the informer returned to Las Vegas and told Webb, who proceeded to round up Rudabaugh, Goodlett, Smith, Combs and Muldoon. They rode to Mora and sought out Sheriff John Dougherty in whose jurisdiction Buean Vista lay. The posse rode to Antonio's home with a search warrant. He pointed out the room where the wanted men were sleeping. Webb called out to them and told them to come out with their hands up. House said they would surrender peaceably if Webb would promise them protection. On the strength of his promise they gave themselves up and were taken to Mora. A. P. Branch did all in his power to make them comfortable. He suspected Webb and Rudabaugh and was firmly convinced that he would never see the prisoners again. Thomas Walton the hotel keeper provided them with food.

Meantime the Masonic Fraternity in Las Vegas gave Carson a grand funeral. Randall they ignored. Carson was a native of Rome, Georgia, and drifted into Dodge as a buffalo hunter. He had a fourteen-year-old daughter in school at Nashville, Tennessee. After his funeral the wife left Las Vegas for Chicago. Webb, Rudabaugh and Hoodoo Brown confined the prisoners in a cell and then went about gathering together the vigilantes. It was arranged to meet at 2 A.M., march to the jail, and take out the culprits and hang them. Despite their disguise and masks, Webb and Rudabaugh were recognized as the leaders of the mob. Webb first marched the men to Sheriff Romero's home. They did not find him in but his brother was there and they demanded of him the keys to the outer door. He refused. They promptly dressed him to the jail, making sure he had the keys. After he opened the outer doors the vigilantes dismissed him. Webb then shot two shots to awaken the jailor, who refused to come out. Webb called for battering rams and the vigilantes hammered away at the doors until they gave. The jailor confronted the mob, a six-shooter in each hand. He was told to put them away or die like the prisoners. He put them away. A rope was placed about the necks of the three prisoners and they were led out, Rudabaugh holding the ends of two, while Webb held the end of the third who limped because of his wounded leg, thus retarding the proceedings. Webb appointed two men to carry him. He howled and wailed, pleading pitiably. Henry turned to him and said:

"Jim, be quiet and die like a man."

Henry was half dressed and shivering with the early morning cold. He smiled as he turned to the man nearest him:

"Boys, you are hanging a mighty good man."

They were now at the old windmill in the Old Town Plaza.

"So you're the fellow who threatened to collect together a group of cowboys and burn us out?" Webb was working with the rope to make sure it would hold.

"Might have succeeded if it hadn't been for Carson."

"Got any folks?" asked Webb.

"Yep, up in Pueblo, Colorado. It's pretty rough to be hung. I wish someone would write to my folks."

"It will be taken care of," Webb assured him.

"Then I will stand the consequences and die like a man." He gave his age as twenty-nine.

Lowe was the first to be hung. His last words were: "Boys, button up my pants." The vigilantes must have really been in a hurry. In their haste to lynch the other two something went amiss and they had to be cut down. They were shot instead. Tom Henry fell at the first shot but crawling to the side of the platform he said:

"Shoot me again. Shoot me in the head."

Each body was placed in a separate box and the three given one large grave.

Hoodoo Brown insisted on knowing each shipment of gold that left the Adams Express office. How much information he got from Webb or others we do not know, but he hounded Webb with all the cruelty of a blackmailer. Webb had evidently done some dirty work for him and they were constantly seen often in each other's company.

Into Las Vegas, feeling high and mighty, came one Michael Keleher. He let it be known that he carried vast sums of money and was looking to buy a cattle ranch. Hoodoo went in search of Webb and asked him if he would not pose as a rancher willing to sell to Keleher. Webb was not interested. Hoodoo took Keleher around to a few saloons and finally deposited him at Close & Patterson's. Again he sought out Webb. This time it was arranged that the constable would arrest him for disorderly conduct. Keleher would resist and Webb was to shoot him for resisting an officer, at the same time reach into his coat pocket and take his money. Keleher had drifted into Goodlett & Roberts' saloon. Webb picked on him and arrested him for disturbing the peace. Keleher resisted. Webb shot him and in the act of searching him for weapons took the wallet. It was so obvious to the on-lookers that they couldn't believe their eyes.

For two days they talked it over and after burying the

stranger they decided that Webb had murdered him and went to Hoodoo Brown to ask him to place Webb under arrest. Brown had skipped town. The vigilantes took over. They surrounded the rooming house where Webb was staying and captured him. He still had five hundred dollars of the money on him. When Rudabaugh heard that Webb lingered in jail he took Johnny Allen along with him and the result was the death of the jailor. Webb refused to avail himself of the opportunity of escape. A trial was held and Webb sentenced to hang. At the last moment the governor commuted his sentence to life. As no attempt was made to bring Webb to the Territorial prison at Santa Fe he was kept in the Las Vegas jail where Rudabaugh found him following his trial at Santa Fe. Webb did not refuse the second opportunity at escape. He went to Dallas for a short time, where he again encountered Rudabaugh. When Rudabaugh was arrested in Dallas Webb went on to Kansas. Rudabaugh as usual escaped the Dallas jail. Leaving Kansas, Webb worked in Nebraska and Arkansas as a teamster for J. D. Scott & Co. He gave his name as Samuel King. (His mother's name was King. At Winslow, Arkansas, he contracted small-pox and died on April 22, 1882. Before his death he disclosed his real identity. Several persons were captured as Webb but always released. During the fight for Royal Gorge Webb lost a left eye tooth and had it replaced with one of solid gold. This saved a lot of innocent persons from hanging.

Not only was Black Jack Ketchum successfully hung; he was also successfully beheaded.

BOOK NINE

19 20 21 AND DEATH

(Porter Stogden)

The service was over. The clergyman walked over from the lowly frame church to an even lowlier dingy parsonage. This morning he was well pleased. The attendance was larger than usual and even a few cowboys that he had repeatedly asked to the prayer meeting had shown their faces. The collection, too, was good. Fort Worth was growing. He had faith in the little community, so much so that he turned down the offer of the pulpit over at Dallas. At the door he met Irma, his oldest girl. The sun played with her hair as she stood there, giving it the appearance of ripe, golden wheat. She was a short girl for a Texan but pretty. There was a minister from over Waco way interested in her and he thought it ought to make a nice marriage. How could he ever forget the day the Comanches killed her mother as they drove up from Castroville? Big Foot Wallace and some of his hunters saved the train that day but it was bitter to lose one who had been such a companion.

Irma was a quiet girl with dull eyes, although there were times these lit up with intensity and excitement. She looked so much like her mother now, the way she cocked her head as if listening for something that seemed far off. He once told a parishioner that her pale blue eyes had the tragic look of death. She stood there as if she had something important to say but didn't quite know how to begin.

"Good morning, daddy."

"Good morning, Irma. Is there something wrong?"

"No. Nothing. There is a young man in the study waiting to talk to you. Porter Stogden."

A thin, blond youngster of medium height was sitting in the room. He jumped off his chair with a quick nervous movement when the minister entered. He had a pointed chin and a knot at the edge of his jaw as if he nursed a wad of tobacco. Upon closer inspection it proved some sort of growth. He was handsome in an outdoor sort of way and looked about twenty. His face was leathery as if he lived to break the wind and still the tempest.

"Good morning." He had good, strong, white, even teeth.

"Sit down," said the minister when the formalities were over. "What can I do for you?"

"Sir, I want to marry your daughter Irma."

"What?" It was an exclamation rather than a question.

"Irma and I feel that we ought to be married." He added nothing more, waiting for the minister to carry on from there.

"How long have you known my daughter?"

"Since that Thanksgiving Day affair over at Talbot's. I cowboy for Talbot."

The minister sat back a moment. He remembered Stogden now. He had spent the day with Talbot and they had discussed plans for a new church. Irma had much of the day to herself and the cowboy had been in and out of the place several times during the day.

"I don't have much to offer, but some day I'll have my own place. I am sure I can make her happy."

"Irma," called her father aloud, "Come in here."

She looked pale and tiny as she tip-toed in.

"Irma, be honest with me. I had no idea. We had never any secrets from each other. Why didn't you tell me?"

No answer.

"Do you really love him. I had such plans for you. But this . . ." His voice trailed off. He looked from Stogden to his daughter, realized what he said, blushed, folded his hands together and looked at his desk.

"There is a cattle drive up to Ellsworth, Kansas, this spring.

If you feel she should have time to think it over, I'll wait until I get back. I'll come over and ask you again."

This seemed fair enough to the minister and a look of relief stole over him. Porter sensed that the clergyman then and there resolved to change his daughter's mind. All he succeeded in doing was to make Irma even more intent on the marriage. Stogden left a prospective bridegroom; he returned a prospective bridegroom, and a killer.

As far as the meat industry was concerned the years 1865 to 1879 were unlike any other ever before witnessed. The land between the Missouri and the Rocky Mountains boomed as never before and would only do so again with the rise of gold mining camps. The immense cattle drives opened a romantic chapter in the West during the post war years such as no gold rush to Pike's Peak could do, as intriguing as it was. It linked hands with the building of the railroad to give rise to Wichita, Ellsworth, Dodge, Abilene and a host of frontier false front towns whose only claim to fame, if we are to believe readers and writers of two-gun folklore, was that they were hallowed by the presence of such gunfighters as Doc Holliday, West Hardin, the Thompson Brothers, Mysterious Dave Mather, Allison, Rudabaugh, Webb and others whose deeds of daring baffle our poised, complacent Twentieth Century minds so that we enshrine them with reverence since we cannot emulate them in deed. More boys play at being Billy the Kid than Pat Garrett. More movies have been made of William Bonney than will ever be made of the sheriff. The only movie to my knowledge that mentioned the name outside of the Kid pictures was Four Faces West.

Texans took advantage of the opportunities offered them when the East clamored for longhorn beef. The army helped keep the supply line open with its numerous frontier posts from Fort Dodge to Fort Griffin. Texas was a vague name to many until the opening of the cattle trail as a steady source of employment for many of its youth. Texas beef became a household word in practically every home east of Kansas. And the Texans who steered this beef to the stockyards were long remembered. After a few drives a regular trail was established, usually called the Eastern Trail, the Loving Trail, the Chisholm Trail, the Goodnight Trail and several others, depending on the starting point and the route taken. Almost a decade before the Civil War a fellow from Illinois fighting in the Mexican War of 1846 saw the possibility of bringing cattle to the Eastern markets. Tom Candy Pointing was the pioneer who showed the way. Richard King, Mifflin Kennedy, Joseph McCoy, Jesse Chisholm, Shanghai Pierce, Loving, Goodnight, Chisum and many others by their employment of the cowboy did much to alleviate the situation in Texas.

In 1867 thirty-five thousand cattle were driven into Abilene and from there shipped east over the newly-opened Kansas-Pacific which had the foresight to give the cattlemen lower rates and threw in stockyards in the bargain. Rival railroads were quick to move westwards to open new markets that received the quaint name of "cow-towns"—Kinsely, Newton, Wichita, Baxter Springs, Ellsworth, Dodge City—moving ever westwards in the hopes of monopolizing all that Texas, Colorado, New Mexico, Nevada, Utah, Arizona and California had to offer. That the business was profitable is evidenced in the bee-like activity of Texas cattlemen pushing herds up the trails to the cow towns. Men scoured the country contracting for herds of longhorns to be delivered in time for the next spring drive, buying horses by the hundreds, for no cowboy rode the trail without at least two or three extra mounts; hiring riders by the dozens, while here and there companies were organized to obtain capital for investment. If the financial panic of 1875 had not checked the golden age of the cattle drive who knows to what extent the market would have been flooded. Several years later, due mostly to the constant pressure of the railroads and the rise of cattle barons, a new outlet for the drive was established up the Pecos River Valley of New Mexico into Colorado.

Every cowboy hired to trail cattle admitted that it was an adventure frought with danger. From central and even southern Texas the start would be made about the First of March, the riders or brush-poppers as they were called, usually gathered together cattle of many brands for which they gave a very loose accounting. It wasn't until much later that a state system of trail brands at different points before the Texas boundary was crossed that division of proceeds became a careful procedure. The men toiled incessantly, often going for days without food and there were sleepless nights when wind, rain and rustlers made cattle as uncontrollable as the northern blizzard sweeping over the plains. There were the ever pesty Indians ever alert to cut out the horses from the remuda or temporary corral that roped in the tame extras. No, the life was not an easy one. It hardened the men, which accounts for some of the rough things they did. It also accounts for the "hurrahing" of a town on payday. All that pent up feeling against unseen Indians, rustlers, howling wind, thirst, hunger, sleepless nights, sun-scorching days—they sure let go on a wild spree when they arrived at the end of the trail.

Like all rapid-fire progress, huge herds developed. To hold on to the ownership of his stock the rancher relied primarily on the old Spanish custom of branding but more hopefully on his riders. It was the daily task of the cowboys to "side-sign" around the area recognized as their special range and to turn back any cattle that went astray. Every spring after the timothy had grown lush and the heifers were fat enough and ready for branding the round-up began. As the range in those days seemed common property ranchers would group together in this undertaking on a co-operative basis. For this work a group of cowboys selected from the various ranches met under a captain and he ruled the roost. Such cowboys came to know each other very well—very much after the pattern of buddies in the two World Wars—and whenever the captain was through in one place they followed him to wherever he would lead them, sometimes becoming powerful enough to defy the law as organized cattle rustlers if they skipped the traces, and taking the law into their own hands to lord it over the non-rustler. Saturday night was their night in town. They came thundering in like a charge of cavalry after fleeing Indians, shooting up the place, drinking all the liquor in town, dancing, loving, gambling, killing, fighting. "Hurrahing the town" they called it. It was the birth of "boot-hill." As most of the cowboys were Southerners and had participated in the Civil War, they resented the Northerners—it was like biting the hand that fed them although they failed to see it that way—and many a Rebel yell was the signal for an all-out fight that a movie fan would have thrilled to have seen. Such affairs brought to our language the familiar words of "stiff," "boot-hill" and others. Of all the cowboys the Texans had the reputation of being the most fearless riders, the keenest masters of the ways of the half-tame roving cattle and certainly the most adept and skillful with the lariat. More than the northern cowboy they fancied the pleasures of the bottle, gun-play, brawls and boisterousness. Of necessity they were hardy, muscular, wiry, self-reliant, often confusing recklessness with daring, and were noisy and truculent when under the standard of their leader, especially on the first Saturday following pay day. They had a sense of humor not quite agreeable to some of the characters they met up in cantinas and homes of Cyprians, and the result was usually gun-play. Sometimes it was petty pride to prove themselves quicker on the draw.

If such traits made the cowboy out to be a ruffian it must be remembered that he had to be tough to survive to go into some other field of endeavor. His social life, too, was pitched to a key of conflict that there was not a day in which he wasn't fighting something or other whether it be the elements, rival factions, Indians, rustlers, dudes, gamblers, rivals in his affections for a dance hall girl, a painted cat, nestors, builders of the barriers of barbed-wire fences that cut down horses and cattle as no Indian or rustler would. There were no barriers on the range—the cowboy was free thinking, free loving, free working, free killing, perhaps because the wide open spaces made him free as a bird.

On the other hand, drink, song and gaming tables are what these "cow-towns" had to offer. Here they found the habitats of vice; here the more popular resorts were saloons, gambling dens, bagnios, dance halls, billiard parlors that sheltered a dissolute and desperate breed of men and the proprietors were ever ready to prey upon the society-hungry cowboy with money burning a hole in his jeans and the taxes levied on such establishments built the first schools, court houses, libraries that generated a second generation of men of worth, education, culture and refinement that brought sudden death to the places that gave them life. A happy merry-go-round but a fact nevertheless.

Caught in the vortex and fascinated by it all was Porter Stogden. He was prepared for it as he rode the trail, regaled by the stories of his comrades as to what he would find at Dodge, Abilene and the frontier towns reaching out for the cattle and for his money. He practised incessantly how to draw, aim and fire so that soon he was as handy with the six-shooter as was the best of them. He knew the Rebel yell as no rebel did and his easy going ways made him acceptable to the gang. He got to know Dick Brewer, Ben Thompson, Doc Holliday, Clay Allison, Dave Rudabaugh, Wilson, Pickett and others whose names appear and reappear wherever frontier gunplay history is told.

In the midst of a thousand square miles of gamma grass, on the right bank of the Smoky river, as seemingly flat as the plain on which it stood, was the northern terminus of the Texas Trail, answering to the sweet name of Ellsworth. In the year 1873 it boasted a stable population of three hundred and a fluctuating population of hundreds more. Life in this community centered about a plaza without benefit of a tree for shade nor for hanging. You walked in dust or mud depending on the season. Skirting one side of the town was the railroad, newly arrived, with its standard fixtures of shack ticket-office and freight house. Across the plaza, running parallel to the tracks, was the business district. Within the circumscription of the plaza this street was wider than the rest of the thoroughfare in order to provide hitching space for cow ponies and wagon teams on either edge of the roadway. About the square were assembled the frame structures which housed the commercial aspects of the frontier town. Beyond and reaching out to the lonely prairie were the shacks and sod houses boastfully known as the residential district. Stretching from the railroad near the river edge were strung the warehouses, corrals, dance halls, saloons and a few frame hotels that accommodated the cowboys and cattlemen, who preferred them to the tent city on the prairie where they usually pitched camp at the end of the drive, a bank, a newspaper office, six stores, twenty-seven saloons, gambling houses, and good time establishments. Fifteen hundred cowboys milled the streets that summer looking over these last twenty-seven places that were ready to receive him and part him from his hard won earnings. Tethering pony to the hitching rails was as much a parking problem then as cars in a crowded business district today. They usually slept six and eight to a room in the wind swept hotels. The plank walks rattled under the weight and clanking of spurs of the hundreds of cowboys making the rounds.

    English born Ben and Bill Thompson took rooms in the Grand Central Hotel. They were quick on the draw and quick on temper. They played a fast game of faro and played on the Southern sympathies of many of the youths, gathering them about their gaming table with honeyed works about the Lost Cause and rallying around the Stars and Bars as a protection against the grasping Northerners and railroad men. With such loyal partisans clustered about them they soon controlled Ellsworth. Behind this dictatorship were the guns of George Peshaur and his cow-pokes. Stogden often visited Ben and played at his gaming table. Thompson developed a special liking for him and taught him many gun tricks he knew. Peshaur also took him under wing and convinced him that the only way to survive was to beat the other fellow to the draw. He was in with Cad Pierce, John Good and Neil Kane. Porter witnessed the shooting of Sheriff Whitney by Bill Thompson and decided that perhaps the side of law and order was not so right after all. Marshall Wyatt Earp forced Thompson to give himself up and anyone loyal to the gambler had to show his contempt for Earp. Peshaur was hoping that Porter would take upon himself the honor of shooting Earp. Porter refused. Another cowboy taunted him with cowardice and one word leading to another Porter told him to draw. This was his first killing. Ellsworth put the dead cowboy in a hole on Boot Hill and went about its business.

    Peshaur was proud of Stogden and told him that any man as fast as that on the draw should stand high among gunfighters. The proof would come in the killing of the marshall. They had a few drinks, left the Grand Central, entered another bar where a few more drinks made Porter absolutely fearless and indestructible. He would kill Marshall Earp. He was placed in the ranks of Peshaur's experienced fifty who rustled, gambled, hurrahed, and held up stages and were a terror to their enemies. All the time Peshaur was priming him to meet the marshall.

Meantime the summer passed quickly enough and Stogden found himself as broke at the end of the season as the first day he hit town. It was now time to return to Texas and to the flaxen-haired minister's daughter. Empty pockets would not convince her father. Neil Kane noted his worried expression.

"Something wrong?" he asked.

"Just about everything. Going back to get myself hitched but no money to do it with. Could use some cartwheels."

Kane looked at Peshaur. They were planning on a Wells Fargo hold-up near Hays City.

"Does it matter how you get it?"

"No."

At the hold-up Stogden shot one of the guards. He received a goodly share of the profits, and head erect, he rode for his bride, all thoughts of killing the marshall forgotten for that season at least.

To Irma's father Porter Stogden was like Poe's Raven, "a thing of evil." Gloom and presentment hovered about him. He couldn't quite put his finger on it, but there was something about the lad that foreboded disaster. It terrified him. To top it all the son-in-law got gloriously drunk on the night of the wedding. He babbled about Thompson, Peshaur, Kane and others whose names in his books were on the savory side of life and not the kind of people he wanted his son-in-law associated with, much less his daughter.

All through the long, hard winter Porter was the ideal husband and the minister was beginning to believe that he had misjudged the youth and everything would adjust itself after all. Much of his time was spent in target practice. In the spring he left for the cattle drive. Wichita had replaced Ellsworth as the shipping center, and added to cattle was the new industry of buffalo hides. On the corner of Main and Douglas, Ben Thompson set up his faro bank and Keno House. Peshaur was there also with many of the boys from last year. Earp also moved in as deputy marshall. Again the proposition was brought to him to rid the boys of this enemy once and for all. Peshaur kept Stogden away from town so that he would not be known and to keep him practicing on the draw. Peshaur had been given a severe fist thrashing by Earp and wanted him out of the way. On the day appointed for the killing Peshaur took Stogden to town, loaded him with liquor and prepared the scene. The marshall came by to see that everything was in order. Stogden called to him. The deputy turned to face a forty-five.

"I'm going to kill you."

The law enforcement officer stood rigid. To make a play for his gun would prove fatal. Stogden, as fogged and beclouded as he was, realized that he had the upper hand. Elated with his triumph, he began to berate Earp which was just what the marshal was hoping for. Keep him talking, he said to himself. Quick as a flash he drew and nicked Porter just behind the thumb, near the wrist, a superficial flesh wound, but serving the purpose of making the would-be killer dropping his gun. Shamed at the humiliation that was the outcome of so many weeks of training, Porter left Wichita and Peshaur, never to return, guessing rightly that he had been but a pawn in Peshaur's hands. He doubted if he would have received the thousand dollars promised for the killing of Wyatt Earp.

In Dodge, Stogden ragained his self respect and his confidence. He gathered a few cowboys about him, strutting through the streets, stamping spurs and high-heeled boots against the board walks to command attention as they made for saloons, full of arrogance, liquor and defiance. They shot at glasses and lamps, broke up variety shows, forced their ponies to drink hard liquor at the bars, held up a gambling den, crossed the street and spent it on the dance hall girls. He killed a man who opposed him and made off for Hays. There he found that his reputation had preceded him and he resolved to become the greatest gunfighter of them all.

At Hays he ran into his friend Clay Allison, who told him that he was doing nicely in New Mexico. Stogden resolved to buy a piece of land near Cimarron and go into the cattle business. He brought his wife up from Fort Worth, built a cabin and was doing nicely until the death of Parson Tolby. All during these days when Allison ran Cimarron, Stogden stuck by Allison. He moved to Elizabethtown for a time to try his luck at prospecting, but he was essentially a rancher and gave it up to return to Cimarron only to find out that Allison turned his share of the ranch to his brother John. He had difficulty with a gambler in Cimarron and added another victim to his fast growing list. He skipped town for a time and returned when he felt the incident was forgotten, which meant a few months at best.

In October 1876 Stogden had been making the rounds as usual. He no sooner left Lambert's bar when he was confronted by Juan Gonzolez.

"You are a sneaking coward." Juan seemed to be quite angry about something.

"And to what do I owe this sudden outburst?" smiled Stogden.

"Last night while I was out, you made an attempt to enter my house because you knew my wife was alone and would not be adverse to your attentions."

He became abusive and threatened. Stogden didn't think it a matter of laughter any longer. He drew and emptied the six-shooter into his accuser, killing him instantly. He sought to escape but was captured and thrown in jail. As much as he pleaded self defense the Justice of the Peace refused to listen to him. Word reached his brother Ike up in Colorado that Porter was in jail. Ike was just as notorious as his brother. He was wanted for cattle rustling and depredations committed in Dodge, Abilene, Trinidad and Denver. He lost no time in coming to Cimarron. He rode up to the jail and demanded an audience with his brother. As he stood with the jailor before Porter's cell, he placed his six-shooter at the head of the keeper and insisted on the key. He released his brother who dashed out of the cell, jumped on his brother's horse and rode away. Ike picked out a horse close by and followed his brother. A posse went in pursuit of them but failed to find them. Porter sent word to his wife to join him at Trinidad.

Before long he had another man to his credit. The posse high-tailed after him, chasing him towards Wooten's toll road. As he climbed the steepy grade one of the posse got close enough to fire but missed. This unnerved the horse and he threw his rider, stumbled and both horse and rider went over the mountain side.

"It's too dark to go down there for the body," said the sheriff. "We'll get it taken care of tomorrow."

They rode back to Trinidad.

The undertaker and a few men came back the next day but found only the dead horse. They came upon a bloody trail and following it they found Stogden sitting on a rock trying to make bandages of his shirt to tie up his wounds. He was brought back to Trinidad and locked in jail. Again his brother Ike came to the rescue and he was a free man again. He took his wife with him, settling at Rico, the county seat of Dolores county. Sheldon Shafer and Joe Fearheiler had discovered gold here in 1866 and it became quite a mining community with all the rip roaring raw life that made a frontier town. Even today a string of false-front frame buildings along a rutted street gives it the appearance of one of the last out-posts of the Old West. As late as 1922 horse thieves were active in the region and were tracked down by posses riding automobiles and on motorcycles.

Stogden made a timely appearance. Rico was looking for a marshal quick on the draw and unafraid. If he would promise to uphold the law Rico would forget that he was wanted in Trinidad. Before long he had the lawless breed of men under control and soon had many working for him, holding up the stage near the Needle Mountains on the way to Durango, rustling cattle along the Rio de Animas. A rancher stopped Stogden on the street one day.

" 'Pears like I've seen you somewhere."

"Is that so? Think hard."

"Yes, those rustlers along the Animas. Sure 'nuf saw you."

"Are you sure?"

"Come to think of it, yes."

" I think you are mistaken."

"I don't mistake the matter of rustling."

Stogden lifted the shotgun he carried and blasted off the man's head from the forehead clean to the back. Scalping would have been a neater job. The Stogdens were on the move again, this time headed for Santa Fe. After a time there he went to the Chisum ranch in the Pecos valley. Mrs. Stogden took to visiting Mrs. Bowdre and the two became very good friends. Charles Bowdre impressed her as a gentleman with his neat clothes and dark complexion. Mal Pais and White Oaks were beginning to make mining news. Mrs. Bowdre told Mrs. Stogden on her last visit that a man was killed somewhere along the road and two sacks of gold dust stolen from him. When she went home to get supper ready her husband was sitting at the table, two small sacks before him. He was tighter than a drum. He said he struck it rich. Of course she believed him. She had no choice.

Again on the move, they settled for a time at Springer and then Raton, two railroad towns that began their careers when the Santa Fe railroad moved over the Raton Pass. Mace Bowman, the deputy sheriff, made it clear to Stogden that it would be best if he shook the dust of Raton from his feet and moved on. He did. Mace Bowman was the fastest man on the draw that ever lived. Others claimed that distinction and when a biographer for Bowman makes his study the fearless deputy will come into his own.

In northwestern New Mexico the little community of Farmington, unable to strike it rich as a mining camp, suddenly found itself as a farming center. Stogden decided to settle here. He built a cabin, bought some land and hired as cow pokes two former pals of Dodge days. Joseph Garrett (no relation to Pat Garrett) and Dison Eskridge also joined him in rustling expeditions. As this was about Christmas time, the three decided to celebrate somewhere and found out that rancher Francis Marion Hamblet, six miles down the cow trail from the Stogden place, on the San Juan River, was giving a Christmas Eve dance at his ranch. The desperadoes brought along a five-gallon jug of Taos Lightning, that potent drink that sent a man plumb loco, and by the time they arrived they were so well heeled that Graves, a neighbor, told them that they would do better to go home and sleep it off.

"We want no sand fired up by whiskey here," he told them.

"This is a party, ain't it?" Stogden wanted to know.

At this moment Oscar Puett and James Brown, guests at Hamblet's, sensed that something was wrong. They came to the door and joined in with Graves in asking the three to leave. Hamblet also came to the door and insisted that they leave at once.

"We want in, and in we git." Stogden was not to be put off. Graves feared gunplay. He was worried about the women and children.

Stogden went to the fiddler's stand, pulled out his six-shooter and wielding it like a baton kept repeating to the strains of the music:

"19—20—21 19—20—21 19—20—21." On and on. He admitted in Raton that he had eighteen victims to his credit. He now decided on Graves, Puett and Brown. Garrett and Eskridge followed Hamblet about, cursing him and tempting him to draw on them. They chuckled the girls under the chin, kissed them, danced with them and made themselves positively obnoxious. Hamblet asked a few of the boys to help him put them out. Quicker said than done, the three found themselves outside looking in. The dance went on. Puett passed in the light of the window. Stogden shot, yelling at the same time: "Nineteen." Garrett and Eskridge now poured a steady stream of lead into the house. Stogden waited for Brown to show himself and when he came to the same window with a shotgun to shoot it into the darkness outside, Stogden shot again, crying out: "Twenty." The return fire from the house became too heavy and the desperadoes rode off into the night.

That night the vigilantes organized at Farmington. A reward of one thousand dollars was posted for the capture of the desperadoes, and the town went on a clean-up campaign. All criminals infesting the Lower Animas country were told to "git or be gotten." All thieves, murderers, gamblers and rustlers were given twenty-four hours to "Git." Drums along the San Juan. Every nook and hiding place was ferreted out. There would be no more bloodshed at Farmington except the blood of resisting outlaws.

January 10, 1881. The vigilantes conducted a meeting wherein it was decided to march on Porter Stogden's cabin. Here they expected to pick up Garrett and Eskridge also. Three ropes were made ready. They fanned out to beat the brush should the desperadoes be in hiding. While thus engaged Stogden came to the door. He saw Graves.

"I wanted to drink your blood for Christmas, but it's not too late to drink it for the New Year," he called to Graves.

He asked him what he was doing on his property. Furthermore, he had something more to say to Graves and if the gentleman would step forward he would tell him what was on his mind. Graves walked out from the brush and stood in front of the house, just a short distance from Stogden. He was aware that the desperado held a six-shooter.

"This is as far as I go," said Graves. "If you have anything to say, say over." His voice was trenchant and could be heard clearly by the other now gathering about him. Stogden opened a tirade of abuse and called Graves a "D— liar."

"Why?" Graves was surprised as he expected Stogden to shoot rather than talk.

"Aren't you the one spreading rumors that I may have had something to do with the recent hold-up near Durango?"

"That's a lie."

"You said that I rustled the Torres cattle over near Costilla."

"That's no lie." Graves never could explain why he said that, staring into the muzzle of a six-shooter as he was.

"Is it true that you spread these stories?" demanded Stogden of Graves.

"Yes, I spread them but they ain't no stories."

"You're a —liar, and d— you, I'm going to kill you."

Raising the revolver which he had dropped to his side during the conversation, and Graves was thankful that he did, he was too slow in following the action with the threat. Graves fell flat to the ground, firing his Winchester as he fell. The shots sounded simultaneous. Stogden fell in his doorway.

Graves was the foreman of the Thompson & Lacy outfit and quite handy with a gun. Stogden was dead before anyone could reach him. Irma came to the door, Winchester in hand.

"Don't move—any of you. I aim to avenge the death of my husband."

One of the vigilantes fired at the rifle to unfit it for its murderous work. The ball struck the stock, completely shattering it, but the lead glanced off and struck Mrs. Stogden in the breast. She fell over the body of Porter.

The shot from the foreman's Winchester was found to have broken Stogden's neck, killing him instantly. Irma was taken to Hamblet's and cared for. She lingered a few days then joined her husband. Said the Las Vegas Gazette (January 16, 1881)

"Mrs. Stogden is said to be the daughter of a well known Texas clergyman and her family highly respected. She is a nice looking, well appearing little woman who has endured a great deal from Stogden, who left her for days nearly destitute. She is a very conscientious person and always refused to dance, believing it to be wrong. How she could live with such a bad man is a mystery, but it is said that she does not believe he ever killed any men only in self-defense. Stogden was a man about twenty-seven years old who came to New Mexico about eight years ago and made for himself an unenviable reputation. His own boast was that he killed eighteen men, but at any rate he has been the means of putting quite a number of men under the sod. He mixed up in the Lincoln County War (as one of the gunfighters for the Murphy faction) and after that was over, began depredating in the Indian Nation. For the past year or more Stogden has been stealing cattle in the Lower Animas country and it is gratifying to write the obituary of such a desperado. . . . He died with his boots on."

Over in Fort Worth the old clergyman opened the mail: "Dear Sir: I regret to inform you that your daughter Irma passed away this morning following an accident. . . ."

Clay Allison. His face will soon be as familiar to readers of frontier outlaw doings as that of Billy the Kid.

Book Ten

WHEEL ON MY NECK

(Clay Allison)

The wind was beating and whirling like a baby cyclone. Gusts of snow whipped up against the Brick House Saloon in Cimarron, where throngs had gathered to celebrate Christmas Eve. At the piano sat a one-time minister of the Anglican denomination. His flock failed to support him so he decided to follow the crowd to Elizabethtown for gold, finding none, he settled down to being a musician at whatever bar would hire him. Far into the night the drinking, gambling and shouting continued. Suddenly the door opened. Six-shooter in hand, lines of determination mingled with disgust on his features, the tall man in the doorway walked to the bar.

Silence.

"Has it occurred to anyone that this is Christmas Eve?"

No response.

"A Saviour came into the world on such a night as this. All over the world every community remembers—everybody but us. Now we shall remember. The piano player will remember his sacred calling of the past and lead us in prayer and hymns."

So, the Brick House Saloon became a church that evening and Bethlehem as Clay Allison, at gun point, kept the memory and sacredness of the season alive. No one was startled nor surprised. This man was that way. At times religious, at times as drunk as they come, at times the hard killer, but always mighty handy with a gun. He never missed. And fast, too. He had such masters as Mace Bowman, Lee of Texas, and others who found him an apt pupil. This was the man who held Cimarron against all odds after Parson Tolby was murdered. Clay Allison, the mightiest gunfighter of them all, who supercedes Billy the Kid in deeds but not in legend.

Clay Allison came from a good family living at Waynesboro, Wayne county, in thee State of Tennessee. He was the oldest of three children — Clay, John and Mary — the son of a cotton agent and buyer. Born in 1840, he attended the Lane School and was considered a remarkable pupil. During the Civil War he served for a time with Hardee's Corps at the Battle of Shiloh, as a spy, and as an Intelligence officer under General Forrest. Captured behind the lines in Federal uniform, he was sentenced as a spy and awaited the death penalty with calm. One guard watched over him. Allison waited until the custodian slept, crawled up to him, grabbed his gun, shot him and fled. Back at home he found the house being turned upside down by Union men in quest of food. One fellow was particularly abusive to his mother, relishing the sport of breaking her best chinaware just to watch her squirm. Later he sought out the soldier in town, put a bullet through him, escaped and identified himself with guerilla warfare until the end of the conflict, after which he decided that home wasn't much of a place to come home to the way the Union soldiers destroyed it, so he headed for Texas, suddenly awakened to the possibilities of cattle markets.

This was the age of cattle barons. Scotchmen, Englishmen, Germans, Dutchmen and Texans were buying up vast tracks, forming powerful syndicates to corner the meat market. Unsettled in Tennessee, Allison decided on cowboying in Texas. He trailed herd for some of the biggest names in the industry: Loving, Goodnight, Pierce and others, saving his money, buying cattle on his own to someday make a dream come true. He would be a rancher. In Cimarron on a deal between Goodnight and Lucien B. Maxwell, he noticed how lush and plentiful the grass and streams appeared to be and decided that this was the place to have a ranch. He bought property from Maxwell near the site of what was to be the ghost town of Otero, sent for his brother John, brought in a few cowboys he had worked with in Texas, and became one of the earliest settlers of the region. Legend gives another reason for his coming to New Mexico.

On the ranch next to his in Texas, lived a short, squatty, powerfully built rancher by the name of Johnson. They were good neighbors for a time until enmity broke out over a water hole. Affairs went from bad to worse. The story goes that Allison invited Johnson to dig a grave with him, after which both would enter armed with just a knife. The one to emerge victorious would bury the other. Allison buried Johnson but skipped the country in fear of reprisals from Johnson's relatives and friends. It makes a nice story but how do we account for the fact that Allison brought his stock into New Mexico? Trailing a herd was a slow process, even a small herd such as Allison owned. Johnson's avengers had ample time to meet up with Allison. Miguel Otero, who became acquainted with Allison shortly after his arrival in New Mexico, said of him:

"When sober Clay Allison was well mannered and extremely likeable, but under the influence of liquor he was a terror to the whole neighborhood and a good man to avoid. Gradually, his name became dreaded in the whole section. He actually killed so many and was so keenly aware of the readiness of friends or relatives to 'get even' that he never stood or sat in a room with his back to a door or window."

Allison, at the time he settled in Northern New Mexico, was six feet two inches tall, weighed one hundred and ninety pounds, blue eyes, a large boned, square-set face so often seen in pioneers, hunters, scouts and outdoor men, he always created the impression of one ever ready to spring into a saddle and lead a caravan westwards. He had a prominent Roman nose and wore his hair long in the fashion of the day. He was blonde. At times he wore a mustache which he permitted to grow so long that it drooped below his chin. At times he permitted his beard to grow but never beyond two or three inches in length. He walked with a limp due to his own carelessness with a gun that went off when cleaning it, the bullet penetrating the right foot, coming out at the heel. His right eye was slightly crossed so that the iris seemed to be just off the bridge of the nose. His ears were large and stuck out from his face a little but he managed to conceal this somewhat with his long curly hair which he parted from the right almost from the center of his head. His upper lip was thin but did not curve at the corners which created the impression of a rather large mouth. His lower lip was thick and protruded a little, causing a shadow to appear at times over his firm, round chin. He wore expensive clothes, usually in fashion, and never resisted buying a shirt every time he was in town. He fitted into a neck sixteen.

Today, as one drives peacefully along Highway 89 on the way to Raton, a few miles south of the city, he will be on the old Allison property. If he can T-V the scene as it looked to him shortly before the coming of the railroad he will see the tall graceful rancher astride a pony rounding up his cattle for Dodge and the stock yards. He will see Allison's dugout used as a shelter during branding time and in the round-up. Here also were stored provisions. Among Clay's supplies one always found whiskey—five-gallon jugs. It was customary every evening for the men to wash up, eat his supper, and for want of a better way to while away their time hugged the jug and cut the rug. As there were no women within miles of the camp they danced with each other. Sometimes they did an Indian dance around the fire, now and then letting go of a Rebel yell rather than a war whoop. It was more interesting when the jug was empty and they were full.

The cook was rather obese and he detested nothing more than dancing with these too merry men who used him for a bulwark rather than for a partner. One evening he managed to escape far from the maddening crowd, hiding in the tall grass near the river. There he bedded down and slept the sleep of the guiltless. For an hour he slumbered in peace until Clay Allison decided that he wanted to dance with the cook. He bellowed out. No response. Where in the world did he go to? Allison decided to hunt him up. He stumbled upon the corpulent cook in the grass and the fellow was compelled to become a ballerina by the light of the moon—at gunpoint.

After a time Allison sold his holdings at this particular

spot and formed a joint partnership with his brother John up along the Vermejo near the village of Cimarron. The sale of the Maxwell Land Grant did not particularly disturb him and he dealt with the Maxwell Land Grant and Railway Company with the same disinterested attitude that he dealt with Lucien B. Maxwell himself. As far as I can make out he was never a guest in Lucien B. Maxwell's home before the sale of the Grant nor in Sherwin's or Whigham's after the sale. He had occasion to visit the Maxwell Mansion and probably had a drink or two there, but most of his visits were confined to business. He made several attempts at striking it rich along Willow Creek and Elizabethtown, but failing in every effort, he decided to stick with the cattle business. He was very friendly with the Utes and Jicarilla Apaches that roamed the area, although he made it quite clear to them that he did not want them running off his horses nor slaughtering his beef even though they often complained to him about the quality and quantity of the rations they received at the Indian Agency in Cimarron. For a time he visited the Bishop girl and when her mother shooed him out with a broom stick, the Holbrook girl, who told him he drank too much to make a loving husband. He was always shy of women but, also, always respectful towards them.

During those frontier days of adjustment, westerners handy with a gun sought fame by seeking out a noted gunfighter or desperado and challenging to a drawing duel. If he was victorious it added to his fame and meant free drinks for everybody in town. No cock crowed louder than he did, until another gunfighter with a quicker draw not only deflated him but usually accompanied the remains to boot-hill. One such character was Francisco Griego, better known as Pancho. He had been brought to Cimarron by Boggs, whose job it was to find workers for Maxwell on his Grant. He was particularly interested in married men because it would help carry out the proscription of the Grant that demanded colonization. Pancho was a native of Santa Fe and had served as deputy sheriff until he followed the lot of the bad man. He had several children and thought that Cimarron would offer better opportunities for starting anew. It has been said that he served as deputy in Cimarron, but I have not been able to verify this.

Pancho was an excellent shot and horseman and resented the attitude of the Texas cowboys about the place, who walked about as if they had been there from the dawn of time. Pancho would argue that Santa Fe was old before anyone ever heard that there was such a place as Texas. He thought that if he killed Clay Allison it would take these cowboys down a peg. He had his adherents and as a gang they raided and rustled. He told Clay Allison that he was going to kill him. They went into Lambert's bar to have a drink over it. Allison noticed Pancho fanning himself with his sombrero, and as it was the dead of winter this was rather an odd thing to do. Stealthily, Pancho reached for his gun, but his overcautiousness was his undoing. Without seeming to move, Allison already had his gun out and shot him. He then sought out the Justice of the Peace and had himself acquitted as acting in self-defense. Commented the editor of the Santa Fe New Mexican:

"On the night of November 1st, Francisco Griego was shot and killed by C. Allison. Both parties met at the door of the St. James Hotel (Lambert's), entered, and with some friends took a drink, when the two walked into the corner of the room and had some conversation. There Allison drew his revolver and shot three times. The lights were extinguished and Griego was not found until the next morning. Francisco Griego was well known in Santa Fe, where his mother lives. He has killed a great many men, and was considered a dangerous man; few regret his loss."

In 1924, C. N. Blackwell, a prominent citizen of Raton, wishing to more fully understand the stirring events that took place following the murder of Parson Tolby, wrote to Lawyer M. W. Mills, living in Las Vegas who had been a long-time resident of Cimarron. Mills wrote the full story in a long letter, a copy of which fell into my hands. Among other things Mills said:

"I think that it was on Saturday, September the 12th, 1875, when he made his usual trip on horseback to Elizabethtown, and on Sunday held his usual church service, that he left Cimarron. On Monday morning he started back to his home. The contractor of the mail route was named Florence Donahue, who had employed a fellow by the name of Cruz Vega to act as his mail carrier from Elizabethtown to Cimarron. This mail carrier started out a short distance behind Tolby that Monday morning, on horseback also, so that when the minister got down about six miles from Elizabethtown, Cruz Vega was about a half mile behind him as appeared from some evidence later on in court. About two miles further on, at the mouth of the Cimarron Canyon, Tolby was shot and his body drawn into some brush and his horse tied to a tree. Vega must have passed not far from Tolby's horse, without seeing the horse, or he murdered Mr. Tolby himself, according to the evidence that was offered. A little later in the day some men found the horse and the body. Afterwards Vega was arrested and charged with murder. At the time Tolby was murdered the District Court had adjourned at Cimarron and gone to Taos for the purpose of holding Court there. I remember very well someone coming over from that neighborhood and reporting the murder. None of them seemed to take much interest in making inquiry about it except me.

I think a reward was offered for the arrest of the murderers and this reward was about three thousand dollars. It was offered by the Masonic Fraternity. About two or three months later I was in Trinidad, Colorado, applying for an injunction before Judge Wells in a mining litigation. A number of telegrams came to me from friends in Cimarron, advising me not to return because a mob was gathering there by the hundreds, from all parts of the country, and that it was charged that I had some complicity in the murder of Tolby, along with Dr. Longwell, Florence Donahue, Francisco Griego and others. These telegrams seemed too absurd and ridiculous to me so I took my team and buggy and started to go back to Cimarron. I ran my horses over thirty miles until they were too exhausted to overtake the coach that went up to Cimarron.

When I finally caught the coach, I turned my team loose on the prairie hitched to my buggy. When I got to Cimarron and the coach rolled into the plaza, a thousand men or more jerked me out of the coach and had the rope all ready to hang me to a telegraph pole. Some of my friends had a lot of Indians arrayed and staked out, who threatened to shoot the mob if anything was done to me. The mob agreed to appoint twelve men to take charge of me, which was done. My friend agreed that they should have twelve also, so I had twenty-four guards of me until the soldiers arrived from Fort Union. They came suddenly upon the mob, who dropped their guns. It was demanded that I be given up to the soldiers, who notified the surging, excited mob that I would be held upon the order of a properly constituted command of the Court. A mob trial had been ordered and hundreds, if not thousands, of witnesses were summoned. Days were given to hearsay testimony. At that time Judge Henry L. Waldo, a young lawyer at Santa Fe, was sent up to look after my defense.

Previous to my arrival at Cimarron, Dr. Longwell, who had been charged as an accessory to the murder of Tolby, fled to Fort Union for protection. He started back from Fort Union with these same soldiers that had been sent from the garrison to restore order at Cimarron, but he became frightened and turned back and went to Santa Fe as fast as a relay of stage coach horses could be given him. He landed safely in Santa Fe, although pursued by some of the same mob. The mob trial lasted four or five days and was made up of the Justice of the Peace and two of the mob men. These men determined that I should be set at liberty since I had no connection with the murder, so they turned me loose and shot a man by the name of Cardenas whom they were taking to the jail.

There was a printer working in the office of the Cimarron News at the time Mr. Tolby was murdered. A man by the name of McMains, who took an affidavit that had been forced from Cardenas by Harberger and others at Elizabethtown. This affidavit charged Cruz Vega as the actual murderer of Tolby, being paid for it by Florence Donahue and Francisco Griego, who in turn got their money from Dr. Longell. It also stated that M. W. Mills was the lawyer employed and knew and advised them about the murder.

O. P. McMains also claimed to be a Methodist preacher.

He took the Cardenas affidavit and rode over the whole country reading it to the people, fixing a day when they should gather together and avenge the death of Rev. Tolby. The day I arrived in Cimarron was the day that the mob gathered. A few days previous to this time, McMains got Cruz Vega and gave him five dollars to husk some corn on the Ponil Creek for him. One night while he was there the mob took Cruz and hung him to a tree. At the trial afterwards of McMains, for murder, the evidence was that he ordered a rope about Cruz Vega's neck, pulled him up to a tree, let him down and asked him to tell who had given him the money to murder Rev. Tolby. Vega said that no one had given him the money and that he had not murdered Tolby. They pulled him up and then let him down, asking him if Donahue and Griego had given the money and Vega said—No. They pulled him up again, choked him almost to death and then let him down and this time he said—Yes. . . (End of quotes from the letter.)

The leader of the mob was Clay Allison. McMains did not need much persuasion to convince the tall rancher that this was a holy war. Clay was very friendly with Rev. Tolby and his death came as a shock to him. He led the mob to hunt down Tolby's killers because he had deep respect for the man not because of McMain's persuasive powers although the Anti-Grant Arch-Agitator was inclined to think so.

"Clay Allison, so well known in Colfax county, is in Las Vegas, and on Wednesday (May 12) said to the reporter of the Las Vegas Optic that he wishes emphatically to deny that he is in any sort of sympathy with O. P. McMains in his incessant agitation of the Maxwell Land Grant question." (Live Stock Journal of New Mexico May 14, 1888)

His brother John as well as David Crockett were with him during the capture of Cimarron when Clay Allison and his mob took over to avenge the murder of the minister. The year following the events related above, the two brothers were in Las Animas, Colorado, to put in a large order at Otero's Mercantile Store. Following their purchases, they decided to make the rounds. Before long they were supporting each other as they sang their way from saloon to saloon. That afternoon

Frank Riggs, a whiskey runner, arrived in town. Unfortunately he met up with the Allison boys and the trio began by toasting to Clay's health. He gave the proprietor a five-dollar bill, saying that he would call for the change as soon as he fetched his valise, which he had left at the dug-store. Once out of the saloon, he hopped a freight and was never seen in the town again. Realizing, despite their condition, that Riggs had deserted them, the two continued drinking and killing time till the evening dance. While the dance was in progress they put on their own version of a strip tease and in order to keep the crowd moving and dancing they fired off their six-shooters every now and then. Sheriff John Spear decided that they were disturbing the peace. He called his deputy, Charles Faber, and between them they rounded up twenty men. At the dance hall Faber ordered the brothers to put on their clothes and to stop shooting off their guns. The music continued playing, the dancers continued dancing and the Allisons continued shooting. Faber fired on the two men, wounding John. Clay, believing that his brother had been killed, fired at the deputy, killing him instantly. Crying like a baby, Clay gathered his brother into his arms, trying to dress him and rush him to a doctor at the same time, hoping that perhaps he had not been killed. He was surrounded and taken prisoner. Some of the posse got John to a doctor and Clay was relieved to find out that his brother was alive and the wound was superficial. Allison was taken before the Justice of the Peace, but acquitted because it was proven that Faber had fired without warning and had secretly hoped to "get" the Allison boys in order to acquire a reputation as a frontier marshall.

Over at Palo Flechado Pass, near the western end of the Maxwell Land Grant, one Charles Kennedy, who came to the country as a trapper, built his cabin and was served by a native woman he took to wife. They had one child. The woman was from the little adobe community nine miles north of Taos called Arroyo Seco. Her name was Dulcinea Maldonado, but she called herself Mrs. Kennedy. In those days you didn't ask a man where he was from, you merely asked him for a drink if he was a drinking man or you left him alone if he was not.

That was the code of frontier friendship. If you were not a drinking man you were invited to table. The rest was his business.

One wintry night, Allison, Goodall, Heifner and others were caught in a storm at Elizabethtown and decided to wait it out at John Pearson's cantina. Pearson was later to move to Glorieta and trouble because of Rattlesnake Sam. Crockett was from Gibson county in western Tennessee originally, out of which was cut Crockett county with Alamo as its county seat to honor an illustrious son both of Tennessee and Texas. While this particular Davy Crockett proved a maverick, on this blasty night he showed some instincts for decency. When a woman came tumbling into the bar with a weird story of murders and burials it turned his stomach. Dulcinea had run away from Kennedy because she could not stand to see him murder any more. Every stray traveler on the way to Taos was invited to the cabin. If he had pelts and horses, during the night Kennedy would manage to put him out of the way and bury him under the dirt floor of the cabin. On this particular day Dulcinea made an effort to warn one traveler, but Kennedy caught her at it. In punishment he killed her child after killing the traveler. He then drank himself to sleep. Making certain he would not wake up, she slipped out of the cabin and made for the nearest town which happened to be the mining camp of Elizabethtown. As a result of the horrors she related, Allison, Crockett and Heifner led a group of miners to the cabin, took Kennedy and hung him to a tree. Allison cut off his head and asked Henry Lambert to put it on a spike in front of the St. James Hotel in Cimarron. After a time it was taken to the farthest corner of the corral fence and when dried out an interested party sent it to the Smithsonian Institute in Washington, where science was saying that skull formations made the criminal. It is possibly there to this day. That is how killer Kennedy got to Washington. Said one old-timer reviewing the past at Cimarron:

"It was at Cimarron that many desperadoes attained prominence. One was Clay Allison, from Tennessee, who had killed Chunk Colbert, Griego and others. He sought with a mob at one time or another to kill Mills and it seems a few hours later said he was wrong and led another mob to rescue Mills because a gang of men were approaching his house and had a rope ready for the purpose of hanging him. Clay always boasted he had saved Mills' life. Allison had much power and personal following and he was immune for arrest for many years, but the federal authorities finally sent aid to Sheriff Rinehart in the person of a few companies of soldiers. These surrounded his house one morning and arrested him. He afterwards made his escape, but was not bothered since."

Allison often made trips to Dodge and Hays. He was at Dodge when several friends of his pleaded with him to put Marshall Earp out of the way. Earp was too good a marshall and a wet blanket on a lot of their fun, especially when they wanted to Hurrah the town. Allison said that he had nothing against Earp. If he would only put Earp in a position for them to get at him it would not be necessary for Allison to do the shooting. Clay always maintained that "he never killed a man that didn't need killing." This is important to understand in explaining why Allison permitted the marshall to get the drop on him. Clay Allison came out of Wright and Beverly's. The marshall stopped and leaned against the wall of the Long Branch cantina, just west of the entrance. Clay came along the walk, turned, as if to enter the Long Branch, and halted abruptly.

"Are you Wyatt Earp?"

"I am Wyatt Earp."

"I have been looking for you."

"Here I am. You've found me."

"I believe you killed a friend of mine the other day."

"What if I have?"

"I ought to kill you. I am pretty loyal to my friends."

By this time Allison was leaning against Earp and before he knew it the marshall felt a six-shooter digging into his ribs. This was a moment of triumph for the marshall's enemies. They were watching from the saloon windows. Suddenly Allison took his hands off his revolver and placed them against his waist and Earp took advantage of the moment by digging a gun into Allison's ribs. Earp tells the story fifty-five years later, making it out to be that Allison was in holy terror of him. But old timers will tell you that Allison was a faster man on the draw than the marshall and could have killed him that moment at the doorway of the Long Branch Saloon. But as he felt that he was not in Dodge to do anybody's dirty work, he let the opportunity go by. All he wanted to prove was that it could be done. Earp's enemies did not take advantage of the moment because directly across the way ready to light into them with a Winchester was Bat Masterson. To prove to Earp that the whole idea was not his but rather a frame-up, Allison got a separate hold of Bob Wright.

"Bob, tell the marshall how you sent for me at Las Animas. Tell him you had something important to discuss with me. You know what it was."

Wright said nothing. Earp understood that his life was spared, but he insisted on bragging years after Allison was dead that he put the Fear of the Lord in Clay Allison. Earp and Allison met several times after that and Allison always attended his business with cattle selling and buying, never molesting Earp in any way. No matter what Earp says, Allison was the only man to hold a gun to his ribs and thought enough of law and order not to pull the trigger.

Several miles south of Raton to the west of the site of the original Allison property, one comes upon a marker placed there by the Tourist Bureau giving the story of the old Clifton House. It stood off to the right of the road and was a stopping place for the Barlow & Sanderson stake. Chunk Colbert came in one day and asked about Clay Allison. He was plenty handy with a gun and decided it was time for him to wear the crown of No. 1 Gunfighter. Here would be the most logical place for the encounter since Allison often frequented the place and usually came without his cowboys. Chunk was a good cow poke himself and knew how to drink and gamble. Like the man whose blood he sought, he did most of his shooting after fortifying himself with a few hair-shrinking drinks. He also bragged a lot. The two had a nodding acquaintance with each other, having met at dances given at the Clifton House. Following each affair it became apparent to Allison as well as to Colbert that eventually they would tangle.

Chunk owned a Kentucky sorrell, a gift from Tom Stockton, builder of the Clifton House, with whom he now cast his lot as a cowboy. Allison had a fine white Texas pony. Colbert noised it abroad that his sorrell was the fastest horse in the West and he would match it against any horse, even Allison's pony. Clay got wind of the challenge and rode to Clifton House to argue the point with Colbert. The discussion became quite heated but no guns were drawn. Allison had a twenty dollar gold piece and a five dollar bill. If Chunk could match it, he would have a chance to see what his sorrell could really do. The race was to be run on a quarter mile straight track at the Stockton place, just south of the stage stop. Two Englishmen from the rooming house were chosen as judges; one to stand at each end of the track. At the end of the race the judges decided upon a tie in the hopes of avoiding bloodshed. One the way home from the track, Allison told a friend of his by the name of Gillespie, that he felt certain that Colbert would not rest until he had his gun play with him. Chunk went to the bar at Clifton House, ordered drinks for all and boasted that his father was a famous killer, having sent twenty-two men to Boot Hill. He himself had killed only seven, to which, when Allison heard it, he had no intentions of being the eighth. Colbert was of the opinion that the eighth had to be Allison.

The following day, at noon, a little party was gotten together to celebrate the winning of the race, although no victor was named. Colbert said the party was in his honor as winner. Allison begged to differ with him as he was the victor. Very few of those invited actually attended because they felt that this was the show down and they wanted to be as far away as possible when the lead started flying. The dinner was not served in the dining room of the Clifton House, but in a small cafe close by where short orders were served people in a hurry and where one could get a steaming bowl of chile prepared by the native cook since Mrs. Stockton was not acquainted with dishes peculiar to New Mexico. Ranchers, trappers, scouts, natives, often came by for the savery dish of tamales, enchiladas or the stomach warming fiery chile.

The tables in the small cafe were tiny, booth-like affairs hinged to the wall. The rivals sat at one table. The two men, facing each other, and by mutual consent recognizing this as "It," placed their guns in their laps, keeping them cocked. The coffee pot was at Allison's left elbow. Colbert had already downed his first cup and decided on another. He reached across his plate with his left hand passing his cup to Allison, who as a gentleman, would lift the pot and pour. This would mean the use of both his hands as the lid was one of the falling kind and had to be steadied. Allison smiled at the idea as quite childish. He refused to pour. Chunk then made a quick movement for his gun, firing with an alarming quickness. Too quick. The muzzle did not quite clear the table. The bullet passed through the table board and ranged upward over Allison's head. At the same time Allison brought his gun into play, the bullet entering Colbert's head just above the left eye. He was buried in the small cemetery on the slope behind the Clifton House.

Clay arranged his own time for meeting Sheriff Rinehart. This sheriff was a German Jew who began life in Cimarron as a miller. He went to Elizabethtown where he made good until the camp folded up. Then then opened a general store at Tascosa in the Panhandle of Texas, changing his name from Isaac to Ira. He built the Rinehart addition in Tascosa and Rinehart street was named after him. He out-lived Allison by several years. He had no heart in his work as sheriff and would have gladly resigned it had it not been such a lucrative position, especially when it came to collecting fines, taxes and other income, a commission from which always accrued to the man in office. As Court was in session at Taos, the sheriff and Allison rode over there to see the judge. At Taos Allison called to all around the plaza to witness the fact that he was under arrest. Asking the sheriff for his hat, he entered a saloon, filled it with beer, forced the sheriff to put it on, yelling gleefully to the laughing mob:

"Look, boys, I'm under arrest," much to the discomfiture

of the sheriff. The judge ruled the killing of Colbert as a plain case of self defense.

Allison married Dora McCollough and the couple seemed quite content. A daughter came of this union who was quite sickly. Allison babied her and took her to every doctor he thought could help her. A doctor in Denver effected a cure and the girl lived to marry and have children of her own. She married into wealth, but lived quietly in Fort Worth, Texas.

It has been said that the only man Allison feared was Sheriff Mace Bowman, who held that office shortly after Rinehart. Bowman proved to Clay on several occasions that he was quicker on the draw than the cattleman. Allison always marveled at the strange way Bowman reached for his gun and had it in your ribs before you could flicker an eye-lash. He asked Bowman to teach him how he did it. Allison had the same type of draw as John W. Hardin, John Ringo and Wild Bill Hickok, only his arm action seemed to be slower. He pulled the hammer back in the motion of drawing, and the gun was fired as the muzzle dropped to level. When Allison thought he had mastered Bowman's way he challenged him to a test with empty guns. Three times he tried it, each time Mace having the bead on him before he quite got the gun from his side. He admitted that the peace officer was a quicker man than he was and ever afterwards held him in deep respect.

On March 3, 1877, Clay sold his share of the ranch to his brother John for the sum of seven hundred dollars. He went to the Washita in Hemphill county in the Panhandle of Texas. While in Texas he made frequent trips to Hays and St. Louis. He spent several months in Missouri in the hopes of living there as a country gentleman but his cowboys bungled up the ranch so much that he gave up the idea. The Dodge papers and the Hays papers kept the public informed of his movements. "Clay Allison of the Washita was in the city this week" (Dodge City Times February 28, 1880). On March 2, 1880, the Ford County Globe carried this letter written by Clay Allison:

About the 26th of July there appeared in one of the St. Louis papers an account of an altercation in which account there appeared several gross mis-representations which I desire to contradict. First: It was that I was the murderer of fifteen In answer to this assertion, I will say that it is extremely false; that I stand ready at all times and places for open inspection, anyone who wishes to make inquiries of any one of the leading citizens of Wayne county, Tennessee, where I was born (Clay's niece told me that he was born in Jackson and have so stated in writings elsewhere until I came upon this letter. I stand corrected) and raised, or of the officers of the late rebellion on either side may do so. I served in the 9th Regt. Co. F, and the last two years of the service was a scout for Ben McCullough and General Forrest. Since then I have lived in New Mexico, Texas and Kansas, principally on the frontier, and will refer to any of the taxpayers and prominent men in either of the localities where I have resided. I have at all times tried to use my influence toward protecting the property holders and substantial men of the country from thieves, outlaws and murderers, among whom I do not care to be classed. It was also charged that I endeavored to use a gun on the occasion of the St. Louis difficulty, which is untrue and which can be proven by either Col. Hunter of St. Louis or the clerk of Irwin & Allen Co. It was also stated that I got the worst of the fight. In regard to this I do not claim to be a prize fighter, but as an evidence of the correct result of this fight I will say that I was somewhat hurt but I did not squeal, as did my three opponents. My present residence is on the Washita in Hemphill county, Texas, where I am open for inspection, and can be seen at any time.

Allison's brother John also sold out in New Mexico and joined his brother in the Panhandle of Texas. When a Townsite Company became interested in their land, they sold out, Clay going to Seven Rivers in New Mexico, John returning to Tennessee. That was in 1883. While on one of his cattle drives, Clay got a toothache in Cheyenne (in July 1886, just one year before his death.) Here is what the paper said of the incident:

"Instead of applying a little creosote to Clay's aching tooth he got him into his dental chair and proceeded to bore a hole in one of the cowman's best teeth for the purpose of filling it, which it didn't in the least need. He was a clumsy quack and inadvertently broke off about half a tooth. Clay got mad and left and went to another dentist who repaired the damage at the expense of twenty-five dollars. He told the victim that he had been treated by an errant quack who evidently wanted to make money out of him. This fired the blood of Mr. Allison, who fairly thirsted for revenge, and he got it, too. He proceeded to the quack's office, seized a pair of forceps, threw the man down on the floor, and in spite of the yells of the victim, inserted the instrument in his mouth and drew out one of his best molars. Not content with this he grabbed for another and caught one of the front teeth together with a large piece of upper lip and he was tugging away at it when the agonized shrieks and yells of the poor devil, upon whose chest Allison was pressing his knee, drew a crowd and ended the matter." (Las Vegas Optic July 7, 1886)

1886 was also the year that the city of Canadian in Hemphill county was founded. Allison was living at Pecos, Texas, at the time, having sold out in New Mexico. He decided to come up and celebrate. When he had enough drinks in him, he divested himself of his clothing, wearing only his sombrero and six-shooter and gun belt. He rode up and down the main street in this scant attire until the sheriff decided to do something about it. Allison paraded the sheriff into a saloon and at gun-point made him drink until he just couldn't hold it any more. After this he returned to Pecos. When taking in a load of wood, something went wrong, and Allison jumped from the wagon to see what the matter was. He failed to set the brake properly, and as it was on a small incline, he no sooner unhitched the mules, when the wagon gave before he could quite straighten out. As he was bent quite close to the ground, the wheels went over his neck, killing him instantly. That was in July 1887. Said the Ford County Globe (July 26, 1887):

"Clay Allison knew no fear. To incur his enmity was equivalent to a death sentence. He contended that he never killed a man willingly but out of necessity. He was an expert with his revolver and never failed to come out best in a deadly encounter."

CHAPTER ELEVEN

BIG SHOT SMALL TOWN

(Rattlensnake Sam Johnson)

Samuel Johnson. Like David Crockett, hearing the name would bring to mind anything but a desperado. While Crockett stirs the ashes of the Alamo, Samuel Johnson brings a picture of the Literary Club, Eighteenth Century England, Coffee Houses, Joshua Reynolds, Oliver Goldsmith and far away places that have no link or connection with a desperado in the little hamlet of Canoncito near Santa Fe where he lies buried, the bullet from the gun of an imposed upon bar-tender still lodged in the reposing frame.

Our Samuel Johnson was Kentucky born. As fiery as the bourbon that made his State famous, he walked about with an air of indifference that amazed his school mates who recognized in him a tendency to fight, bully, terrorize and play the part of the hooligan with frightening success. He had no love for Yankees and maintained a steady, overt confidence in his physical prowess and strength. He was overbearing because he was oversized. He was tall, raw-boned, strongly knit, shoulders massive and a little stooped, he wore his curly sandy hair long after the fashion of frontiersmen. Brown-eyed, he was never relaxed and always seeking to rule and dominate with fists and brawn rather than by personality and good-will. The Civil War left him stranded and mal-adjusted. Nothing satisfied his restless spirit nor was anything right with the world. He drifted to Texas as so many others of his day with cattle-baron ambitions, only to end up riding herd for the more fortunate, which did nothing to soothe his "world owes me a living" attitude.

Still, the vast profits derived from the ride of the longhorns to Kansas gave him hope that someday his ship would come in. Railroad gangs, the steady concentration of industrial areas, the extinction of buffalo herds, the rise of prosperity gave him hope that he would ride the bandwagon to equal Goodnight, Chisum, Pierce and others as one of the mighty of cattle-land. He began by cowboying for A. H. Pierce, better known as "Shanghai" Pierce who was building an empire for himself at Rancho Grande. He sent many herds up the trail, and his brand was as well known in Kansas as it was in Texas. Perhaps Johnson would have amounted to something had he not been consumed with his own importance and carried a chip on his shoulders. He believed that he was destined to rule and he would do so if he had to beat every hired hand into submission and loyalty to him. Pierce was made aware of his tactics and ordered Johnson to move on. He next worked for the La Quinta outfit in the southern part of the state, then in a repentant mood asked to return to Pierce's place, where he worked in silence planning a way to cut out cattle as a rustler since he felt he could get to the top no other way.

For a long time he relied on his massiveness and strength rather than a gun, springing on his opponent like a tiger to crush the breath out of him and won for himself in the camps the name of Tiger Jack. Later on some thought his manner was more like the uncoiling and sudden dart of a rattler, so that he went by a second name of Rattlesnake Sam, either one of which he went by to the end of his days. For a time he associated with Sam Bass until he found out that he could not rule the roost. He drifted into Fort Griffin where he worked as a bar-tender—manipulators they called them in those days. Here at the frontier headquarters for buffalo hunters and principal supply station along the Dodge Trail, he took to practising more and more with the six-shooter, but try as he might he could never master any type of draw. In a gunfight in the cantina he killed a cowboy but that was only because the other fellow was slower on the draw and drunk to boot.

Rattlesnake took up freighting for a time, but it was not to his liking so he organized a buffalo hunter party of his own. He was constantly fighting with his men and the outfit died in infancy. He next cast his lot with Mannen Clements, cousin of John Wesley Hardin, and, of like manner born; killers both of them actually enjoying it like a professional boxer enjoys the squared circle. With Mannen rode his brothers, Gyp, Jim and Joe as well as his cousins, Simp, Bud and Tom Dixon. At the Cowskin Creek Camp this gang joined George Peshaur, who dreamed of working over Marshall Earp as Clements dreamed of working over Wichita.

Named after the Wichita Indians who had established a little village near the mouth of the Little Arkansas river, it would have been doomed to oblivion had not James R. Mead and Jesse Chisholm, the half-breed Cherokee, established a trading post near the village in 1864. Just after the close of the Civil War Mead sent Chisholm into the Southwest with a wagonload of goods to exchange for buffalo hides. While returning he ran into a heavy storm and his wagons cut deep ruts into the mud that dried as the Chisholm Trail, over which the subsequent years brought the herds of Texas to the Kansas rail heads. The settlers at Wichita began to provide accommodations for the herd-driving cowboys. Mungar built his hostel, restuarant, saloon and dance hall; a second settler built his "First and Last Chance" saloon to accommodate thirsty cowpunchers for their first drink coming up the trail and their last drink before returning to Texas. Sometimes a fight ensued and their first drink proved their last. When the railroad came to Wichita in 1872 the town boomed. In came the Cyprians, dance hall girls, gamblers, cantinas by the car load. Scouts, Indians, soldiers, frontier lawyers, loan sharks, cow pokes, cow punchers, bullwhackers, teamsters, mule skinners, buffalo hunters, hide skinners, sweet girls, dance hall girls, plainsmen, homesteaders, cattlemen, Spanish Americans, gamblers and deputies rubbed elbows along the crowded streets for they had read the sign on the outskirts of the town: Anything Goes in Wichita. Leave your revolvers at police headquarters and get a check. Carrying loaded weapons is strictly forbidden.

Clements and others objected to Wichita's becoming a "Goody Town" and blamed Marshall Earp. Nobody paid attention to checking in their guns and life went on pretty much the same. Shooting usually occured in the evening when there was more time for gambling and frolic although most places ran a twenty-four hour shift—eight hours each with bands going at all hours so that there was never a time of the day or night a person could not dance or drink or gamble. Like the drinks and the music the painted ladies were available at all times. Reforms were coming too fast and quick to suit characters like Clements and Rattlesnake Sam and they decided to do something about it. In town at a certain establishment kept by Ida May, Rattlesnake often served as a bouncer in return for the favors of one of the belles of the house. He offered to marry the girl but she knew his moods and tenses and wisely put him off. Sam was to be at a certain spot on a certain day for the march on Wichita.

Clements was aware that the most quiet time of the day for the cow capitol when there seemed to be a lull in the day's occupation, was at eight in the morning. It was decided to attack the town at that hour and catch the lawful element by surprise. If their six-shooters spoke loud words, their mouths shouted even louder and all Wichita was aware of the day and hour of the raid. Rattlesnake was especially vindicative especially since he had been thrown out of a cantina by Earp and clamped in jail for wearing side arms. Clements was hoping that Rattlesnake would shoot first and ask questions afterwards, provided he got the marshall before the outraged outlaw.

On the flat across the river the brigade marched as to war, the Clements brothers in the lead. As they clanked across the bridge they were confronted by ten riflemen fanned out across Douglas Avenue. Johnson looked in vain for Marshall Earp. The invaders decided on a conference before opening fire. They came to the conclusion that it would be safer for them to fight on foot. Ten men were chosen to guard the mounts; forty advanced on the town. Rattlesnake, brown eyes ever alert, looked for his enemy. To kill Marshall Earp would rank him among the greatest gunfighters of all time. Suddenly from behind one of the false front buildings stepped the marshall. Behind him stood several men. He was unarmed, save for a six-shooter still hidden away in his gun belt.

Clements stopped. He eyed the rows of houses that lined Douglas Avenue. How many Winchesters were behind those windows and out of sight? Behind him were the horses and open prairie. To the sides the river. Every one of his men was covered. This he sensed rather than saw. To open fire now would be to make this bridge their monument. He ordered the men to put away their guns. They turned and marched back to Cowskin Creek Camp. It was the only humanitarian act of his life and only because his life would be forfeited otherwise. He had no fear of the marshall and either he or Rattlesnake or any one of a dozen men there would have killed Earp that morning but they were not willing to barter their lives to make Wichita free for a lot of people who would not so much as say Thank You over their graves. He was not so interested in strife as of life. Rattlesnake Sam was a little rattled. Clements, despite his blood-lust, was not the man to shoot in the back; Sam was. He wanted to turn suddenly as he jumped on his horse and send some lead after the form of the retreating marshall. Clements would have none of it.

Over on the trail into Dodge was the stage stand of a quaint character known as Hoodoo Brown. Here whiskey, tobacco, six-shooter shells, and other comforts of Western life might be bought, a friendly game of poker might be played, and if you knew Hoodoo real well, a hold-up might be staged. Here Red River Tom, Dave Rudabaugh, Tom Pickett and men of like stamp assembled and talked over the possibilities of a new holdup, a rustling job, a bank robbery and other such affairs that made their lives interesting if not dangerous to live. Here Rattlesnake aligned himself with Dave Rudabaugh for the Kinsley robbery, but was jailed when Dave turned State's Evidence against him. Whether he escaped or was given a short term, we find him in Dodge again working as a "manipulator" as bar-tenders were called. He continued his relationship with Hoodoo Brown and when the latter pulled stakes and moved to Las Vegas where he was elected Justice of the Peace, Rattlesnake joined him there. He was in on the stage robbery at Tecolote and one on Raton Pass. He joined the gang that rustled government horses and mules at Fort Union and government beef belonging to Fort Union at the Tecolote feeding grounds. When Las Vegas decided to clean up, Rattlesnake decided to clean out for the vigilantes mentioned him by name and gave him until sundown to decide between a rope or to shake the dust of the town. He next located in Arizona where he was busily engaged in rustling cattle and selling them across the border. When the law caught up with his activities there he returned to New Mexico in Santa Fe county.

Just to be in New Mexico was dangerous. He was wanted for killing a sheep herder at Loma Parda near Fort Union, and for the death of a stage coach driver at the Raton Pass robbery. When he brought some rustled steers up the Vermejo a cowboy questioned their brand and he killed him. The Territory of New Mexico wanted him dead or alive. The Maxwell Land Grant Cattle Company offered a reward for his capture. He was notorious and this elated him. "He strutted about," said one old timer, "as if he were Mr. Peacock himself." The people of Southern Colorado and Northern New Mexico sent out posse after posse after him but he always eluded them. When he took to robbing the Barlow and Sanderson stage he shot first and demanded the strong box afterwards. He was as slippery as an eel. He had more hide-outs than Coe before him and Ketchum after him. He gambled away his money only to replenish his resources at various points along the line. Wells Fargo sent a detective to trace him down but his search proved fruitless.

Single-handed he entered saloons, lined up gamblers against the wall, took all the money in sight and vanished into space which was quite a feat considering his bulk. Pay day at the "end of track" was a busy one for him. Sometimes he saved the pay master the trouble of counting it out; sometimes he waited until it was paid and all the men were gathered at a bar in a spending spree. Even when the paymaster had guards to protect him, Rattlesnake coiled in and out without warning to strike and they had heard enough of his ruthlessness to drop their guns and rifles when he asked them to. There were more rewards offered for him dead or alive than Billy the Kid ever dreamed existed.

Eighteen miles out of Santa Fe at Glorieta Pass two hamlets made their bid to fame in the frontier manner of Dodge, Tombstone and Las Vegas: Glorieta and Canoncito. The latter was an older settlement having been colonized by farmers out of San Miguel del Bado, Pecos and Santa Fe. Here the Santa Fe railroad had a freight yard and stage coach station which still stands to the side of Highway 85 and looks very much as it did when transfers were made out of Las Vegas and Santa Fe while the railroad was building its regular stop at Lamy. It is a long, adobe building coated with yeso that glares against the brilliant New Mexico sky. Up the road from it was the Santa Fe camp and the baggatele that follows an "end of track" town. Saloons without number offered competition to a sister town near by known as Glorieta. This is a famous land mark of Civil War days. Here Rattlesnake took into his confidence the Pearson boys who folded up at Elizabethtown after the lull in the mining industry. They had a nice cantina when gold was an all important item before the coming of the railroad. But gold ceased to flow and business slowed up.

Rattlesnake frequented the Rhodes & Hogan saloon in Canoncito and exacted tribute from its owners. The Pearson cantina was in Glorieta where Sam often found refuge from the law. Word soon reached the sheriff that Rattlesnake was hiding at Pearsons. As he also wished to question the brothers concerning another incident he decided to pay Glorieta a visit. The desperado was warned in time.

"To what do we owe this visit," asked the older of the Pearson boys.

"I want Rattlesnake Sam."

"You don't see him, do you?"

"Is that saying he isn't here?"

"I am not saying one way or the other. You're the one that wants him."

"I'll take a look in the restaurant." His was in another part of the same building.

"Help yourself."

"You could be arrested for harboring a criminal you know. And from what I hear of you boys you could stand a little investigation yourselves."

The younger Pearson got behind the officer, reached for his gun, picked it out of the holster and threw it behind the bar. Those drinking in the place put down their drinks and made a mad scramble for the door. The brothers unfastened their gun belts and set upon the sheriff very much as Rattlesnake himself would have done. They broke three of his ribs, his right arm and opened a head wound with a bottle. They told him to go back to Santa Fe and leave Glorieta to the Pearson brothers. Nobody in Glorieta dared ride out to Santa Fe for help. As much as they would like to see the Pearsons and Rattlesnake dead, they would rather leave it to someone else. They kept the law officer at their place all night. In the morning they put the sheriff on his horse and told him to keep going until he reached Santa Fe.

Over in Canoncito, Rattlesnake was on a gun toting spree. He shot out lights, made dudes dance, entered saloons and forced customers to wait on him at gun point. If anyone showed signs of displeasure he made him drink until he couldn't stand up. A deputy came in from Santa Fe. Never having seen Sam nor the Pearson boys who were celebrating with Sam and at the moment were playing poker with some railroad hands at Rhodes & Hogan's, he made no effort to arrest them. One of the workers was brave or foolish enough to tell Sam his dealing wasn't quite in line.

"Are you calling me a cheat?"

"You are not honest, if that's what you mean."

Sam coiled, sprung and grappled the fellow around the waist and began sqeezing. Then he landed a hay-maker, knocking the fellow to the floor and digging his boots into him.

"That's about enough," said the deputy. "You're under arrest for disorderly conduct."

Sam laughed until the tears came. He went over to the bar.

"Pour me a good one. I'm a little tired but have some unfinished business."

He downed the drink; threw the glass at the deputy and went over to finish the railroad worker.

"You're under arrest."

"We'll talk about that later."

"Now is as good a time as any." He was a persistent fellow. He approached Sam drawing out his gun as he did so.

"Hold it," commanded Joe Pearson.

They took the gun away from him and gave him a worse going over than the sheriff. They sent him back to Santa Fe to join his boss. The bar-tender quit. He wanted no part of the fireworks that were bound to follow. Frank Page somewhat of a dandy but an adventurer withal, came in from the East and accepted the job. Sam came in and asked for a drink.

"That will be two-bits, please."

Sam looked at him a moment refusing to believe his ears.

"What?"

"Two bits, please."

"I don't pay for drinks. I run this berg."

"You may run the berg, but I run the bar. Pay up."

"Listen, Yankee—stay healthy."

"I'm not a Yankee. I feel fine. Now, pay up."

"No, you're not a Yankee. You're a s - - -."

"Whatever I am, you still owe me two-bits."

One word led to another. The mistake of so many desperadoes. Talk. Threats. Page turned around. Behind some bottles for such eventualities he had hidden a pistol. Swinging back while Sam was still cussing him, he fired, hitting the victim right through the heart. You may see his grave, off in a corner in unconsecrated ground of the tiny cemetery on the hill above Highway 85. Said the Santa Fe New Mexican for December 6, 1879:

"The killing of Rattlesnake Sam is confirmed and now comes the rumor that the Pearson boys attacked and severely beat an officer who was attempting to quell a disturbance at

Canoncito." Two days later after sending a reporter to get the facts—evidently the officers were ashamed to give the press the stories of their beatings—the same paper said:

"Rattlesnake Sam, a notorious desperado for whose body, dead or alive, large rewards have been offered, was killed at Canoncito on last Thursday by one, Frank Page, lately from the States. Page was clerking in the saloon of Rhodes & Hogan. Rattlesnake Sam came in and demanded a drink in a very insulting manner, refusing to pay for the same. Words ensued and threats were freely made by the deceased. Page secured a pistol and, without a word of warning, fired, the ball passing directly through the heart of Rattlesnake Sam. The murderer soon afterwards gave himself up to the officers of the law, who have him in custody. Thus endeth the chapter and New Mexico is rid of a bold, bad character."

"The sheriff of Santa Fe county visited Glorieta a few days ago on business connected with his office. He entered the saloon and restaurant of the Pearson boys, not unknown in Las Vegas, for the purpose of arresting them. They immediately set upon him, beating him unmercifully over the head and other parts of the body and breaking his arm in the fracas. The sheriff was kept prisoner overnight in their saloon. They are not at large but will probably be caged for their brutal and unlawful attack upon an officer in discharge of his sworn duty."

Poor Frank Page. Not one red cent did he receive for fulfilling the requests of so many who wanted Rattlesnake Sam, dead or alive. Garrett was luckier with Billy the Kid. Indeed, Page had all he could do to ward off a murder rap. It was finally decided that he acted in "self defense" but only on condition he claim none of the reward money. Such is life.

Everybody seems relaxed—even poor Gus Mentzer. From where he hangs he questions their right to do this to him.

Book Twelve

INCIDENT IN RATON

(Gus Mentzer)

Raton is the gateway to New Mexico. This was recognized as far back as General Kearny when he marched his troops over the stupendous mountain for the unbloody conquest of New Mexico. It was also recognized by the Santa Fe railroad in its fight with the Rio Grande for the right of way along Uncle Dick Wooten's toll-gate road. The village of Otero to the south was abandoned for a new "end of track" town, where the railroad built its round house and drifters followed in the wake of merchants, lawyers, butchers, grocers and painters to build their saloons, gambling dens, dance halls and bawdy-houses, most of the latter to the satisfaction of the law abiding element of the town being located on the other side of the tracks in an area called Chihuahua but actually a quasi-village with the quaint sounding and appropriate name of Buena Vista.

Into the alembic fabric that made up the melting pot of those first years came two partners, up from Texas to hope for one touch of Midas then retirement. To bring about a realization of this dream they opened a glass palace saloon that was the admiration of the quick and the morally dead alike. The partners were William Burbridge and Gus Mentzer. Said the Raton Guard, February 10, 1882, concerning their wonderful establishment:

"Mr. William Burbridge has rented Cook's new building and will fit it up as a model bar and billiard hall. It will be the showplace of the town and the proprietor intends to spare neither labor nor capital to make it complete in every detail.

The counter was made here by Mallett and Lawlor, and is a fine piece of workmanship. Three side boards have already been received from Cincinnati which cost nearly a thousand dollars, and everything else will be gotten to correspond. When open, the whole room will be principally marble, cutglass and French mirror, and will be tony in every respect. If men will drink, we wish the new house success."

In his own sight, Burbridge was every inch a gentleman and wished everyone else to look upon him as such. The worst crime in the world for him was to appear in public with a stain on his cravat, or a stray hair out of place and for soup to form tear-drops along the fringles of his handle-bar mustache was an unpardonable sin. He was courteous to all his customers of necessity, for it was good business but he expected all to keep and maintain their proper distance. Not that he was cold by nature but he had political aspirations and reasoned that if other cities could elect saloon keepers mayors how much more so Burbridge who ran a place that would be envied even in Denver. There was one exception to his rule of life—one man he favored and that was more because he was under obligation to him rather than because he felt the need of his companionship. Rather if he could do so he would shed it.

It began in Texas. Burbridge and Gus Mentzer pooled their meager finances and opened a saloon in Dallas. Business was good and the place quite popular. One day a customer walked in and, ordering a few drinks, began to abuse Burbdige as each drink made him headier than the last. He came to the point that he insisted on looking upon Burbridge as his mortal enemy and would be satisfied with nothing less than his blood. He challenged the tavern keeper to a duel, but the meticulous William would have no part of six-shooter affairs which only served to pour hot coals on the head of the abuser and he called Burbridge all the names in the book and a good many not in the book. Mentzer, several years younger than his partner and not adverse to gun-play, walked over to the belligerent character and invited him to a table for more drinks. As they both drank the customer continued his efforts to draw out Burbridge, hoping that he would reach for a gun so that he would have a pretext for shooting him. Mentzer was aware of this and was ready for the customer. Eventually when the customer was so far gone with drink that he reversed his opinion of Mentzer and told him he was just as cowardly as his partner and that he was going to do in both Burbridge and Mentzer, the latter accepted the invitation to shoot it out. The customer was carried out as Mentzer coolly blew into the barrel of his smoking revolver and told his partner that he had saved his life, a fact that Burbridge readily recognized. Gus then took a couple of witnesses before the Justice of the Peace and they testified that he had killed in self defense. After that all went along smoothly until the railroad came to New Mexico via Raton Pass and the pair thought they would make a fortune in the new town. In this respect Burbridge's foresight was far better than his hind-sight and he might have become mayor of Raton if he had left Mentzer behind.

As the discrepancy between the ages of the two was apparent, the townspeople called Mentzer The Kid to distinguish him from his partner and most of the business was discussed with the older man. This caused Mentzer to suffer qualms of jealousy and gradually he took consolation in drink. Now William was seriously worried about The Kid's drinking. With the new cantina catering to the elite, it was not good for business to have a drunkard about. Customers getting tight in the place was not the same as having one of the proprietors of the place under the weather. He was trying hard to make a gentleman of Gus but he just wouldn't play ball. He warned Mentzer that if he did not stop drinking he would dissolve the partnership. To which Gus would invariably reply that the business was his by right for if he had not saved William's life in Texas he would not now be putting on airs in Raton. When Burbridge had about as much as he could stand, he dissolved the partnership and had Mentzer thrown out. This hurt his pride as much as his seat. He re-entered the saloon.

A short distance away the Wallace Sisters, famous actresses of their day, were giving a performance at the McAuliffe & Ferguson Hall. They had previously engaged to play at Cook's Hall but at the last moment the plans were changed. It was early summer and they were catering to a large audience. Suddenly the sound of shots was heard above the voices of the players. The show must go on. Dramatically they carried on as the audience emptied the hall. No reflection on their ability, merely the fact that people were more interested finding out what the shooting was all about. The Bank Exchange Saloon was having a drama all its own.

Burbridge would not accept Mentger's invitation to come out into the street and shoot it out. The duel, much to the distaste of both, since the mirrors would have to be shot up and they were so expensive, would have to be fought in the cantina. R. P. Dollman, who ran the Little Brindle Saloon, was also deputy sheriff. He happened to be at the Bank Exchange when Mentzer came in and invited Burbridge to fight it out for the ownership. The deputy yelled in warning to William because he was aware that Mentzer was drunk. Burbridge misinterpreted his yell as a warning to him that he was taking Mentzer's part so he turned to the drawer behind him, picked out a six-shooter and shot at Dollman. Patrons ducked under the tables; others made for the street. Glasses, water system at the bar, and other things were hit in the three-way exchange of gun fire. One bullet struck Mentzer without doing serious damage. Seeing that he accomplished nothing he took to his heels. The patrons came from under the tables and joined forces with the crowd from the theatre and under the leadership of Dollman went in search of Mentzer. All the buildings were searched; the boxes and packing cases lined along the streets thoroughly examined, but no Mentzer.

There was a hawkeye in the crowd and he spotted the culprit. Mentzer was hiding behind some packing cases at the railroad depot. A shout went up and the man-hunt was on. At this juncture the evening train pulled into the station. Fearing that Mentzer had boarded it, the mob took it over, looking behind every seat, in the wash rooms, even under the train. No fox was ever better hounded. Dollman came to the conclusion that Gus was in the woods some distance beyond the tracks, and as it was already quite dark, the search was called off for the time being. A posse would be assembled in the morning in the hopes that Gus would sleep it off somewhere in the vicinity. Back went the human beach-combers to the Little Brindle to drink to Dollman's health and to celebrate his narrow escape from death. This cantina was but a few doors from the Bank Exchange and across the street from the depot.

So, for an hour the deputies of the brass rail re-lived the incident and tall stories of other deeds and events made the rounds. The drinks piled up as the incident calmed down. With imaginations fired up of other shootings and stomachs fired up by Dollman's generosity, the mob decided to re-visit the Bank Exchange to condone Burbridge and drink to his health. Several, seeing that no blood was spilt, went back to watch the Wallace Sisters finish the the drama of *Lord Louie*.

The drinkers near the entrance of the saloon stiffened. Into the cantina walked Gus, who planked himself against the Bar and voraciously called for a drink. What he got was a volley of lead, none of which struck him. He seemed to bear a charmed life. The mob now closed in on him but Gus took the defensive and began throwing a little lead himself at which the mob beat a hasty retreat. The Kid fled across the street into the railroad yards just above the depot lawn. The switch engine had just pulled in. Engineer Mulvaney had just taxied his wife up to town in the engine from their box-car quarters a mile down the tracks after her purchase of groceries from the mercantile company that separated the two cantinas. They were in the store when the shooting began and Mulvaney decided that it was no place for his wife to be.

To Gus the return of Mulvaney spelt salvation. He disappeared behind the engine and climbed aboard. Hugh Eddleson, partner of Moulton of the Moulton House hotel, spotted Mentzer in the locomotive. By this time the fugitive had shaken off the effects of drink and had no other thought in mind but his safety. Rather than have Eddleson bring the mob on him, Mentzer sent a bullet through him. But Hugh had already yelled: "There he is," and the sound of the shot directed the posse to his hiding place. Seeing Eddleson in a prone position, the mob decided to investigate the extent of his injuries before closing in on Gus. This only served to give him time to work at the controls in an effort to ride the engine towards Raton Pass and safety. But Mentzer was no engineer and no matter what he pulled the engine refused to budge.

S. H. Jackson, who forsook the bar-tender's job at the Little Brindle to get in on the kill, climbed the engine to grab for Mentzer. He fell to the ground dead from a bullet as Mentzer fired at him point-blank. Deputy Dollman arrived by this time to see Jackson, his brother-in-law and co-owner of the Little Brindle, fall to the ground. Mentzer's gun was now empty. Taking advantage of his opportunity Dollman crowded the killer and the mob stormed in to subdue him. Part of the crowd carried Eddleson to Dr. J. J. Shuler's office on Park Avenue off First Street for medical attention. The larger part, feeling that more was to be played in this drama, accompanied Dollman and Mentzer back to the deputy's cantina. The law officer decided to shackle Gus lest he escape and cause further disturbance. He was just about to clamp on the shackles when in walked Harvey Moulton.

Moulton first appears in outlaw history as the defender of Billy the Kid in his fight against a blacksmith. When the blacksmith later had the advantage of Moulton in a fight at Silver City little William Bonney remembered the man who befriended him, pulled out a knife and ran it to the hilt through the smithy. This, according to legend, was the outlaw's first murder. Moulton remained for a time in Silver City then went to Kansas, Trinidad and the coming of the railroad to New Mexico decided him on his hotel at Raton. Added to this he was an engineer for the Santa Fe, a Justice of the Peace, a relative of Eddleson, who was his partner in the hotel business, and the first person in Raton to dig for water. Moulton Avenue in Raton is named for him.

News of all the shooting was not long in reaching Moulton, who was especially more bent on justice since his partner was involved. He decided that Mentzer was to be hung then and there. The mob seconded his decision. Dollman, although his brother-in-law had been killed, was in favor of holding Mentzer for trial by jury. Moulton would have none of it and demanded the custody of the prisoner. Dollman, seeing that he availed nothing, left the Little Brindle in the hopes of securing others who would come to his way of thinking and disperse the mob. The Justice and mob left the saloon for a moment, leaving Mentzer alone with deputy William Bergen. The only possible explanation for this action is that the Justice wished to hold court legal like and went outside to hear testimony in order to pronounce Mentzer guilty of death. Whatever the explanation, the deputy and the killer were alone.

Moulton returned and told Bergen that he found Mentzer guilty of death and he proposed to take him out then and there to hang him. Bergen told him that he was a justice and not a judge; therefore he had no right over life and death. Moulton insisted that he was going to hang Mentzer. And that was that. Bergen told the Justice that he would have Mentzer over his dead body. He was here to up-hold the law and there was nothing lawful about Moulton's demand. The Justice ignored him and reached for Mentzer. Bergen, seeing that he would lose his prisoner if he did not act promptly, pulled his six-shooter and shot the Justice. Just as Moulton fell he crossed his hands and grabbing his gun returned the fire, sending a bullet through Bergen's stomach. Mentzer stepped over the wounded men, sought the back entrance and escaped to Williams & Frick's butcher shop. The crowd had forgotten him for a moment in administering to Moulton and Bergen. The deputy they carried to the office of the Raton Coal & Coking Company, where he died the following morning (Tuesday).

When butcher Frick saw Mentzer all he could do was stare in amazement. Finding his voice at last he said:

"Why Gus, we have been looking for you all evening."

Mentzer pleaded for help and that he be hidden away somewhere in safety until he could skip town. The butcher picked up a rope that a customer left there when he led a pig to the shop to be butchered that very afternoon. He threw it to the mob that now came to his shop when he cried out that the desperado was within. Dollman came in and took the prisoner. The mob told him to stand back. Mentzer was in their hands. The rope was placed about his neck and he was dragged out to the First Street boardwalk. They sure had a time with him, for he fought like a tiger. He was conducted to the front of the Raton Bank on the corner of Clark Avenue and First Street. The rope was thrown over the bank sign, but the sign crashed under the weight of the killer. A boy was boosted up to the post on which the sign rested. He fastened the rope over the top. Up went Mentzer. He struggled for a moment with the rope about his neck. His strength failed. The body hung there until Tuesday morning to greet the incoming train and give the travelers a vivid view of frontier justice. Mallet and Van Harem had coffins for all five. Bergen was buried at the coal mining camp of Blossburg. Mentzer, Moulton, Eddleson and Jackson were buried in Raton. If you go to the far end of the cemetery to the right you will find their graves. The whole town was out for the funerals. All work was suspended for the morning at the Santa Fe shops. Rev. O. P. McMains, the Arch-Agitator for the Anti-Granters in the Maxwell Land Grant Bubble preached the funeral oration for Moulton and Eddleson. Rev. Callen preached at Blossburg at the Bergen funeral and later at Raton for Jackson. Mentzer was simply buried.

On July 6, 1882, eight days after these bloody events, Dullman resigned as deputy sheriff and devoted all his time to the Little Brindle. When saner minds reviewed the affair it was found that Mentzer, who was twenty-six at the time of his death, had been influenced by a gambler by the name of Turner. He was ambitious for the Bank Exchange and hoped that by instigating Mentzer against his partner who would kill Burbridge and Turner in turn would kill Mentzer. It was found out that Turner handed Mentzer the guns for the blood letting. Turner was arrested at Las Vegas, but nothing came of it as he was not actually implicated in the killings. The evening following the killings irate citizens banded together and twelve hundred organized into vigilantes. E. Parson was elected chairman; J. Osfield, secretary and law and order changed the history of the railroad camp. Burbridge never did get to be mayor.

Book Thirteen

MURDER FOR CHRISTMAS

(Baca of Socorro)

A. M. Conklin was born in Ohio in 1841. When but a lad his family moved to Westfield, Indiana, where he received his education and from which town he volunteered in the war between the States when he attained his twenty-first birthday, serving on the side of the Union. After the war he married and raised a family. As newspaper work was his forte, he decided to work for the Las Vegas Gazette in New Mexico in the hopes of one day owning a paper of his own. Opportunity came when the Socorro Sun was for sale. Taking his children to Westfield and leaving them at a boarding school there, he returned to New Mexico with his wife and bought the Socorro paper. He found a few members of the Presbyterian church, with which he was affiliated, banded them together and invited Rev. S. D. Fulton to come in as pastor. That was in October 1880. Christmas Eve of that year the editor was dead.

His story runs parallel to that of lawyer McSween of Lincoln county which adjoined Socorro county. Both were religious men; both came to New Mexico for wealth and health; both stopped bullets; both started local wars which stirred hatreds that last to this day. When Christmas time of the year 1880 rolled around, Rev. Thomas Harwood, who had done much work for the New Mexico Protestant Missions, decided that all the Protestants in Socorro should get together and give the kiddies a Christmas treat. As he was living in Socorro at the time and was well known, he received generous support for the project. One of the men he invited to assist him at the affair was the Elder and editor Conklin. Years after these events he recorded his life in New Mexico in two volumes. As the newspaper man was present upon his invitation he felt the impact of his sudden death for many years. As an eyewitness to the murder he relates it in his *History of the New Mexico and Spanish Missions:*

"Christmas Tree at Socorro—This was December 24, 1880. The Presbyterians had come in, a few of them—and the Rev. S. D. Fulton was their pastor. We all held services together in our chapel. All was very harmonious. Mrs. Harwood taught the principal and only school in the place at the time (I believe he meant for the town, not for the religious group). It was a union Christmas tree held in our church. Mrs. Harwood has charge of it. It was well attended. A new thing for the place, and as the school would have many Mexican children, special pains were taken to have something on the tree for each child, and for fear that some might be overlooked a barrel of apples was brought in. The program was beautifully rendered. In the afternoon of December 21 (a few days before the peaceful scene described above) Mrs. Harwood and myself were privileged to be the guests of Mr. and Mrs. Conklin of Socorro. They had for some time desired to have all the preachers of Socorro and their wives make them a visit. Accordingly, the time was fixed and the following named persons were present and spent the afternoon of the above named day: Rev. Mr. Fulton and wife; Rev. N. H. Gale and wife, from Albuquerque; Rev. M. Mathieson and wife, and the writer and wife. The afternoon was pleasantly spent with profitable conversation, avoiding the too frequent neighborhood gossip. At six o'clock supper was served. It was a well spread table. All formalities were forgotten, and the occasion rounded up into an old-fashioned farm-like social and joyous visit. I had never seen Mr. Conklin so cheerful. How little did we think of the sad fate that would soon befall him!

'Mysterious fate, that night bade us part,
But left his memory sacred to our heart,
Oh, tell us, can this world a hopeful thought bestow

To friends now weeping at the couch of woe?
Oh, no; but hope soothes the last adieu,
And sorrowing one, hope speaks to you:
"Weep not," she says, though death in terror comes,
'Twas but the gate to his eternal home.
No more of sorrow here, no more of pain,
Our brother's death, though sad to us, to him is gain;
In heaven we'll meet no more to sever
Where friendship sweetly glows forever.

"How quickly our joys that Christmas Eve were turned to deepest sorrow! The meeting was almost out. As we said before, a barrel of apples had been brought in. At or near the close, Mrs. Harwood asked that the apples might be distributed. She then requested me to ask: 'Has every one in the house an apple?' I did so. No one said he had not. Mr. Conklin was standing near the door with a large apple in his hand about half eaten. I asked: 'Mr. Conklin, have you had an apple? At which he held up the half eaten fruit and a ripple of laughter passed over the congregation. A few parting words, the doxology and benediction and Christmas greeting and nearly all were gone except Mr. and Mrs. Conklin and a few of their friends. I had noticed a little disturbance in the congregation a little before this and stepped back to the door and asked him what it was. He told me briefly what it was. As soon as he stepped out he was attacked. I was with him trying to stop the trouble. It is the greatest wonder that I was not shot as it was in the dark after the first pistol shot and the lamp went out. I eased Mr. Conklin down, otherwise he would have fallen heavily for he was a large man. I heard him say distinctly: 'God have mercy on my soul.' His wife told me later that they had prayed together just before coming to the Christmas tree service. The funeral was largely attended, assisted by several preachers."

Just that. No names, no incriminations. Socorro did more about it than that. So did the press. It was an incident to focus the national spotlight on Socorro for the next few days, and it looked like Socorro was going to have a nice little war of its own, an honor which the town of Lincoln was then enjoying. The murder had far reaching effects and stirred up hatreds that exist to this day, and very likely will continue as long as Socorro exists. Certain things have to be clarified, and the scene reset in order for the reader to understand what actually took place. Mind you, I am impartial. I was not there, and those who were are so confused after the lapse of so many years, and the repetition of the telling, that only court-house records, letters, newspapers can be relied on for the actual facts.

The Bacas were members of an old, megatherium family whose traditions and ripeness were time-honored before Coronado stepped into history. Of royal vintage, they played a tremendous part in the colonizing and settling of New Mexico, to the very days of the Santa Fe Trail, the invasion of the Texans, the march of the Americans, the rise of the cattle barons, the rides of the vigilantes. They were prominent in Socorro from the very beginning. Their escutcheon was to be found with every Conquistador who sallied forth from Mexico City in the name of the Crown and Christianity. They were hildagos, peacemakers, Indian-fighters, Conquistadors striking taproots along the trail, permeating the country with Spanish culture, Spanish pride and Spanish trade. Unsung heroes, for the most part, they set the stage for the advance of General Kearny and the forces of Occupation. One branch of the family settled down at Socorro building up the great ranch house, putting into it all the splendor of their heritage and tradition as their fathers knew it before them. Castilian hearts wrapped in Kearny's flag. That they wished to be Americans they proved in the fact that they refused to follow the migration to Mesilla and south when given a choice between Mexican or American citizenship. As Santa Fe traders they were acquainted with the world beyond New Mexico. They even sent their sons and daughters as far afield as St. Louis and New York to imbibe American culture and education. Their roots were in the soil and they loved New Mexico with warmth and passion, ready to sacrifice their lives for their homes. Steeped in tradition and drilled in heritage, their pride made them quick to interpret the slightest remark as a slur on their nobility, a degradation in the eyes of their peons. This, more than anything else, brought about the Yuletide slaying of the newspaper man, and its aftermath of vigilantes and bloodshed, even though in 1880, they were not blessed with worldly goods as they formerly had been.

Over and above that was the moving tide of changing and fusing cultures rapidly engulfing Socorro with the tremendous influx of miners, soldiers, ranchers, gamblers, lawyers and all that went to make a melting pot and cosmopolitan area. Slap on to this the mistaken idea that despite all this a family with such a heritage was untouchable, and all he did above reprimand. Indeed, no inferior especially was to question his conduct. Report it to his father, yes, and have his father dole out the punishment. That was the custom. Nowhere else in the United States do customs die so hard as in New Mexico. You have but to attend a wedding, or a baptism, or a funeral to find this out. And it is good. He was subject only to the "jefe de la familia." While Protestantism was not really new to him due to his contacts abroad, and with the traders and soldiers, he was never able to understand it as a creed as fully covered by the Constitution as his own. It has often been said that what a man doesn't understand he ridicules. What brought the youthful Baca and his cousins to a church not his own, at a time when his own church was making elaborate preparations for the Mid-Night Mass? Whatever it was never found its way to the records. They could have spent the night in carousal in some saloon, or dance-hall. While not a fitting preparation for Christmas it would have prolonged their lives and that of the newspaper editor. It couldn't have been a desire for diversion, for a church is the last place to look for it. Perhaps they were there because of some senoritas, quien sabe? They were there, and were out for trouble that night no matter where they were. Here assembled in this little church were many people responsible for their changing world. If a peon no longer doffed his hat at their approach it was because of the philosophy of democracy coming from people such as these. Perhaps it was merely curiosity to see how these

Christians celebrated Christmas Eve in comparison with the old San Miguel mission.

So, Antonio, son of Don Antonio Maria Baca, hidalgo of Socorro, set out under the twinkling stars that frosty Christmas Eve, for a little troublesome fun but not with murder in his heart, and wound up at Dr. Harwood's service. Accompanying him were his two cousins, Onofre Baca and Abran Baca. Perhaps, in passing the Methodist church they heard the caroling of the children. On one side of the edifice was the Yuletide tree. Nearby sat the Rev. N. H. Gale and his wife, and the Rev. Mathieson with his wife. Methodists, Presbyterians, Baptists, and other denominations united in the unity of the season. There had been prayers, readings, speeches. Presents were distributed, and everybody relaxed with the satisfactory feeling that it was Christmas, that humanizes the banker, the butcher and the candle-stick maker. Naturally, at a gathering of this sort, ushers were appointed to seat people and preserve the orderly atmosphere that pervades a church. The men chosen for this task were Judge Shaw (the former Baptist preacher) and A. M. Conklin, editor of the Socorro Sun.

There they sat, refusing the aid of ushers, in a bench directly behind some young ladies. By some queer quirk which a man will not explain in a thousand lifetimes, Antonio put his boots on the seat in the front of him, getting the points between the seat and the young lady's dress. Just as impulsively, he pressed upwards, much to the embarrassment of the señorita. When Conklin passed by she attracted his attention and complained of the annoyance. Noticing that this distressed her to the point of taking the joy out of the celebration, the editor turned to Antonio and whispered for him to remove his feet from the bench. He refused. If the young lady was so bothered, why didn't she move? But Conklin had a mind of his own. He reached across Onofre and pushed Antonio's feet down. Crimson, then pale. If only his cousins hadn't been there to witness the insult! How dare, he whose family background, whose presence in Socorro was of recent date, whose prestige, position, heritage could never equal Antonio's, presume to reprimand him! Immediately he asked Conklin to step outside and settle the matter as an affair of honor. Conklin merely laughed. Who wanted to fight at Yuletide? Antonio was fit to be tied. Anger is a mild word for it. He called his two cousins, lapsing in his excitement into broken English: "Come me out."

All this in a matter of seconds. The congregation for the most part was totally unaware of the by-play. The meeting broke up about nine o'clock that evening. (Evidently this was not at mid-night possibly in consideration of the children, not accustomed to such late hours.) After a number of the congregation dispersed, Rev. Harwood spoke to Conklin, asking him if he did not deem it advisable to take along some friends as an escort for he feared reprisals in the way of a personal attack—not murder—on the part of the injured party. Conklin told him that he didn't anticipate any trouble but if it would ease the minister, he would take along a bodyguard.

So, out the door he went; his wife on one arm, a Dr. Munger on the other. The two young McFarland brothers, one on Mrs. Conklin's right, and the other on the doctor's left. No sooner out the door when Antonio caught him by the arm. At this, the editor turned to the doctor and told him to tell the youth in Spanish to let go of his arm or he would be compelled to use force. He refused to loosen his grip, which was rather strong, for Antonio was of slight build, weighing one hundred and twenty pounds, while the newspaper man was closer to two hundred. Conklin then turned on him, caught him by the arms and forced him back several feet towards the entrance of the church. At this juncture, a pistol shot was fired, without effect. The Rev. Thomas Harwood approached at this point and shouted: "No shooting. No shooting, please!" No sooner were the words out of his mouth than there was a rush from behind that corner of the church and two more shots rang out, breaking the stillness of the night. One shot entered the editor's left breast, passing through the apex of the heart, in nearly a direct line. It was later removed by Dr. Sowers. It had lodged a little to the left of the backbone. The wounded man fell forward on his face. As he fell he uttered: "God have mercy on my soul." One of the McFarland boys pulled

Mrs. Conklin away to the left, out of the line of fire. After her husband fell, all gave him their undivided attention, which left the Bacas free. Taking advantage of the opportunity, they sped away on horseback. A crowd gathered, but the man was already dead. No action was taken until Saturday evening, the day after Christmas, when fifteen witnesses were called in before justice Blackerton who questioned them until eleven o'clock that evening. Both Anglos and Spanish-Americans testified. The justice handed down the verdict that the deceased came to his death by a pistol shot from the hands of one of the three Bacas.

The whole town attended the funeral. The service was conducted by Rev. Fulton of the Presbyterian church.

Assisting at the services were Rev. Harwood, Rev. Gale, Rev. Mathierson, and Judge Shaw. The Rev. Gale held up a pencil for the people to see, saying: "This was found on his person when he died; this could have been his only weapon of defense; this I will cherish till the day I die."

The widow was heartbroken. A thousand times the story circulated, from house to saloon, to store, to hotel. The sheriff did nothing to arrest the culprits.

Then the fireworks began.

Juan Maria Garcia was sheriff at the time. Even that exhalted though precarious position did not ease his mind, for not only was he related to the murderers, but how could he go about arresting the son of an hildalgo? From his mother's breast he was fed on class distinction. He wished himself anywhere else in the world or with any other position. He could have resigned, but the position was too lucrative. Word spread around that the sheriff was doing nothing to set the wheels of justice in motion. Colonel Ethan Eaton decided to do something about it. He sent word to the sheriff to do his duty. The colonel was the commanding officer of the local militia. He had a ranch outside the city limits and was not aware of the killing until he had returned for his Christmas dinner. His messenger returned with the information that the sheriff was nowhere to be found, although he was believed to be in hiding at the home of his deputy, who was also his son-in-law, Felipe, also closely related to Antonio. The colonel decided to force him to do his duty. As he went, word spread that the tall, determined Eaton was on the march to Baca's to pick up the sheriff and bring him to Don Antonio's house and have him arrest the Bacas. From the houses, as he passed, men, rifles in hand, took their places behind him. At that moment the vigilantes of Socorro were born. True, they had been milling around a couple of days talking about it, but it took a leader like Eaton to act rather than talk. The sheriff and his son-in-law were caught sneaking out the back door when they were apprehended and brought before the colonel and his marchers. They were brought to the Baca house, but were told that the men they wanted had already left.

"Just you open the door and let us find out for ourselves," demanded the colonel.

From somewhere within, a voice replied:

"Take our word for it, they are not here."

Someone from the back of the crowd yelled:

"Bring on the dynamite, and blow the door open."

The sheriff who was now thoroughly alarmed, pleaded with Don Antonio in Spanish to open the door. Finally, he said:

"Compadre, open or be blown open."

So, Don Antonio opened. The first in line was Abran. The sheriff kept a poker face. The colonel, on his ranch for the most part, did not know Abran. If he ever saw him before he never associated him with one of the men wanted. He let him by. The mob was either on too good a lookout for Antonio, or just wasn't sure who it really wanted. The McFarland boys were not in the crowd. The ministers were not expected to be; the widow much less. Abran got away. One young woman they let by who immediately got on a horse but the action was so swift that the dress lifted to expose a pants leg, and when the shawl fell, a man's hair-cut was exposed. Hands reached up and Antonio was in the hands of the mob. Of Onfre they saw nothing.

That day a Vigilance Committee was formed. By December 30 they were organized enough to elect Colonel as president, and an executive committee. Every American refusing to serve was imprisoned. What the vigilantes eventually turned out to be was not the fault of the colonel. The plundering, robbing, hi-jacking, stage-coach hold-ups that followed may have been others wearing the masks of vigilantes, or may have been vigilantes under the protection of the masks. They exacted a pretty penny of saloon keepers, dance hall girls and gamblers if they didn't want their places of business destroyed. No one knew where they would strike next. Colonel Eaton realized that it became too powerful a thing for him to destroy, for he was always out for law and order, and only with the re-organization of the militia, without masks, did he finally wipe out the renegade vigilantes whose deeds were anything but on the side of law and order.

Brown and Manzanares, merchants, were called upon by the Anglos (I use this term to separate them from the Spanish-American population) and compelled them to turn over thirty rifles and two-and-a-half dozen pistols in their store, leaving only three rifles to the merchants in case they needed them. There wasn't a street that didn't have its armed vigilantes, with itching fingers, hoping that the natives would start something. At three o'clock on Tuesday morning they again marched to Don Antonio's house in four companies of over fifty each. Again they asked that he surrender the murderers into their custody. Again the sheriff made his appeal. The old man wasn't napping either. He had sixty armed men to defend the fortress against the invader. At that moment one man slipped, discharging a pistol, the bullet passing through the fleshy part of the hip of the man in front of him. The discharge of the gun was the signal for a regular fusilade by the excited crowd which started firing in all directions. Fortunately, no one was hurt. Two were surrendered by Don Antonio, but it was later found that these were not the men wanted. He felt that since they would not take no for an answer it would be better to give them two men, and when they cooled down they would realize that the men they sought were already gone. Twenty-five guns and fifteen revolvers were taken from the Baca house. On Tuesday afternoon all the Bacas were bound over to keep the peace. The sheriff and his deputy were bound over to the tune of five thousand dollars, each to appear before the next district court to answer the charge of malfeasance in office. Dionicio Amarilla and Esteban Baca were bound over in the sum of twenty-five thousand dollars, each to appear before the district court as accessories. Whose faces were red when they proved they were not the parties wanted? All the prominent Spanish-Americans related to the Bacas (and that took in quite a a few) were granted their liberty only on peace bond. Young Antonio was remanded to the Socorro jail, where he was closely watched to frustrate any attempt at escape. One day his beautiful sister brought him a lunch basket. The guards were courteous, and even inclined to a little flirting. As they opened the cell door, she smiling remarked: "Mal a ea quien te parió." (May the one who bore you have hard luck). Well, their war was not against women. Besides, they thought she was thanking them for permitting her to bring her brother some food. Too bad a cute senorita like that was the sister of a murderer. They shrugged their shoulders and walked away.

About nine o'clock that evening, Jack Ketchum and two others were sent to the jail to check up and see that all was well. Confronting them with a .38 calibre pistol was the prisoner. The ball hit Ketchum in the left side, penetrated a rib, glanced upwards, lodging in the body. He carried that bullet for the rest of his long life. In the excitement that followed, Baca received a bullet in the head, killing him instantly. Again the vigilantes went on the march. Arrangements were made to use the Park Hotel as a hospital and arsenal. With young Antonio dead, it meant open warfare for there wasn't a man in Socorro who didn't know that Don Antonio would let them off easy. Help was telegraphed for by the vigilantes who knew they could rely on San Marcial in an emergency. A railroad town thirty-two miles away, to the south, this short-lived beehive was to have as hectic a time as Socorro. But that is the story of San Marcial. They sent forty well-armed men on a train pressed into service for the purpose. But they returned that evening rather down in the mouth when they felt they were not needed. A company of troops was sent from Fort Craig, south of San Marcial, to patrol the town. They remained ten days. Court was held, and the justice of the peace gave the verdict over the shooting of Baca as follows: "Come to death by a pistol ball wound from parties unknown."

The Albuquerque Daily Journal for December 30, 1880, remarked:

"The trouble at Socorro, caused by the sheriff's refusing to act in the case of the Conklin still continues. Troops arrived here this a.m.; they are guarding property. Last night, one man, a prisoner named Antonio Maria Baca, shot the guard who was stationed over him; the prisoner was then knocked down and killed. Quiet now, but more trouble anticipated."

So men lined the streets, Winchesters and derringers in hand. One Baca was dead; two still at large. Tempting rewards were offered as bait, and descriptions posted everywhere. Down at Isleta del Sur, James B. Gillette of the Texas Rangers passed by Judge Baca's home. On the porch were two handsome Spanish-American youths talking to the judge. Immediately he associated them with some posters seen at the Ranger station. Upon inquiring he became aware that the judge was related to the Bacas of Socorro. He took the two young men into custody. Up to Socorro he went, with his eye on the reward. One proved to be Abran; the other was released.

Ranger Gillette was pleased with his reward. He reasoned: If Abran was at Isleta del Sur, then Onofrio was not far off. This he kept telling himself until he was convinced that a search around the area would uncover the man. Here and there he angled feelers in the hopes that some one would bite and reveal the hiding place of Baca. A month went by: no results. Finally, one day he stumbled on a lead. He was told that there was a new man employed as clerk at the Mercantile store in Saragosa five miles south of the border. This might be the man; again, it might not. As a Ranger, and a sergeant at that, to hazard the chance without proper authority might have repercussions all the way to Washington east, and Mexico City south. Evidently he had either convinced himself that this was the man wanted or perhaps someone had identified the clerk as the same fellow whose picture was on the Wanted poster. In a dilemma, he consulted George Lloyd. Together they decided to risk it. They made Saragosa safely enough. Baca was measuring some flour for an old lady customer when they entered. Gillette went up to him, grabbed him by the collar, pointing his pistol in his face. The old woman graciously fainted. Then bedlam broke loose. People running and screaming all over the place. Baca hesitated a moment. He demanded to know where he was being taken. He was told to El Paso. Some quick-witted individual started ringing the church bell; some in nearby homes started shooting towards the store, high in the air—not to kill, for there were too many women and children about, just to frighten, or perhaps because they were frightened; after all there were so many political factions about that every sunrise seemed to ring in a new president. The Ranger put Baca on Lloyd's horse, but when the animal began lagging, he was exchanged to ride behind Gillette. They managed to beat their pursuers to the Rio Grande boundary. Captain Baylor was a bit curious. How come—wet men, sweaty horses? There was quite a storm when they told him. He finally consented to let Gillette bring his man to Socorro, keeping his fingers crossed that he wouldn't have to answer to Washington for disturbing the international peace. Gillette wired Socorro that he was coming to collect. However glorified the account seems in Gillette's book, *Six Years as a Texas Ranger*, the Albuquerque Daily Journal in its March 31, 1881 issue had this matter-of-fact report:

"The last of the murderers of Conklin, the former editor of the Socorro Sun, Onofrio Baca, was arrested by Sergeant Gillette, of the Texas Rangers, several days ago and delivered to the sheriff of Socorro county. This morning, at an early hour the prisoner was forcibly taken from the county jail by unknown parties and hung. On awakening from their slumbers, the population found him dangling from a gate frame in the courthouse plaza. A party of about one hundred and twenty-five Americans was formed in old town about 3 a.m., who routed up every American they could find in the town and proceeded to the depot to meet the prisoner and escort. Baca, who had taken unto himself a wife since the shooting of Conklin, was accompanied by her and his mother. (They must have received word indirectly of the arrest and managed to elude the marchers at the depot, for they were able to speak briefly to the prisoner. Some old timers say that the young wife brought a little baby along which the father saw for the first, and last time. Whether this is merely a human touch, or the actual case, I have not been able to find out. So you will have to accept their word for it. If you interview the few survivors that marched to the depot that night no two will give you the same account. So you take them all and divide by the reporters' accounts and the result will be nearer the truth). It has been reported that Baca's friends telegraphed the governor of the Territory to issue an order for the train not to stop at Socorro for fear of the vigilantes. The governor telegraphed Gillette to bring the prisoner on to Santa Fe, and on no account to stop with him at Socorro. The train did stop at Socorro and was promptly boarded by a band of armed men who overruled the governor's command. While on the return from the depot to the old town with the prisoner, the party stopped about half-way and would have hung Baca to a cottonwood tree had it not been for the appeal of Sergeant Gillette, who did not wish to be implicated in the affair. So the party continued on their way to old town and delivered the prisoner to the sheriff, and the sergeant and party were seen safely to bed."

Gillette collected the reward. He didn't feel too good the next morning when Baca's relatives, hats in hands, asked for the keys to remove the shackles from the dead man's legs.

All during this time Abran lingered in jail. His trial was pending. His case was set for the fall term of 1881. Why he wasn't hung by the vigilantes remains a mystery, and you can bet your bottom dollar it wasn't from lack of intention. His lawyers were R. E. M. Farland, Moore and Shaw. The prosecuting attorney was Colonel J. Francisco (Pancho) Chavez. As all the members of the jury were Spanish-Americans, Chavez naturally addressed them in their mother tongue, much to the dissatisfaction of the vigilantes who were expecting the verdict to be none other than guilty. When they were surprised with a not-guilty verdict, Baca was let out through a window to a saddled horse outside, and away. The vigilantes were then in favor of hanging Chavez. He was told never to show his face in Socorro again or a noose would be awaiting him. To which he replied that he would return whenever he had business in Socorro.

For a while Mrs. Conklin carried on the newspaper with the able assistance of the former editor's assistant editor, as writer of the editorials. Another newspaper in town, the Socorro Miner, criticized her attitude during the trial. Another newspaper of the day remarked:

"Mrs. Conklin, widow of the murdered Socorro editor, was in Albuquerque last evening and gave her views quite freely in regard to the trial of Baca, the supposed murderer. She says that there were only two persons, the Rev. Mathieson, formerly stationed in Socorro as missionary, and his wife, who could positively identify Baca as one of the assassins, but neither was present at the trial. Whether they had been subpoenaed she did not know, nor is she aware of their present whereabouts. As for her own absence at the trial, she was under the impression that it was not to come up for another two months, so she went east to get her brother, A. E. Hawley, an attorney at Beaver City, Nebraska, to assist in the prosecution. She was not sub-poenaed as a witness, and the first intimation she had of the trial was a few days after the acquittal of Baca. She attaches no blame to the prosecuting attorney, Col. Chavez, as her testimony had been taken at the preliminary hearing examination, and had but little bearing on the case, except the influence of her presence may have exerted some response from the jury. She is highly incensed at the insinuation of the Socorro Miner that she had purposely absented herself. She says that the Miner attacked her for personal reasons, and that one of the editors of that paper was a sworn enemy of her's. A libel suit will be at once instituted as she desired to vindicate herself at the bar of justice." (Albuquerque Journal December 9, 1881)

Here ends the case of the man killed as a result of a disturbance in church. The further feud between his widow and the editor of the Socorro Miner dimmed as time went on, and sight of it lost completely. Nothing seems to have resulted in the libel suit and it was dropped.

About this time the gamblers and dance-hall girls decided to do something about their souls. They attended church every Sunday, forming a choir. They had angelic voices, although they de-angelized on Monday. Some members of the congregations raised arched eyebrows and the ministers were asked to request that these choirs either change their methods of making a living, or stay away. They stayed away.

When the editor of the Socorro Sun (hands in pockets, near the door of the Sun office) went to a Christmas service after posing for this picture, he did not suspect sudden death at the hands of youth standing on barrel to far left of picture.

Book Fourteen

AFFAIR IN SPRINGER

(Dick Rogers)

When Dave Rudabaugh made his escape from the Las Vegas jail, one of the four prisoners refusing to take advantage of the opportunity for escape was a former Texas cowboy by the name of Richard Rogers. He was imprisoned for cattle rustling. In jail too, he came to know another unwanted character known as Red River Tom. Tom was on the list of those who would be given a neck-tie party if the vigilantes found him in town after sun-down. Whether because Rogers was not found guilty, or because Las Vegas was tired of hangings, he was given his freedom with the injunction to stay away from the Meadow City. With Red River Tom he shook the dust of the city and landed a job cow-punching along the Vermejo and in the Raton area.

The Colfax County War was in full swing at this time between the squatters and the Maxwell Land Grant Company. The squatters contended that they were justified in settling on the land since it was government property by right of the unbloody conquest of the American Occupation. The Maxwell Land Grant Company insisted that they were violating private property since Congress already settled the issue that the Miranda-Beaubien Tract came into the hands of Lucien B. Maxwell properly and the Maxwell Land Grant and Railway Company paid Maxwell a good price for it. The Maxwell Land Grant Company was an outgrowth of the land and railway company. The company would gladly let them have the land for a nominal fee if they chose to remain. McMains, who took up the cudgels for the settlers, told them to stay put and not pay a cent. Thus the war was on. This was the way the situation stood when Dick Rogers and Red River Tom rode into the Vermejo country one day and asked for a job. Shortly afterwards the pair were trailing herd for the Cow Creek outfit.

Meantime McMains made every effort at obtaining the Cow Creek ranch for himself. He even hinted at compromise if the Maxwell Land Grant Company would turn over the property to him—free of course. They flatly refused. Instead, they ordered him off the Grant property and promised him a nice term in jail if he continued to arouse the squatters. Rather than leave the area he bought a printing press and started a campaign against the company that was to make a crusader of him. He preached violence and bloodshed. He rode up and down Colfax county soliciting the allegiance and guns of the cowboys working on the ranches within the limits of the Maxwell Grant. Rogers and the boys working with him were in accord and joined the vigilantes obtensively to clean out Colfax county but really to bring the Maxwell Land Grant Company to its knees. Rogers, who was just twenty-two at the time, was already the leader of a gang of cowboys.

Richard Rogers was born near the site of Fort Griffin in Texas in 1859, the year a band of Comanches ran off his father's horses and cattle. Despite the efforts of his father and several of the ranchers he collected together in pursuit of the marauders the stock was never recovered. Then came the Civil War and the elder Rogers joined up with Baylor, then with Hood. The family carried on during his absence fighting off Indians, milking cows, planting and harvesting. By the time the war was over Dick, as he was commonly called, knew how to shoot, ride, chop wood, weed gardens, ride a horse, take care of stock and himself. He had very little schooling, simply because there was no time for such matters. As more and more cattle were being shipped to Colorado and the railhead in Kansas in the years following the war, Dick's ambition was to follow the herds to Abilene, Dodge, Caldwell and other cow towns in the plains area. Even as a young lad he was able to supply the family table with turkey, rabbit, grouse, venison and antelope. At twelve he was a remarkable shot, an excellent rider and a fearless hunter. Blonde, blue-eyed, slim but sturdy, he gave promise of being tall in the saddle. At fourteen he made his first trip over what became the Chisholm Trail and tasted the wildness of frontier Ellsworth and liked it. There he remained with fifteen hundred other cowboys guarding cattle against rustlers, for despite the panic of 1873 there were more cattle in the stock yards awaiting shipment East than the railroad could provide transportation for.

Rogers came to know Cad Pierce, John Good and Neil Kane, whose yen for a fight in every cow camp made their names by-words. They organized a new sport known as gunfighting. A man quick on the draw sought out another man quick on the draw and the victor sought out another, very much like a modern fighter making his way to the top for the championship. Rogers attached himself for a time to George Peshaur and associated with such gun men as John W. Hardin, Billy Helfridge, Alex Barrickman, the Millgians and the Cunninghams. Such company brought him to acts of cattle rustling and stage hold ups. No doubt he was involved in a killing or two, although we have no record of the number of men he actually killed. Some old timer in Raton said that when he was a boy he heard his father say that Dick Rogers was known to have killed eleven men. We do know that in Colfax county he was wanted for killing Miller, Smith and the shooting of Hixenbaugh.

Because he was a good cowboy he was hired by ranchers in Colfax county. McMains had sold his newspaper to enter politics. Failing to be re-elected to the Territorial legislature, he bought back his paper to carry on his fight against the Maxwell Land Grant. He changed the name from *Raton Guard* to *Raton Comet* and in his first editorial stated the purpose of his sheet: Here is the Comet again with the same old motto—Open War Against Secret Fraud—The Fraud: A towering majestic 2,000,000 acres, is the Maxwell Land Grant. It is fed on fraud; fraud will kill it. Its demise, however, can be hastened by a newspaper as well as legal treatment and hence the Comet will go for the diseased and unwieldly corporiety of the Maxwell Land Grant and heavy ... (Opening lines began: Greetings to our friends, defiance to our foes—Raton Comet July 14, 1882)

Another newspaper published at the time in Raton was the New Mexico *News and Press* formerly published in Cimarron. Unceremoniously dumped into the river by objector Clay Allison, most of it was salvaged, new parts added and printing continued under the direction of Morley and Springer. With the coming of the railroad they showed more interest in the Iron Horse than in printer's ink and the press went to the highest bidder in Raton. As editor George F. Ganis came up from Las Vegas where he worked with the Las Vegas Gazette and was the enemy of Conklin who later bought the Socorro Sun. Canis and Conklin came to blows and a duel was to be fought but it never took place as the editor of the Sun was killed in Socorro before it came off. Conklin would have been content just to horse-whip Canis. As rival of the Comet, Canis was very uncomplimentary to McMains. Osfield, who admired the leader of the Anti-Granters, wrote a letter chiding Canis which was published in the Comet. Reviewing the effect that the struggle had on Raton's future the editor said:

"From several events reported to have happened in town during the past few months it would appear to outsiders, or rather to those not acquainted with our town, that Raton is a terrible bad place and that life and property is considered of no importance by the blood-thirsty inhabitants of this burg. This impression has gone abroad through the disjointed, garbled, maliciously false statements found in several newspapers and in no sense of the word does this sort of thing do justice to our people who are intelligent, upright, and law-abiding citizens as can be found in the world.

"George F. Canis, editor of the *New Mexico News and Press*, is blamed mostly. He published a supplement of seven columns to his paper on October 30, 1882, wherein he charged Rev. O. P. McMains with murder, etc. McMains' friends are a little mad and so is everybody who is opposed to this county being stolen by the millions of acres by the vampires and land-grant pirates of New Mexico. Mr. McMains has had to suffer martyrdom on more occasions than one by this exposure and fraud by which the people of Colfax county were threatened to be engulfed.

"When Parson Tolby, several years ago, was waylaid and shot in the back while performing the duties of his heavenly mission, Mr. McMains nobly came to the rescue and was instrumental in tracing the murderer of his brother minister. (Actually the case is unsolved to this day.) This was an act on his part which has placed him at the mercy of the terrible bad element that infested this country at the time. When McMains went to Canis asking for proof of his statements Canis said that he didn't have them. Whereupon McMains addressed a large gathering, telling them the facts that led to the killing of Parson Tolby and of the arrest of Cruz Vega as the murderer. When he fiinished Canis got up and addressed the crowd and apologized for his writing and promised to write a retraction. Mace T. Bowman, the deputy sheriff, was present. Everybody here knows that Canis did not do this of his own accord, but with instructions he dare not disobey. He was used as a catspaw to pull someone else's chestnuts out of the fire. Instead of injuring McMains it is on the whole the best thing that could be thought of to elect him a representative of the people of this county to the Legislature at Santa Fe."

Then followed a statement signed by a number of witnesses to prove that Canis fully retracted and that no force was used nor any revolvers displayed. But the agitation refused to die. The Pro-Granters, or settlers who paid for their land, felt that they were imposed upon by the Anti-Granters who burned their fences, ran off their stock, burnt their barns and committed other damage in an effort to get them to move off the Grant, so they decided to call in James Masterson, the brother of the more widely known Bat Masterson. Jim, as he was called, immediately formed a company of National Guards, making sure to keep it legal by procuring a signed paper from Governor Lionel A. Sheldon. The Company consisted of commissioned officers and five non-commissioned officers in addition to thirty-five privates. When, however, mustering roll call was published on Monday, February 23, 1885, it was discovered that a number of privates were only on paper; that the company was fraudulently organized and that the governor of the Territory duped into lending his name. Rumor had it that this was actually a secret army raised for the purpose of overthrowing the Anti-Granters. These on the other hand accused the Pro-Granters as raising it to oust them.

Actually no one knew what to believe, especially when newspapers published such item as: "Last week two cases of arms addressed to James H. Masterson, Capt. Co. H, Territorial Militia, arrived at the express office at Raton." (Raton Comet February 18, 1885)

The Anti-Grant men took the offensive. They called together a meeting of all sympathizers and elected representatives to plead their cause before the governor, who, hearing their side of the case, rescinded his order and demanded that the Company be disbanded. Company H dispersed on March 1, 1885. This left Jim Masterson stranded and put him in an ugly mood. He paraded up and down First Street spoiling for a fight.

Before long he became involved in a heated discussion with J. E. Herndon of the opposition and pulled a gun on him. Only the timely intervention of some of Herndon's friends prevented bloodshed. Masterson went to Springer, the county seat, full of threats and fighting words. He resented being called a hired gunman, a killer and an outlaw. At Springer he had himself sworn in as deputy-heriff. Casting about for one to oppose Masterson, McMains singled out young Dick Rogers. His choice was not made hastily. He had watched Rogers coming into town on pay day after pay day to "hurrah" the place. With him were Marion Littrell, Robert E. Lee, John Dodds, Red River Tom Wheelington, Ed King, Garnett Lee, Abe Lowe, John Curry. After their fill of shooting out windows, lamps, bottles, mirrors and top-hats, they would settle down to drink, then move on to the opera house or the Rink. When Masterson was told that Rogers was elected to oppose him he sneered and said that he knew the cowboy from Kansas days and could kill him any time he had a mind to.

Raton at that time was divided into Buena Vista, known

as Chihuahua, Boggstown, also across the tracks and the stronghold of the Anti-Granters, and the town proper. When you had the urge to gamble, dance, drink, pick up a sweet-time lass, or mingle with the rough element, you went over to Buena Vista, especially to William S. Sargent's dance hall where you did everything but dance. Masterson came in one evening and after a few drinks had it noised abroad that he was out to get Dick Rogers. As there were partisans in the cantina they went to the Rink where Rogers happened to be and notified him to be on the alert. Instead, Rogers said: "Now is as good a time as any to settle this."

He headed for Buena Vista, followed by a gathering mob interested in gunplay. Approaching Sargent's place he told the mob that this fight was strictly between Masterson and himself. He entered alone, walked up to the deputy:

"What's this I hear, Masterson? I understand you have notions of killing me on sight. Here I am. Draw?"

Masterson made no attempt to draw.

"I do not come here to kill citizens or to fight citizens but only to kill those people who are continually saying they will kill me on sight."

Masterson pondered this a moment. He was following the old Earp trick of letting his enemy talk long enough to be off his guard. However, he answered:

"I believe there is some mistake. I have a warrant for your arrest. You are wanted for the murder of Miller, the shooting of Smith and the wounding of Hixenbaugh; for the assault of an officer of the law in the performance of his duty. There was no talk of shooting on sight."

The officer assaulted was Masterson who was given a sound thrashing in this very dance hall but two weeks before.

"I'll be arrested when I want to be which doesn't happen to be now. I'll pick my own time and place."

Then he unbelted his six-shooter and whipped the deputy roundly. Telling the bar-tender to throw a bucket of water over the prone deputy, and not to waste good whiskey on him, he re-placed his gun, turned his back on the Masterson sympathizers and returned to the Rink.

On the following Saturday Rogers returned to Raton to hurrah the town. He went to the opera house, enjoyed a play, then presented himself before the authorities and gave himself up. Hailed before the Court for the shooting of Miller, Smith and Hixenbaugh he pleaded guilty and was set free on a $1,000 bail. More than ever Masterson felt he was the laughing stock of Raton.

Monday evening, March 9, Masterson was walking down First Street. Coming by from the opposite direction was D. W. Stevens who had just padlocked his mercantile store for the night. As they passed each other Masterson turned, struck Stevens across the back of the neck with the barrel of his six-shooter, a trick from Dodge City days known as "buffalo-ing" which marshals used in preference to the night stick of the police. Stevens down, Masterson kicked him into the gutter; not a very manly thing to do. Stevens was well liked in Raton and a violent anti-granter. Working for him as a clerk was a nineteen-year-old lad by the name of George Curry, one day to become governor of New Mexico. He was brother to John Curry, who worked with Dick Rogers. When work of Masterson's action reached the clerk he called a mass meeting of the vigilantes. Stevens placed a large sum of money at his disposal and told him to buy up every shotgun, pistol, revolver, rifle, cartridge and shell to be found in the city. Curry sent riders to Cow Creek, Vermejo, Ute Park, Rayado, Cimarron and Springer to round up all partisans from one end of the Maxwell Grant to the Colorado border.

The meeting was held in the Raton Rink. It was agreed that Masterson should be arrested and everyone of his gun-fighters connected with Company H be asked to leave town. Curry went to the Moulton House where Masterson boarded and asked him to turn over his guns. Six hundred had taken over Raton. It was useless for Masterson to resist. Back at the Rink O. P. McMains took over. He placed a motion before the committee that all saloons in Raton be closed. Motion carried and for the first time in history of the frontier railroad town a contingent of men was dispatched to carry out the order. That night every cantina in Raton closed shop.

Curry and a number of armed men escorted Masterson to the Rink. The vigilantes told him he would be spared if he left New Mexico. Fifteen guards were selected to escort him over the Territorial boundary several miles north over the Raton Pass. In order to make certain that Masterson would not talk them out of it Dick Rogers was named captain of the armed guards. Everybody was aware how affairs stood between these two and the selection of the big, raw-boned cowboy was in equity with the proceedings. One hundred and fifty armed men patrolled the streets. Any member of Company H that was picked up was taken to First Street to join forces with Masterson for the grand exodus. After all of them were rounded up three hundred vigilantes escorted them to the Colorado line with the warning that if they ever showed their faces in Raton they would be given a neck-tie party.

James Masterson died at Guthrie, Oklahoma, on Monday, April 16, 1895, of quick consumption. He has been a deputy U.S. marshall for years. He was city marshall of Dodge City in its wildest days, and was considered one of the most fearless men in the Southwest, being in the lead in every chase after train robbers or raids on cattle thieves and outlaws. (Woodward, Okla., Jeffersonian).

To go back to why Rogers was wanted by the law. Jack Miller was deputy-sheriff prior to the call of Masterson. He was a fearless peace officer and quick on the draw. Known in Abilene, Dodge, Deadwood, Las Vegas and Albuquerque, he was invited to Raton to help clean out the lawless element. When Bob Ford, slayer of Jesse James, realized that he was not wanted in Las Vegas, he sold his cantina and opened a saloon in Raton. He relied on his popularity as slayer of the desperado to get him ahead very much as Garrett did. Before long he had difficulty with Deputy Miller. Ford challenged Miller to a gunfight, leaving it to the deputy to select the time and place. Miller picked out a lonely spot along the Folsom highway. The understanding was that if Miller returned alive he would take over Ford's saloon; if Ford returned from the gunfight he was to expect immunity from the other peace officers. Miller was at the spot but Ford failed to make his appearance. Shunned as a coward, his business failed, especially when Miller made known how Ford operated. Ford sold out and went to Colorado. He was later to cash in as an actor on how he killed Jesse James.

It was shortly after this that Rogers came in to hurrah the town. Miller decided to put a stop to this, and when Rogers entered the Green Lantern cantina in Buena Vista, Miller was there as if expecting him.

"I'm placing you under arrest for disturbing the peace," said Miller.

"Not tonight nor any other time," responded Rogers.

"You'll come if I have to take you in at gun-point." He reached for his six-shooter.

"I wouldn't touch that gun if I were you."

Men eased away from the brass rail. The music stopped. Dance hall girls, gamblers, lover-boys, drifters dodged under the tables or made a bee line for the exit. Miller, fast as he was, never quite got his finger on the trigger. He was buried on the site of General Kearny's camp, the place where the officer rested his troops after the arduous Raton Pass climb.

Several weeks later while Rogers was drinking at one of the East Side bars a man named Smith walked in and began making big talk about what he would have done if he had been Miller. Rogers put up with it for a while, then approached the braggart.

"Would you mind demonstrating what you would have done?"

Smith was buried next to Miller. The sheriff decided it was high time Rogers was taken in.

John T. Hixenbaugh lived on the frontier since 1871. He moved to Colfax county in 1877, opening a saloon in the new lumber camp of Catskill. When this burnt down he moved to Raton and had himself elected sheriff on the Democratic ticket. When Rogers learned that Hixenbaugh was in town for the express purpose of arresting him, he picketed his horse near the cemetery above Buena Vista and went in search of the sheriff hoping to bring about a gun battle, kill the sheriff and plead self defense. Failing to run into the law officer, Rogers decided to visit the cantinas on Garcia Street, four blocks from where his horse was tied. News reached the sheriff that Rogers was looking for him and he decided to hunt up Rogers. Taking Deputy Will Lysett with him he went up to the place where he heard Rogers had picketed his horse.

About midnight Rogers, full of the gut-rot Garcia Street had to offer, came for his mount. When within fifty yards of the animal Hixenbaugh ordered him to "Throw up your hands." Instead of complying, he cocked the Winchester he had been carrying and shot in the direction of the voice. His shot shattered the sheriff's right knee. Rogers jumped forward as he fired, upsetting Lysett's aim, which was rather uncertain in the dark anyway. The deputy ran to the horse and grabbed the reins expecting Rogers to put up a fight for the animal. After waiting some time he realized that the desperado had duped him, fleeing back to Buena Vista under cover of the night. He now turned his attention to the howling Hixenbaugh, placed him on his own horse and took him to Dr. Kolhausen for medical attention. The sheriff was eventually to have the leg amputated in St. Louis and to spend the rest of his days in some county office or other. He lies buried in the cemetery almost near the exact spot where he was shot by Rogers.

When Rogers next came to town to attend a performance at the Rink he brought over a dozen cowboys with him. No attempt was made to arrest him. After the show he sought out the Justice of the Peace who threw everything in the book at him, to all of which he pleaded not guilty. This nettled the Justice who was at a loss as to what to do so he released Rogers on a $1,000 bail. This the cowboys with Rogers readily paid, caused the editor of the Springer paper to comment:

"There is a gang of fellows at Raton who seem disposed to run things in a light-handed manner to suit themselves and the minions of the law up there seem disposed to turn a cold shoulder to the enforcement of law and order. Bad state of affairs this. The remedy should be searched for and applied hot. Poulticing will not do in such cases."

A week later Rogers saved the life of a deputy by the name of Lee, the man who was to kill him. In order to understand the death of Rogers we must know that Springer was the county seat of Colfax county. The officers of the law there were very much opposed to the manner in which Curry, Rogers, McMains and others ran Masterson and Company H out of New Mexico. Added to this deputy Hixenbaugh was aware of what Rogers had done to his brother the sheriff. These accounts that follow are not mine. I take them from the accounts of the day for their quaintness and because eye witnesses can do a better job of it than I can.

Yesterday afternoon one of the Dick Rogers party from Raton, a fellow named Dodd, was arrested by officer Jesse Lee, a deputy-sheriff with a warrant for his arrest. The prisoner immediately telegraphed Dick Rogers that he was under arrest and Rogers came here (to Springer) this morning (Monday) with a number of men who first attacked a constable, beating him severely over the head and ordered him to leave the country at once. They then went up to the county jail. A hard fight with guns ensued, in which Rogers, John Curry and Red River Tom were killed by the plucky officers on the inside of the jail. The remnant of Rogers' party then left the town and are said to be awaiting re-inforcements to come again and attack the victorious officers at the jail. When they arrive it is thought that another severe fight will ensue and many will be killed....

Yesterday afternoon Dick Rogers and three of his pals, one of whom was the somewhat notorious Bob Lee, a shooter from Raton, were at Maxwell Station, twenty-four miles north of Springer. They were all armed to the teeth and presented an ugly array as a passenger train pulled by them. Rogers stood a little apart from the rest of the gang and as the platforms of the cars moved passed him he dropped his Winchester down into position as if looking for somebody to shoot at, or to intimidate the passengers and made it appear to them that he was really the bad man his past career would indicate him to be.

After this performance at Maxwell Station the interesting quartette were re-inforced and rode their cow-ponies to Springer and there is where fate overtook the hapless Rogers and left him dead on the gory field of his own selection. The citizens of Springer are in sympathy with the officers in this trouble and a number of brave men have volunteered to stand by them. Excitement is intense and much uneasiness is felt for the approach of night, for no one can foretell what it may bring forth. (Springer Stokman March 14, 1885)

The Las Vegas Optic decided to investigate the affair and carry the full story. This is what it came up with on March 18, 1885:

The other side of the story told us today is that Jesse W. Lee, acting sheriff of Colfax county (Rogers incapacitated Hixenbaugh), was ordered out of Raton with the bogus militia company, but he begged off with the promise to leave the country so soon as he could arrange his matters to this end. It is also stated that Dick Rogers, the victim of Lee's deadly aim, also once saved his life by placing his thumb under a trigger which was intended to snap him into eternity.

There was no arrest, nor was there a member of Rogers party in jail at the time of the reckless and fatal shooting. Johnny Dodds, in the employ of the Maxwell Cattle Company, went to Springer and behaved badly. His carousal lasted all day Saturday and Sunday. He pounded up Jim Carter, a constable, and made numerous other bad breaks about the town. Lee, the jailor, was appraised of what was going on but made no attempt to arrest the man.

Soon after the attack upon the constable by the drunken cowboy, Jeese A. Lee, W. L. Kimberley, Jim Carter and Duce Hickenbaugh, brother of the sheriff and in charge of the jail, took refuge therein. Dick Rogers, Tom Whealington, familiarly known as Red River Tom, were at Maxwell Station. They were telegraphed to come down and use their influence in quieting down Dodds, who was running things in a high-handed way. The pair started for Springer, arriving there after dark on the Sabbath evening. They found Dodds in all his glory and set about to pacify him. It is claimed that neither Dick nor Tom took a drink nor fired a shot while in town. On Monday morning they prevailed upon Dodds to consent to an arrest, pay his fine, and leave with them. With this arrangement in view, Dick Rogers remarked that he would go to the jail and arrange the matter with Jesse Lee, provided some one would accompany him. Jack Williams, a deputy U. S. Marshall, and late candidate for sheriff of the county, said he would go and together the men started for the jail.

Approaching the jail they were ordered to 'halt,' which they did, both throwing up their hands and Rogers remarking 'we are here for peace only.' Williams was told to step aside and almost simultaneously with the order came a volley of bullets from the jail and Rogers fell to the ground pierced through and through with many balls. Jack Williams, who took to his heels for life, was fired upon many times but fortunately was not struck. The clothing of Rogers caught fire and Red River Tom rode up to the dead body of his comrade to put out the fire. He alighted from his horse and threw his Winchester away from him a distance of at least fifteen feet to show that he was not disposed at the moment to avenge the death of his bosom friend. The men in jail asked him if 'he wanted any of this' and he replied that he did not. One shot was fired at him from the jail without effect, and he started to run. Another shot took effect in his shoulder and as he turned to look back, the fatal shot pierced him in the eye and went crashing through his head.

Dodds and John Curry, who were within one hundred and fifty yards of where Rogers met his death, were aroused by the reports of the Winchesters and naturally concluded that the boys were in for a lively fight and they must lend a hand in the bloody business. However, Dodds was the only one that returned the fire from the jail, he firing off his Winchester but once. Curry was mortally wounded, dying soon after he was shot. Ed King was reported to have been killed while bending over the body of Rogers, did not arrive in Springer until after all the shooting was over and was not hurt.

Excitement is running high at Springer and upwards of one hundred cowboys are on the ground. However, the presence of the troops seems to hold them in submission for the time being. This morning acting governor Losch arrived from the siege at Springer in order to open telegraphic communications with President Cleveland relative to the handling of the detachment of troops at the Springer jail. It seems that the Springer office was cut off from telegraphic service last night and repeated efforts on the part of the acting governor to get into communication with the outside world were futile. He arrived in Las Vegas at 8:45 and sent telegrams to the president and to the department commander asking for authority to handle the infantry detachment the same as he would a company of New Mexico Territorial Militia. As the members of the latter organization are too far away for immediate service the troops have to be depended upon entirely. Lee, Kimberley and Hixenbaugh in the county jail in Springer have been very anxious to get out and leave the place, but being prisoners of war they must abide by the commands of the captain in charge. Losch told a reporter this morning that by removing the prisoners to Las Vegas things would quiet down in Springer, and that is what is wanted. He then saw Superintendent Dyer for a special train to run to Springer and return for the purpose of getting the officers and troops out of town. Mr. Dyer granted the request readily and as the governor had gotten permission to move the soldiers, the expedition started for the scene of the siege at ten thirty.

Conductor Markle and Engineer Filower were in charge of the train. On board were Governor Losch, Judge Axtell, Major Sena and Supt. Dyer. The train was an extra freight carrying empties eastward. A day coach stands at Springer, having gone there with Fort Union soldiers Monday night. The running time should place it at Springer at 2:45 this afternoon. The plan is to have the soldiers—and there are only twenty of them—form a square around the trio of besieged officers and march them down through town to the depot; then load them into the car and whirl away as a special train to Las Vegas. An extra guard of six men will be needed to accompany Lee's party to Las Vegas as the soldiers leave the train at Watrous and the three prisoners are to be placed in the Las Vegas jail pending a hearing for the killing of the Rogers gang for which they must stand formal investigation before the courts. Supt. Dyer yesterday received an order to issue transportation to Lee, his colleagues besiged at the jail and the witnesses required to hear the case. It is the desire of Lee to be heard in Las Vegas as he can hope to find more favor here than at Springer.

The special train out from Las Vegas arrived in Springer at 2:45 this afternoon and Governor Losch proceeded at once to the jail. The soldiers drew up in line and surrounding the three prisoners—Lee, Kimberley and Hixenbaugh—started for the train which had meantime turned about for Las Vegas. The line of march was not through the municipal streets along which were great crowds of cowboys and citizens. Many people were on the roofs of buildings and box cars at the railroad. The triumvirate of officers were safely placed on board and the train pulled out for Las Vegas at 3:20, troops and all. The soldiers will not stop at Watrous, but will come direct to Las Vegas, arriving here at 7 P.M. this evening. Lee's party will be conducted to the county jail on the West Side and there held for trial. Governor Losch, Adjt. Bartlett and Judge Axtell are on the train. (End of Las Vegas Optic quotes).

The paper then gave a summary of the affair. Added all up it amounted to this: On Sunday night Dick Rogers, sporting two revolvers, came to Springer with Red River Tom, Bob Lee, John Dodds and John Curry. They decided to stop in for a drink and entered Bob Stepp's saloon. There they saw James Carter, a constable they had no love for, especially since he assisted Jesse Lee in the arrest of John Dodds but a short time before. Dodds had been released and at liberty to come and go as he pleased without interference from the officers of the law. He thought that Carter and Lee were unnecessarily rough with him even though he had been drinking heavily and making a nuisance of himself. Carter was having a beer with W. C. Corbett when the cowboys entered Stepp's place. Dodds, seeing the constable, ran over to him and struck him over the head with his revolver, knocked him down, and gave him a working over. When Dodds was through Carter calmly got up, went to a wash stand and washed the blood off his face and head. This only served to rouse Dodds the more. He said to Carter:

"I will give you this for arresting me yesterday." He

pointed his gun at the constable but did not fire. Rogers then approached Carter:

"You are under my charge now. Get yourself over the New Mexico line into Colorado or I will put you over at the point of my pistol."

Dodds then said that there was another fellow in town by the name of Jesse Lee who should join Carter in the march over the Territorial border. Rogers told him that there was plenty of time to take care of Lee in the morning as this was Sunday and they should enjoy themselves.

"I shall put Lee out of New Mexico in the morning and that long-legged Martin (editor of the Springer Stockman) must leave also."

Word of the threat reached the editor. He dared not saddle his horse for a get-a-way. Instead he left his office in his shirt sleeves and entered a neighbor's house as if for a visit. He slipped out the back door, headed for the railroad tracks and walked twenty-five miles to Wagonmound, where he got someone to take him to Las Vegas. There he sent a telegram to Santa Fe asking the governor to come up to Springer as some desperadoes were taking over the town.

On Monday morning shortly before nine o'clock Rogers and his gang went to the home of the Justice of the Peace to denied. All during the siege Anthony kept saying: "I hope they kill you, I hope they kill you." As Curry wished to pay Dodds' fine which amounted to $6.50 and costs. A crowd of sympathizers had gathered and asked Rogers not to pay the fine until Lee arrived but the Justice said that his presence was not necessary. Rogers then turned to the group and asked if one of the citizens would walk up to the jail with him. Williams was selected. The rest has already been told.

The vigilantes, headed by George Curry, rode in from Raton and surrounded the jail. Besides the trio there were two prisoners: Earnest Anthony, a confirmed horse thief, and Jim McCall, a cattle rustler. They asked for rifles but Lee knew that their sympathies were with the men outside so their request was complete arrangements for his brother's funeral, John McKown and Charles H. Hunt took over the vigilantes. Never for a moment did they relax their command of the jail, the railroad station and the telegraph office. When the soldiers from Fort Union arrived the vigilantes blocked their way. The captain pleaded with them and finally it was decided that a committee be named to talk over matters with him. Littrell, Hunt, Gabble and Curry were chosen. They permitted the soldiers to march to the jail. Frank Springer the lawyer intervened and after the governor arrived it was decided that Littrell, Curry, King and South accompany the prisoners and soldiers to Las Vegas. Over two hundred men with rifles were awaiting the signal to open fire. Curry never gave it. His brother's death sobered him a bit and he wanted no more bloodshed. In Las Vegas Lee felt that Curry had too much influence and asked for a change of venue to Taos. The trio were kept in jail until May 15, 1885. The jury was in session forty minutes and returned the verdict of not-guilty. Tom Catron was the lawyer who won the case for them.

If a crowd turned out for the burial of Mentzer's victims, a multitude attended the funeral of Rogers, Red River Tom and John Curry. Three ministers preached the funeral orations, taking care to being very impersonal in their remarks. Mostly they spoke about the evils of drink and the wildness of the life of a cowboy. The funeral was held on St. Patrick's Day 1885. Over five thousand followed the three boxes to the cemetery above Buena Vista. Several weeks later (April 9) the Las Vegas Optic wrote:

Governor Sheldon offered $1,000 for the capture of Dick Rogers. His reputed surrender to the Justice of the Peace at Blossburg goes for naught when it is told that the governor had no official notice of his capture. Jesse Lee will receive the money. Lee receives his reward for killing one of the worst desperadoes New Mexico ever had.

Rogers got into a fight at a dance at Blossburg in 1884. He killed the fellow he had the argument with and went to the Justice of the Peace pleading self defense. He fined Rogers $2.50 and costs. Too many of Rogers' friends milled about for him to imprison the killer. Uncle Tom Boggs, one of the last of the old Mountain Men, lived in Springer at the time

Rogers was killed. Called to the inquest his answers are quaint and the whole scene is here reproduced to give an idea of such proceedings during frontier days.

March 31, 1885—Words exactly as used in the preliminary hearing:

Tom O. Boggs, being duly sworn in, is examined by the court and testifies as follows:

How far from the courthouse (and jail) do you live?

About 150 yards.

Is there anything to obstruct the view from your house to the jail?

No, sir. But I don't think you could see the body that was farthest off.

Could you see Rogers' body?

Yes, sir.

I went down to town pretty early in the morning. As I passed by the hotel these cowboys were sitting in there. I don't know what they were doing. I went back up to the house and saw Mr. Williams and a cowboy going by on the street up to the courthouse, up the main street. I got up on the back porch and then the shots commenced and I saw this man fall and Williams ran towards my house. I shouted at him and said: 'Turn and run the other way,' but he went on down the street toward town. I don't know whether he went into town or not.

Were you looking towards these parties when the first firing took place?

No, sir. I had got on the porch and was going over to Charles's house.

Did you see Mr. Williams and this cowboy going up towards the jail?

I saw them before they got behind this brick house.

You didn't see them close to the jail before the firing.

No, sir.

Did you hear any words passing between them and the persons in the courthouse?

No, sir.

After Williams ran past you, what then occurred?

I saw somebody on horseback go up the main street and

he soon passed by the brick house and came in sight again. I think he had a couple of guns in his hands. He rode up close to this body and jumped off the horse. In a few minutes the firing commenced again, and I saw him pitch over.

What did he do when he rode up to this body?

The body was smoking like, and it seemed as though he was beating out the fire.

What did he do with the guns?

They were lying there.

You say there were two guns?

Yes, sir.

You were the first man on the ground, were you?

There was a lady got there before me and she put out the fire. (Mrs. D. A. Clouthier, wife of the leading merchant in town, on her way to her husband's mercantile store)

How many weapons did you see there?

Two Winchesters and six-shooter, if I am not mistaken. They were lying between this body and the body of Rogers. I should say that the bodies were ten or fifteen feet apart.

Which body were the guns nearest to?

They were nearest to the body of Rogers.

When the firing re-commenced and the second man fell, what then occurred?

They were firing from the courthouse and from this brick house. I never went up while the firing was going on. I don't know who did the firing from this brick house.

You say that you saw this man come up on horseback after the first firing?

Yes, sir.

Did you see any others?

I saw some others come up on foot. They came running on foot as fast as they could go.

From what direction?

From town.

Can you give any idea of the length of time between the first shooting and the time these men came up to the brick building?

Not over twenty-five minutes. It was all done very quickly. Probably not as long as that.

Mr. Williams thinks the course he ran was 450 yards or so, and that it took him two or three minutes and he says that a man named Dodds was there firing when he arrived.

It was a little longer than that. Williams stopped running and leaned against a fence because he was give out, and I thought at one time he was shot.

After this firing was over, what took place? What did you do?

This cowboy they call Johnny Dodds came along while I was walking with Mr. Wilson and said: 'Go up there and put out that fire on that man: He is burning up.'

You speak of Mr. Wilson. Did he come up to your house?

Yes, sir.

When did he come up to your house?

Just at the time after this shooting.

After the first shooting?

Yes, sir. I spoke back to the cowboy just this way and says: 'Why don't you go up and put out the fire yourself? You have been making all this trouble.' Then I said I would go and Mr. Wilson came along with me a piece and I told him that he had not go along any further. I hollowed to Lee and asked him if I could come up and put out the fire and he says yes but before I got there there was a woman with a bucket of water and she put out the fire. I saw that the wadding in his coat had been burning. Then I went up to the next body.

That one where the fire was, was that nearest the courthouse?

Yes, sir. I found out afterwards that it was Rogers' body. He was lying on his back.

Then you went to the other body?

Yes, sir. I turned him over to see if he was dead and I saw that he was. I then laid his hat on his face and the woman said: 'That one is not dead.' I went up to see him and he had vomited and was smothering in blood and I took my hand

and rubbed it off his face. I asked him where he was hurt. He thought I was the doctor and he says: 'Turn me over, if you please.' I says: 'I'll go for the doctor.' And then I shouted back to Lee and he says: 'Yes, tell him to come alone.'

Where was that body?

That body was some ten or fifteen steps from the others. It was right south from the courthouse.

How far from that brick house was the body of the wounded man?

A considerable distance. It was very near the courthouse.

Was he half way between the brick house and the court?

Yes, sir. More.

Did you see him fall?

No, sir.

By the Court—What time in the morning was it, as near as you can remember?

About 9 o'clock, I should judge. Maybe earlier.

The only weapons you remember to have seen about the bodies were two Winchesters?

At this last body there were pistols and maybe a gun and afterwards a young man asked leave to get them, and he did get them.

By Mr. Springer—Do you know who it was that went up and got them?

Little Jimmy at Bob Stepp's place. James Sibley.

Is that all you know about the affair?

When I asked Mr. Lee if the doctor could come up, he said: 'Go and tell Mr. Mills that I will turn over to any proper authorities but I won't turn over to the mob,' or something to that effect. Then after the Raton people came they held a meeting and I was at the meeting. They wanted to know what Mr. Lee would do and they sent a paper up to the jail and I delivered it to him and I brought back his answer.

The message was in writing?

The message was in writing and the reply was in writing.

Did he say anything about the shooting?

He asked me if he had not done right in protecting his life?

About the first shooting, I mean.

No, sir.

By the Court—He said that he wouldn't turn over to these Raton people?

Yes, Sir.

By Mr. Springer—Did you hear anything that passed between Lee and Rogers? Or any other men that were shot?

No, sir.

When you examined the body of Rogers, did he have any weapons on?

I don't think there was; I pulled all his clothes up.

You said there was a pistol there.

But it wasn't near Rogers. It was close to the other body right between the two.

Was it a pocket pistol or a little pistol.

It was a holster pistol.

Did Rogers have a belt on?

I don't think he did because I pulled his clothes over to put out the fire.

That is all.

So, Lee got his thousand dollars and freedom for killing desperado Rogers. What about the killing of Curry and Red River Tom? Nobody bothered about them. They were merely two other cowboys. Frontier Justice!

Joel Fowler—The vigilantes took him for a ride from which there was no return.

BOOK FIFTEEN

MOON OVER SOCORRO
(Joel Fowler)

"IT'S A COLD NIGHT FOR ANGELS, JOEL"

NOW who in the world said that? I don't supose it matters much; he is dead, and the fellow he said it to is dead. Not that I particularly mind their being dead: I didn't say that. It was just the humor of the times, and a man had the choice between the rope or his bed, but men like Joel didn't die in bed. They died with their boots on, if that means anything, especially since the boots, like their bodies, were suspended between heaven and the earth. You wouldn't know who passed that remark anyway. He wore a mask like the rest of the vigilantes, as if his face were cold, or he didn't want to be recognized. You wouldn't either—want to be recognized, that is— if you were hanging a man without sanction of the law. Or were the vigilantes the law? Quien sabe? It's too much for me, amigo. But then, I was never a vigilante. And if I were what would I be vigilant about? Being caught? Restoring order without order? Who benefited? Historians mostly, and undertakers. Yes, he wore a black mask that night he went about the grim undertaking of putting a man's neck in the noose. Well, Joel was certainly no angel, but, too, I have never read of an angel's ever having hung anybody. Have you? The Socorro vigilantes were merely performing a self-imposed duty. The prisoner was a short man; five-foot-four, to be exact. He weighed a hundred and thirty pounds. Probably the lightest man of the mob around that tree in Hangman's Alley. He looked innocent enough, and pretty. Girls thought he was cute. Are you going to judge a man by his looks? That depends on whether you glorify a gun-play or merely classify him. Every town in New Mexico during the eighties had one. William Bonney in Lincoln; Gus Mentzer in Raton; Clay Allison in Cimarron; Poncho Griego in Santa Fe; Joel Fowler in Socorro. One account concerning Fowler says he killed a man by the name of Monroe; another says he took hold of a barkeeper and knifed him; McKenna certainly gives an account that makes one believe he dramatized a bit.

But, this fellow that Fowler killed—where was he from? Where is he buried? What was his name? What was he doing in Socorro at the time? Every old timer I've met was the first to see Fowler hanging by the neck, early that Sunday morning. The sums he was supposed to have on him would put DuPont to shame. Actually, he had no money at the time he was hung, although money was the indirect cause of his hanging. Most of the facts are sugar-coated. He was an outlaw. Men were called so for less than he did. Basicly, he was hung for killing a man in or near (depending on your source) the Grand Central hotel which once graced the spot near Gamble's auto store that is now a garage and gas station. A nice little sign welcomes you: Gas with Cook, and Cook with Gas. The place belongs to George Cook. His Dad knew the Vigilantes; George was a wee bit of a lad then, but he was to have enough experiences to fill a book. George has died since this writing.

Joel was a different kind of outlaw. He had book learning. His background was so different. Fine environment to begin with; a wonderful home; a kind father, loving mother. Up Indiana way. Just beginning to be the literary state of the nation when Joel was born. Admitted into the Union in 1816, it was now fast climbing as a center of culture. Joel's father was educated. A lawyer. His mother was educated, too. Naturally, the boy had to follow suit. He was born in the year of the gold rush—and at the time Marcy was writing into his diary his unfavorable impressions of Socorro. He was one of the few better known outlaws (Isn't it wonderful how many outlaws are known to every schoolboy in America as compared to the ugly old sheriffs and marshals who had to shoot them down. The nerve of them.) who had not blue eyes and blond hair. Not that this runs as a type, but the majority of outlaws were blond. Pure coincidence. Joel was not tall, not golden-haired, but he was handsome in a swarthy sort of way. As a grown man he wore a size sixteen shirt, and his pants measured thirty-one inches from the waist to the cuff. Ain't that just ducky? He had a thirty waist. Complexion fair, but on the tanned side; teeth—all of them his own; brown eyes that matched his brown, very dark brown, curly hair. At school he was a model student, and at church he was well mannered and respectful. Everybody knew him for what he was: pious, soft-spoken, obedient, kind, friendly. He was no problem child. He presented no difficulty for his parents who had great plans for his future. When twenty, he married the girl he had his eyes on from the first grade. It's happened before. Not that the romance began then, but that is when they first met. So, Joel settled down to the practice of law. Here his story would have ended and somehow we wish that it did. Just any other American fellow trying to make a living in his chosen profession.

About this time his father's brother pulled stakes and hit the trail for Fort Worth, Texas. His letters to his brother were so full of enthusiasm for the place that they fired the young nephew's imagination. Adventure in the raw. Why sit behind a desk, pencil-pushing? Texas, that was the place. He was going to be a second Daniel Boone to open up the wilderness for his children to come. His young and attractive bride was soon penetrated with the same feeling. They could not rest until they were in Texas roping steers, fighting Indians, blazing a trail. They sold their home, bought a chuck wagon and steered it into the plains country. For a while he carried his luck with him. Everything was rosy. Joel had himself a ranch and a well stocked one at that. All day long he rode the range, probably wondering why he had wasted all these years in Indiana, pushing a pencil. But it was a rather unvarying sort of life for his wife, who promptly eased the situation by pretending that some one else was Joel. Word of this reached the rancher, but he passed it off as gossip. But the grain of suspicion remained. Gradually it took root. Unbeknown to himself he found that he back-tracked to the ranch one day. He couldn't analyze why. Just one of those impulsions. There he found his wife and her lover in a rather compromising position in the bed-room. He pulled out his six-shooter and emptied it into the man before he could jump from the bed. Driven mad by the infidelity of one he loved more than his life; blinded by the rage of what he would like to do to her to make her suffer—killing was too good—he ended up by abandoning the ranch, leaving with just his gun, horse, bed-roll and his savings. Daniel Boone was now to become Billy the Kid. For a while he made himself believe that he hated women. He took to drink. Wandering from place to place, he went from crime to crime. I don't suppose there was a man in Fort Worth in 1875, who would have blamed him for his action. To them it was frontier justice; but to follow through so as to include the innocent, that made him a worse man than his wife's lover. The number of his killings in Texas he took to the hangman's noose with him. It has been said that Fowler was like Clay Allison in that he got nasty only under the influence of liquor. That being the case, why drink? But talk that his jailer overheard one night in Socorro between Fowler and another inmate known to Joel from those Texas days disproves the theory that he killed only because of John Barleycorn. Fowler and his consort were talking of their stagecoach hold up days. French seems to think that Fowler killed between thirty and forty men. Silly. The report that credits him with twelve in seven years is more accurate. He was on the loose for seven years, which made him a young outlaw indeed. Actually, he drifted into New Mexico about the same time as Clay Allison and with the same intention—to settle down to ranching. He was not completely lost, thanks to his bringing up. In 1879 he found the pickings good in Las Vegas and decided on his method of making enough money to buy a ranch. He started a dance hall on Sixth Street where the MacDonald building was later built and occupied by a Mr. M. Barash. To stimulate trade he brought in dancing girls, one of whom soon made herself queen. She was pretty and very popular with all the male patrons. Of this Fowler was not unaware. For the second time he decided he was in love. His background, while not always in the foreground, did now and then assert itself. The dance hall girl was aware that he was a gentleman from back East somewhere. She did not repulse his attentions. Together they decided that there were better ways of making a living. The hall was sold, the couple married and a ranch bought near White Oaks. But those few years of crime had a hold on him. You don't shake off a habit with a snap of the fingers. Leaving his wife at the ranch he sampaned his way to the mining town between Lincoln and Socorro. There he discovered that three cowboys were running the place. He promptly killed two and wounded the third, to be king for a short time. Fear of reprisals put him on the move again. He sold his ranch and bought another at Guadalajara near San Antonio, but this was of short duration. His next ranch was in the Oscuras mountains. Again, luck favored him and his cattle business thrived. Cattle rustlers relieved him of some steers. He accused Jim Greathouse and two companions. Trailing them into the Jornada he came upon them while they were lying in camp and killed them. It has been said that Fowler also met "Pony Bill" and "Butcher Knife Bill" at McGee's ranch on the Cuchillo Negro and wiped them out just for the sake of doing it, but I have found no conclusive evidence to that effect. The gentlemen were found shot, but gossip was not ballistics. Today one could prove what gun fired the bullets; in those days unless one actually witnessed the shooting it was mostly hearsay. If a man killed a few men they presumed that he had a few more on his record. The editor of the Las Vegas Morning Gazette seems to be the only one to credit Fowler with killing these men, but offers no proof. Besides, he had no liking for the rancher, remembering him from his dance-hall days.

While Fowler awaited sentence in the Socorro jail, another man named Barnes was also incarcerated. They were old friends. One night they quarreled bitterly so that they raised their voices. They were so angry that they were unaware that the guard was taking it all in. He heard Barnes accusing Fowler of killing a man in Texas for twenty-five cents. Among other things he brought up the robbing of a stage coach and other desperado deeds that put Billy the Kid to shame. While we have only the guard's word for this, it may be true, for he was a citizen of good standing in his community and not given (over) to fabrication.

Fowler's ranch was a little over fifty miles from Socorro. He sold it to a syndicate for $52,000 cash. In all the reports of what followed nothing is said of his wife, although eye-witnesses have stated that she was registered at the hotel in Socorro with him. There is no indication that she ever visited him during the weeks he spent in jail. Some one has attempted an explanation of this by saying that she had to care for a three-year-old girl, and a one-year-old baby. One man who knew Fowler intimately from the time he bought the ranch at Guadalajara of his dad, told me that Fowler did have two little ones. Nothing on record to that effect. The wife did go off to Texas and was never heard of again. All mention her as a wonderful woman. When Joel sold his ranch for cash she may have been the one to have induced him to come to Socorro to deposit it in the bank. Fowler came to Socorro to bank his money—not to have a good time! Why is it that every author you read seems to want to impress on his audience that Fowler was in Socorro to spend fifty-two thousand dollars. The fact was simply that: He had a lot of money he didn't feel safe in carrying. Socorro had the nearest bank. He registered his family at the Grand Central hotel. On the following day, after his drafts were deposited, he decided to take a drink. He made the mistake of following it by another, and another. After making the rounds, he haltingly and hesitatingly made his way back to the Grand Central hotel. There he found his way to the hotel bar. In the bar he took out of his hip pockets two small revolvers and compelled two traveling men to stand on their heads in one corner of the room. Two guns in the hands of a drunken man at short range made discretion the better part of valor. Fowler then left the room and by his boisterous manner attracted a large crowd, who soon surrounded him, but kept a respectable distance from the guns. A few of the more daring, because of the hazard to women and children, were able to get behind him and take the guns away from him. Feeling he would be better off if he slept it off in jail, they marched him there.

Then came the murder. Nearly all accounts place it as at the bar of the hotel. Reporters of the day (and they should know) place it as on the street near the hotel, as the men led him to prison. Joseph Cale was from Vermont. He was in Socorro to look over the mining prospects, and if successful, hoped to bring his family out to Socorro to live. He had become acquainted with Fowler but a short time before. He was registered at the same hotel. He was on the street when he heard the commotion, crossing to see what was going on. When he heard that they were taking Fowler to jail, he elbowed his way through the crowd to succor, if possible, a friend in need. Fowler, jerking his right arm from the person holding it, took a large dirk knife which he carried under his vest, and in a movement quick for a drunk, plunged the blade into Cale's breast. The victim was carried into the hotel, lingering two or three days before he passed away. Being of the Catholic faith, he was administered the last rites by the pastor of the San Miguel mission, Father F. F. Lestra. When he died he was buried in the Catholic cemetery in Socorro and not shipped to his folks as some old timers have stated. Fr. Lestra registered him as James Cale; the court-house records registered him as Joseph Cale. Take your choice. The San Miguel register of his burial runs thus:

1883

James Cale

Obre 11 di sepultura ecca. en el campo santo al cadaver de James E. Cale adulto hijo que fue de Patrick Cale, del estado de Vermont.

(Signed) F. F. M. Lestra

(On October 11 I gave ecclesiastical burial at the graveyard to the body of James E. Cale, adult son of Patrick Cale, of the state of Vermont)

After the funeral service the town started humming. Sheriff Don Pedro Simpson didn't like the ugly mood of the people. Over and above this, Fowler was well enough liked to have friends who would attempt his rescue, especially if they thought they would get a slice of the fifty-two grand salted away. In opposition were a goodly number of citizens in a hanging mood. The sheriff wired Governor Sheldon for assistance. Col. Eaton and the Socorro militia were ordered by the governor to guard the prisoner. They divided the watch to cover the full twenty-four hours daily. These men had to be fed and paid for their services, all of which added up into making Fowler a very expensive prisoner indeed. Again the sheriff wired the governor asking that Fowler be taken to Santa Fe. He replied that it was possible provided Socorro would foot the bill until the fall term of court. For some reason the transfer never transpired. Day and night the guard never lost sight of the prisoner. Finally, the December term of court came around. The attorneys for Fowler were Thomas Catron of Santa Fe and Niel B. Field of Socorro. Catron received five thousand dollars as his fee, which means that Mrs. Fowler did not get all the money. If you take out Field's fee and other expenses there probably wasn't too much left for the widow and the two children. The jury was composed of natives. Only five of the twelve could read; less could write. It was not their fault but it doesn't speak well for the educational facilities under Spanish and Mexican rule. The Americans, after twenty-seven years in Socorro, hadn't done much better, although Col. Eaton and others were working on it. The first public school in Socorro didn't get under way until after the Fowler trial. Judge Bell presided at the trial. Catron pleaded that Fowler was drunk at the time of the killing and therefore not in his right mind. The jury was undecided. It remained closeted all that afternoon and all that night until ten the following day. Verdict: guilty. Catron then pleaded for a new trial but was overruled by Judge Bell, who sentenced Fowler to be hung on January 4, 1884. Catron and Field then tried to carry the case to the supreme court but it was not to meet again until January after the date set for the hanging. Then one of those behind-closed-doors affairs took place and January 4th went by without the hanging. The people of Socorro did not like it one bit. A whispering campaign started that soon became loud enough for the Vigilantes to take action. Catron was after Fowler's money, went the rumors. Nothing satisfied save a hanging. It wasn't Cale. They didn't know him from Adam: it was the principle of the thing. On Monday night, January 21, the vigilantes decided to enforce the Lynch law. Again, fate intervened. On the following night they gathered together on the outskirts of the town—all masked and armed. At ten o'clock they sent envoys to the jail. Fowler was sleeping. The guards were asked to leave peacefully. A few of them had been guarding the outer door and two others were pacing up and down in the hallway. The vigilantes numbered two hundred. They waited until twelve o'clock, midnight. In a quiet and orderly fashion, like a parade, the ranks of the hangmen beat a path to the jail door, arriving there at 12:20. They were halted by their leader and a committee delegated to wait on the jailer and obtain the keys. In town, the sentries, masked, as the rest, guarded all the exits and entrance to Socorro. No one was permitted in; no one let out. In cases of emergency, such as the doctor who was called to Lemitar to attend a woman in childbirth, an escort was given. Doctor Duncan never forgot that midnight ride to Lemitar. Two masked men stopped him at the place where the postoffice now stands and asked him to turn back. After much pleading he was permitted to go on provided two masked companions went along. They rode one on each side of him without saying a word. If what they were to do that night was so open and above board, why were they afraid that the doctor was seeking an excuse to bring help? Why the masks, and silence? The doctor said later on that he thought the two men were intimate friends of his and the silence was to prevent his recognizing their voices. All through the difficult labor of the woman they never lost sight of the doctor, watching his every move, Winchesters ever ready. One false move and the doctor would be carried back to Soccoro. If the doctor had a telegraph office in mind that was as far as it ever got.

Meanwhile over in Socorro the vigilantes woke up Joel Fowler. Some authors say that the victim fouled his pants in fright when he realized that he was being lynched, but these accounts of men writing their memoirs and trying to make them sell. Some claimed to be eyewitnesses, but I doubt if they were that close. He did yell, pull, plead, entreat, call for help, storm heaven—had to be dragged out of the cell. Realizing the grim determination of the masked men to swing him from the same tree that ended Gordan's career, he ceased struggling, but never stopped his entreaties to heaven. Some wag in the crowd called out:

"It's a cold night for angels, Joel. Better call on some one nearer town."

The prisoner turned to the voice and said:

"As a law abiding citizen you should protest rather than abet such a mob scene as this."

The same voice answered:

"You are in the hands of law abiding citizens, Mr. Fowler, and they will see that you get your just deserts."

The tree in hangman's alley was about two hundred yards from the jail. Today, the place is a vacant lot between McCrutchen and Park streets. Where the big two-story adobe building stands, just forty yards to the right once was shaded by a large cottonwood tree that branched out to the alley. So many men legally or otherwise have been suspended from this tree that the place became known to this day as Hangman's Alley. Arriving at the tree one of the crowd remarked:

"Fowler, this is just your size." A rope was thrown over one of the lower limbs, and the murderer's neck encircled by the dangling noose. Fowler was trembling in every limb. He never ceased his entreaties until he realized that not one in the crowd would come to his defense. Then he became very quiet and said:

"Boys, you are doing wrong, but you will not listen to me. When I am dead do me the favor of sending my body to my uncle in Fort Worth, Texas. Good-bye."

Fowler knew he was going to die. At this point he should have mentioned his wife. Not once during the trial, or in prison or in the death march did he refer to her. Was it that he never quite lived down the unfaithfulness of his childhood sweetheart? When under the influence of liquor, he knifed Cale was there something about the man at that moment that reminded him of the one he saw that day with his wife in Texas? A psychiatrist might hazard an answer. His second wife was a dance hall girl and friendly. Fowler may have been jealous, a disease he developed that terrible day at the ranch house. Cale and Fowler were friends. Even drunk, a man doesn't knife his pal unless some subconscious urge or sense of justice causes the body to act. Did Fowler reveal anything to his lawyers? If he did they took the secret to the grave with them. Why ship the body to his uncle? Why not his family in Indiana, or his wife? This terrific silence concerning his wife has me puzzled. They both seemed on well enough terms when they registered at the hotel. The only explanation I can attempt is that the second wife was a sublimation for the first who was never completely out of his mind or heart despite her conduct. Why didn't he shoot her? He couldn't bring himself to that because his love was stronger than his trigger finger. Possibly at the hotel Cale joined the Fowlers for supper and rejoiced in their good fortune. Being under the influence of liquor and seeing Cale brought the subconscious reaction of seeing the last man who was talking to his wife and associated him with the man who was with his first wife in Texas.

Catron was in Santa Fe the night they hung Fowler. Field was in Socorro. His was the only voice raised in Fowler's defense. When news was brought to him that the vigilantes were on the way to Hangman's Alley with Fowler, he promptly jumped into his clothes, raced to face the mob at the west end of the plaza, where he mounted an adobe wall and spoke to them about law and order.

"If you touch one hair on Fowler's head, I'll shake the dust of Socorro forever. He did. The next morning he was on the first train to Albuquerque where he hung out his shingle. He never saw Socorro again. Who received the balance of Fowler's fortune? What became of it would make an interesting thesis. When Fowler was pronounced dead, the vigilantes dispersed, leaving his body dangling there. Early that Wednesday morning (not Sunday as several old timers seemed to think —there were so many hangings they probably got their days mixed) the news spread about the town and several thousand people viewed the remains before some one had the nerve to cut the body down. Laid out, two silver dollars were placed, one on each eye. Shipment to Fort Worth followed. Legends sprung up, and tales grew with the telling. Men are said to have had target practice with the corpse. All in all these are the simple facts; if they are not gory it is because the deed was gory enough. That Fowler was becoming a legend to perpetuate we read from the following account in the Chloride Black Range for December 12, 1884:

"Kean St. Charles went to Socorro with a load of spuds week before last and on the trip struck a foot racer named Fowler, a printer who works in one of the offices there. A foot race was arranged between Kean and Fowler, to be run on Sunday, November 30, at two o'clock and two hundred yards distance. On the day previous a test race was run for fun for one hundred yards and the two men ran neck and neck, the winner being less than six inches ahead of his antagonist. It has been arranged that Kean should lose the race and get a divvy on the winnings. He informed his friends of this arrangement but at the same time said that he should disregard the compact and win the race and with this pointer the boys bet all their money on Kean. Only one man, a gambler, backed the stranger, but he took all the bets offered. There were several hundred dollars up in wagers when the race was run and in spite of Kean's assertion that he would run the race out on his oppenent, he lost by five or six feet. Fowler beat him just as badly as he wanted it. It is now generally understood that this chap Fowler is really Casad of Trinidad, Colorado, one of the fastest long distance runners in the country, and Kean will never make his backers believe that he did not play the double game on them."

Why the name Fowler? Because he thought the little guy great.

After showing the manuscript on Fowler to an old timer, she said to me:

"There is very little here about Mrs. Fowler."

I told her that it was because very little was known of Mrs. Fowler.

"Little, why I knew Mrs. Fowler very well, not in the sense of intimate friendship, but we met often at our dressmaker's, for she had her gowns made at the same place I did. She was one of the most beautiful women I had ever seen. She had big, brown wide-open eyes, set in a baby face that caused men to look at her twice. She was short and trim and wore nothing but the best. It was a fallacy to say that she returned to Texas after the death of her husband. She remained right here in Socorro. She had to earn a living, and she did. She dealt Stud Horse Poker in Charlie Udder's saloon. She had a title, too, for all her beauty. 'Queen Gambler of the West,' she was called, and her manipulation of cards proved the title was not a vain one. In 1886, when I came to Socorro she was still here, the Common Law wife of one Sam Egginton. The man that told you she had children is mistaken. The Fowlers had no children. Mr. and Mrs. Egginton roomed at the Weaver House Hotel, near where the electric light company now has its offices.

"My husband was here when Fowler was hung. He was not hung in Hangman's Alley as many people believe. He was strung up on a beam across the street from the present Damian Padilla home. There was a gate there with a cross-beam. Fowler was a short fellow, and the vigilantes figured this was just the thing."

I asked if she didn't mind my using her name.

"No names, please. I only tell you this for the sake of history, not for gossip. But it burns me up to read so many lurid accounts of Fowler and vigilantes. After all, Socorro had something better to offer, and people should write these better things also."

The interview ended. I could not help agreeing. The good things should be written, too.

Leader of a gang of cutthroats, his own men put him out of the way for keeps.

Book Sixteen

MAN WITH THE RED BEARD

(Vicente Silba)

THIS NAME WILL COME AS A SURPRISE to many readers because Rudabaugh, Billy the Kid and Webb have overshadowed Vicente Silba in fable, fiction and song that many people of Las Vegas are totally unaware that this leader of the White Caps ever existed. Nor were the journalists of the day annoyed at the shenanigans of Silba's men, for they brushed them away as political moves rather than daring deeds of outlaws and bandits. But as a "shanachie" I must include the story of Vicente if the tale of Las Vegas is to be complete. Intellectually undervitalized, Vicente Silba shrank pathetically from expanding his contacts and never delved into problems which he knew to be beyond his powers. He was always daunted in his civic outlook; that is why he never ran for office. A fine appearing man and a natural leader had he the proper advisors, he would have cut out a place for himself that might have elevated him among the all-time New Mexico greats. As it turned out to be his was a life of unrelieved apprehension, helpless wrath, and dread disillusion which confined his activities to murdering a wife, a brother-in-law, a couple of faithful followers and petty thefts that made him, as far as reporters were concerned, wholly destitute of either circulation or reputation so that he was not considered news by any standards. In his own circle he was considered to be kindly, companionable, fairly democratic, gracious to his friends, adroit in the manipulations of the men he controlled, handsome, and with a winning personality. Up to a point. Actually he was a pulpy, spluttering, timorous, loud-mouthed, domineering character who loved to stand at the entrance of his saloon to greet his acquaintances with ribald jokes, a hearty, boisterous laugh that was more hollow than hearty, and have everybody tell him what a wonderful fellow he was. He had none of the dash of Billy the Kid, none of the verve of Doc Holliday, was neater about his appearance than Rudabaugh, but as a leader of bandits he failed to come within the shadow of the least of them. He lacked the daring of Clay Allison, the strength of Big Bill Williams, the push of Joel Fowler. He boils down to this: He was a proto-type of the Prohibition gangster of the Roaring Twenties. That and nothing more. Being a murderer, well there is nothing glorious or dashing about that. Murderers are born every day, and will keep on being born. That is part of the pattern of the world as old as Cain and Abel.

Yet, to the native New Mexican he is a legend as real, mysterious, momentous, energetic, magnetic and studendous as Billy the Kid, the James boys and as much a part of their folklore as the Conquistadores. Sit down among them of a raw wintry evening as the fire roars on the hearth and they shell pinons. The old abuelo will stare into the dancing flames and think back into the years and he will steer the conversation into the exploits of el bandito Vicente Silba. His eyes glisten as he relives those daring days. The leaping flames are so many horses riding the wind, up and away to carry raiders through the fields to rustle cattle or burn down fences or scatter sheep. White caps they wore and black masks over swarthy faces. The abuelo makes Silba just as real as a rider of the purple sage flashing across the silver screen. Actually, no one really knows what he really did or how to classify him as a gunman. He never even caused a stir in Las Vegas where he lived, planned and robbed. Vigilantes ignored him completely as beneath their notice. Yet, books have been written about him (in Spanish) and some old timer showed me a long epic poem of his misdeeds. If we except Dave Rudabaugh, Las Vegas had no Fowler, Mentzer or Allison as did Socorro, Raton and Cimarron. Vicente Silba will have to substitute. He makes an interesting chapter.

His raids, burnings, killings were nothing noble nor for a noble purpose. They were very ignoble.

Vicente Silba was born in a little adobe hut on the outskirts of Albuquerque in Bernalillo county in 1845. He was a jovial child despite the poverty of his birth and had no time for schooling. Almost from the day he first took his first steps his father took him into the fields to teach him how to plant alfalfa, chili and oats. Shortly after his birth the country passed into American hands, but it made no changes for the Silbas whose lives followed very much the same pattern as before. Another very good reason for not attending school was that there were no schools to go to except the little private school at the San Felipe rectory in Albuquerque and Vicente's father could not afford to send his son to it. This was for the children of the Dons and old man Silba knew his place. When the great bishop J. B. Lamy brought in the teaching Brothers and the Loretto Sisters, Vicente was too big, ungainly and awkward to go to school. He was tall for his age and did a man's work in the fields before he was twelve years old. What he lacked in brain power he made up for in physique. He was sturdy, broad of shoulder, healthy, handsome and a redhead. Being a redhead doesn't mean much to Easterners, but to the Latin American it makes him the Rudolph Valentino of the village. During his teens he developed a grave, poised, almost studied physiomgomy that attracted people much older than himself to him, and he had the natural intuition of sympathy, liberality and agreeableness that commanded respect as becomes a person born to lead.

It is a law of nature that unlike poles attract. One of the girls in the village, two years younger than Vicente, was Telesfora Sandoval. Short, plump, dark with beady eyes and squatty as a Pueblo Indian maiden, she was one of the many who was attracted to Vicente's red hair, but because of her ugliness, the last person in the world to consider herself first in his affections. So his father went to her father and both fathers went to the father of the parish in Albuquerque and the banns were published. From the first the marriage was a success. What Telesfora lacked in feminine beauty and charm she made up for in natural ability and brains. The couple moved to Albuquerque, where Vicente obtained a job as assistant bartender in one of the saloons in Old Town, which at that time made up the little city of Albuquerque. He gave his pay to Telesfora who stored it away in a cup hidden under the dress of El Santo Nino d'Atocha. Telesfora believed this would bring them luck. One cloud saddened these early happy days, Telesfora could not bear children. Perhaps this was the factor behind all the actions that made life so miserable and unbearable in Las Vegas. About this time Vicente learned to read and write just enough to get by on, but never enough to sever the chain that tied him to ignorance. In this respect only is he like Billy the Kid and Kit Carson, although both these knew more Spanish than he knew English. Fortified by the flattery of friends that he was destined for greater things than a helper in a bar, he gathered his wife and savings one fine day and set out for the new mining towns of San Pedro and Golden. Of the two he selected San Pedro near Santa Fe, where he opened a grocery store and charmed the miners into doing business with him. On Saturdays and Sundays he went on hunting trips and came to know the country so well that it was to become his hideout during the early days of the White Cap escapades. Telesfora ran the candy counter and was well liked by all the little ones of the mining settlement, for she gave away more than she sold because of the mother complex. Every little child she saw was a heartache for laughing voices of urchins were not destined for her home. One old timer remembered her as barely able to peer over the candy counter, but as very nice and kind.

Vicente soon tired of life as a grocer in a mining town. He decided he should get into something bigger. Again he moved. This time to Old Town in Las Vegas, where he bought a saloon on the south side of the plaza near the Romero Mercantile Company. It was a combination affair of bar and billiard parlor, and well frequented. Quite a business he built up, our Vicente, enough to keep him busy day and night. Some of them spent freely and often. Where did they get their money? He had to slave for what he had, yet these seemed to have it without any effort whatsoever. When questioned about it they simply smiled and spent more. This was the first step, envy of others. Now he took to studying these customers, to gain their confidence, and the secret of the source of their income. He was going to jump on the band-wagon. One day he bought some gaming tables and his new-found comrades told him that this was a step in the right direction. It was at these gaming tables that he came to know the men who later made up his company of White Caps and the Forty Bandits. After a time his superior personality gained an influence over them and they were doing what they were told.

As an organization the White Caps were not founded by Vicente Silba. It originally started as a group of native ranchers banded together to do some night riding against some unscrupulous squatters from the States who took advantage of the native inability to read and write to register as their land that had already been in the hands of its rightful owners for several generations. Modeled on the terrorism of the hooded K.K.K., its members wore white caps, black mask and rode only at night. They burnt down homes, barns, carriages, crops and fences of those who dispossessed them. One could hardly blame the squatters for wanting the land, for the meadows about Las Vegas were rich and the soil could be made to produce more than onions, squash and corn. This is another instance of bloodshed and terror as a result of a lack of education. After a while the night raiders took to burning the homes of people they did not like so that they became worse than the vigilantes because it was a matter of feeling rather than law and order.

As was inevitable with the native New Mexican, the organization became affiliated with a political party, and a force in San Miguel county to be reckoned with when one wanted to swing votes in his favor. In 1891 the White Caps were reorganized under the leadership of Juan Jose Herrera and Pablo Herrera of Las Vegas, but the burning of houses, fences, and night rides continued. It was not until the Vicente Silba case broke that it became known that these were the deeds of the Forty Bandits. The Herrera brothers were politicians and they organized the White Caps as a third political party. The idea was sound and honest. No more raiding; no more burning; no more masks, merely the white caps to denote their party affiliation. This was a protest against the graft, greed and corruption that dominated the political scene at the time. But too many of the members of the White Cap party frequented the tavern of Vicente Silba which was their second home. Or one might safely say that the cantina was their hearth where the fires of their aspirations were drowned out by the quantity of beer and wine consumed from six in the evening to three in the morning and from nine in the day to five in the afternoon. Pablo Herrera succeeded in being elected to the Territorial legislature and hoped to further the interests of the White Cap party. At the close of the session he created a mild sensation through the delivery of a rather quaint speech:

"Gentlemen: I have served several years time in the penitentiary but only sixty days in the legislature, the present House of Representatives. I have watched the proceedings here carefully. I would like to say that the time I spent in the penitentiary was more enjoyable than the time I spent here. There is more honesty in the halls of the Territorial prison than in the halls of the legislature. I would prefer another term in prison than another election to the House."

He packed his bags and returned to Las Vegas. Upon his arrival, Felipe Lopez, deputy-sheriff, was sent to arrest him on some pretext because Herrera's words did not sit so well with the members of the House. The two encountered each other near the courthouse. Aftr some words the deputy pulled his gun and shot Herrera through the heart. Enough witnesses were produced to vouch for the plea of self-defense. Lopez was never brought to trial. The White Caps would have disbanded but for Vicente Silba. Said the Rev. Gabino Rendon:

"Vicente Silva was a big man with reddish-brown whiskers. He owned a saloon on the plaza next door to Baca, the surveyor. The saloon had a portal all around it and the top of the portal was an excellent spot from which to see everything that went on in the plaza. At that time there was a third political party in these parts and Silba used it to cover up his activities. This party was organized by a man by the name of Herrera. Meetings were held in a blue stone house on Grand Street. No one knew actually what the party stood for and the name White Caps really signified nothing. Silba blamed all his killings, burnings, stealings on the White Caps. He distributed free whiskey to all the men who would listen to him and spread the gossip he dispensed around town to blacken the name of the organization."

Silba was recognized as an inoffensive family man trying to make a living. His wife Telesfora was looked upon by all as a very holy woman. She was constantly in church helping the Altar Society, the Carmelitas, the Guadalapanas. Unattractive and rotund as she was she attracted many to her for advice, help and friendship. She was ever busying herself to keep her home neat and clean and worthy of the man she married. Vicente permitted her to keep her brother with her, whether this was because she was lonely or because he was an orphan I have not been able to ascertain. Gabriel Sandoval was twenty years of age when the White Caps became an organization controlled by his brother-in-law. He did the chores at the saloon as well as at home. He certainly worked for his keep, although we may imagine his sister helping him out now and then with an extra dollar. Later Silba was to take in little Emma, but only after heavy persuasion on the part of Telesfora.

In 1885, John Minner had a livery stable where horses, carriages and wagons, all types of freight conveyances and draught horses could be rented. On the night of March 5, when he went to the corrals to feed the horses, he found a newly born baby left in the straw of one of the stables. Aghast at such cruelty, for March nights in New Mexico are not much warmer than January nights, in this section of the state anyway, he bundled the child in his coat and took the foundling to the city officials. This was a problem indeed. One of the wives took over until the city fathers could make up their minds what was to be done. There was no orphanage; none of the families visited were interested in an adoption; Minner was too busy with his own family and the stables; so they advertised it about town that anyone who wanted the baby could have it provided they promised to provide for her. When Telesfora heard that the child could be hers for the asking she ran to the saloon and told her husband. He was not interested. She said that she would not leave the cantina until Vicente went down to see the officials. He was not to come back without the child. This was several years before he took over the White Caps. When he saw the baby he was as much pleased to call her his own as Telesfora was. He named the child Emma Silva. The child was treated as a member of the family and from the fond attention she received from both Telesfora and Vicente one could hardly believe otherwise. No sooner had Emma learned to walk than Vicente took her down the three blocks from their home to the cantina to show off her blond hair to the customers, much to the horror of Telesfora and the City Fathers. After all, Vicente should have more sense and the child would revert to the city if he were not more careful about her bringing up. Such an environment was hardly conducive for the well being of the child. Emma had her way with both foster-parents that developed a trait which resulted in her tragic end.

Then Silba began his reign of terror. He promoted Gabriel to bar-tender in order to give himself more time to the gaming tables, plunder, meetings and other activities. One thing that troubled the redhead constantly was that after sixteen years in Las Vegas all he had to show or it was a tavern catering to the lowest of the low. He was no richer than in San Pedro, Albuquerque, Corrales.

Association with the characters that frequented his bar evolved into a plan to make himself rich without attracting the attention of the law. He curried the favor of three policemen in Old Town and these became the first members of his gang. So the night riding was renewed. So in 1892, the White Caps called themselves the Forty Thieves. There was no particular reason for this name except that someone must have heard about it from the *Arabian Nights*, for there was no mastermind in the group except Vicente; yet he could hardly be called that; just shrewd. Not one lawyer, nor one member with a grammar school education and less intelligence. There were no

I.Q. tests in those days so we can hardly classify the motley crowd. On paper they were known as The Society of Bandits of New Mexico. It turned out to be that they were neither a society nor bandits. Predators, raiders would be more appropriate. As they confined their activities to a small section of San Miguel county and a smaller part of Mora county, New Mexico could hardly be an inclusive term. The three officers helped in the selection of the others so that when they felt that they were really organized, the roster stood as follows:

Vicente Silba
Julian Trujillo
Jose Chavez y Chavez
Eugenio Alarid
Martin Gonzolez y Blea
   (Alias El Moro—The Moor—because of his dark complexion)
Manuel Gonzolez y Baca
   (Alias El Mellado—i.e. Toothless)
Guadalupe Catallero
   (Alias El Lechuza—The Owl)
Dionicio Sisneros
   (Alias Candelas—The Firebrand)
Antonio Jose Valdez
   (Alias El Mico—The Ape)
Ricardo Romero
   (Alias El Romo—Pugnose)
Jose F. Montoya
Florentino Medran
Francisco Ulibarri
Remigio Sandoval
   (Alias El Gavilan—The Hawk)
Nestor Herrera
Manuel Maldonado
Librado Polanco
Patricio Maes
Procopio Real
Acasio Real

Zenon Maes
Nestor Gallegos
Nicanor Gallegos
Leandro Maestas
German Maestas
Hilario Mares
Marcos Varela
Gabriel Petal
Genovevo Avila
   (Alias El Cochumeno—i.e. Cocoa-skinned)
Cecilio Lucero
J. M. Vialpando
Juan de Dios Vialpando
Tomas Lucero
Sostenes Lucero

This much must be said of them: They were so secretive that no one suspected that such a society existed. They rode at night stealing sheep, horses, cattle. Usually the victim was a friend or neighbor. They carefully avoided getting into difficulties with the Anglos who would be a little more zealous in tracking them down. To take care of the stolen cattle until they could be disposed of with safety, Silva purchased a ranch near the mining camp where he once ran a store. This was in the vicinity of San Pedro, in Santa Fe county, and was known as Monte Largo, a terrain admirably fitted by nature for cattle rustlers. Those were the days when the penalty for such an offense was hanging. We can readily see why Silva was cautious. He wanted riches but not at the risk of his neck. Here was one of the best watering spots in the district as well as good timothy grass and the animals were fattened before shipped out to the buyer, the brand being changed of course.

All went fine for a while and Vicente felt that at last he was on the road to fame, success and wealth. Then Refugio Esquival had the wit to track down some of his stolen horses right to the corral at Monte Largo. Whatever he thought, Silva was the last one he suspected. On March 7, 1891, the Las Vegas Free Press, which seems to have been the only newspaper at the time interested in the deeds of the White Caps, carried

Vicente Silba's name in a news item, but not as a malefactor:

"Last Monday (May 11) the trial of Meliton Ulibarri, charged by Pablo Herrera with insulting him (Pablo evidently liked to argue) with words before Justice Clemente Angel, resulted in the death of a young man by the name of Florencio Sandoval and the fatally wounding of his father Doroteo Sandoval. At this trial, Vicente Silba, in whose saloon the row took place, testified that he had heard no such remarks as Ulibarri was charged with having made. Having given his testimony Silba was on his way out when he was met by Juan Jose Herrera and upbraided for the way he had testified. Silba replied that he was under oath and was obliged to tell the truth. Doroteo Sandoval joined in the conversation and praised Silba for having acted honorably in the matter. At that moment Pablo and Nicanor Herrera appeared on the scene in a buggy. Both brothers alighted. After a few words between them and the other parties knives were drawn and in the melee that ensued Doroteo Sandoval was stabbed. Florencio Sandoval, seeing his father stabbed, ran to his rescue and received a stab in the breast, dying shortly afterward. Billy Green, a deputy sheriff, attempted to quell the disturbance but his revolver was knocked out of his hand and he was badly beaten.

Silba was considered by the court as more offended against than offending.

Refugio Esquivel brought his horses back to Las Vegas, corraled them, and went to the authorities. For the first time Silba was brought in to answer as a suspect, not by Refugio, but by his father who did not like the look of things at the cantina. Vicente put up an injured air and was very evasive in his answers. Someone talked. Who? Why? Was it possible for Refugio to trail the horses all the way to Monte Largo without inside information? The set-up was too air-tight for anyone to guess its existence. At least it was up to now. How could Silba hold meetings night after night and hope to avoid suspicion? As is the way of a transgressor he baited a trap for the informer. Esquivel was anything but friendly. He was a relative of the Herreras; therefore no friend of Silba's. But why did his father specifically name Vicente Silba during the trial? And with such certainty in his voice? He was so sure of his ground in the courtroom that he turned pale with anger when told that the verdict was innocence for the tavern keeper. There was no place in the society for an informer.

October 22, 1892. It was a threatening and tempestuous night. The wind howled, storm clouds gathered, cold penetrated. The night was as raw as Silba's hurt pride. People were better off by their firesides and stayed there. Only a few of the daring ventured out. The politically minded who were conscious of the approaching November elections buttoned up their overcoats and braved the tempest. A county election was more sacrosanct to them than the election of a president. Suddenly the wind ceased, the air warmed and soft white snow covered the streets of Las Vegas. In Silba's cantina this called for more drinks. Members of the gang sat around the gaming tables in separate groups whispering to each other. About midnight Silba announced that the tavern was closed. This surprised the non-member customers, for his place was a twenty-four-hour affair. The last customer gone, Vicente locked his place and made for home. Footfalls in the snow. Crunch overlapped crunch as the members of the society back-tracked to the cantina by way of the side door on Morena street. At last they were all accounted for. This was a council for justice. They were told by their leader that they were assembled to pass judgment on one of the members who had betrayed his trust. Ballots were cast for officers to preside over the meeting. The final count showed El Mellado as president, El Moro as secretary, Romo and El Gavilan as marshals, Silba as attorney-general, and Polanco as the defending lawyer.

Silba stood up and made a speech. He said in effect that some one present had revealed to Refugio Esquivel the hideout at the Monte. This was the unpardonable crime of traitor. The name of that traitor was Patricio Maes. This man not only talked to Esquivel but had the effrontery to go to the Knights of Mutual Protection (a rival organization), enemies of the society, giving information detrimental to the safety of every one assembled. A letter was then introduced by El Moro, the contents of which told the group that Maes was resigning from membership because he was tired of being a White Cap and was in favor of the Republican party. (The White Caps were favorable to the Democrats). He furthermore frankly asked admission into the Society for Mutual Protection. Whether this was actually the case was never proven. The logic is faulty for if Maes named names he was the one holding the stick. Any harm befalling him would certainly reflect on those named. No one ever proved that Maes actually wrote the letter. I am of the opinion that he could hardly write his own name. Silva had a reason for wanting him out of the way and this was as good a way of doing it as any. What actually happened was that Maes was given false promises as to what the society stood for and the benefits that would accrue to him as a member. In his letter he calls the society the United People's Party and seems to have been sincere when he joined, hoping to better his lot as a law abiding citizen rather than as a thief. The letter was probably written by one of the Herreras but spoke for Maes. It was addressed to the editor of El Sol de Mayo newspaper (The May Sun) and written at Rincon de la Tablazon, a nearby hamlet, on October 7, 1892:

"By these presents, I give notice beforehand that I am severing connections with the United Peoples' Party primarily because this organization fails to live up to what it promises as beneficial to the people. It forces on people laws that are prejudicial, of interest to a few, and beneficial only to the leaders. I believe that the Republican party is the only true party of the people. I hereby join that party with all my heart, and I enlist under the banner of the Society for Mutual Protection. Gentlemen of Rincon, look out for your own welfare. The leaders of the People's party are at present selling you old corn, and the quantity is so great that the bag may not hold it." (Signed) Patricio Maes.

Maes jumped up and denied the charges. All he needed was a little time to prove it. Besides, there was nothing in that letter to prove that he betrayed Silba. Anyone receiving El Sol de Mayo could read the epistle a thousand times and never get out of it that stolen horses were over near San Pedro mining camp. El Mellado smiled and merely said that the fate of the culprit was in the hands of the society. Indeed, he was judged before the meeting took place. Cuadrilla was the word El Mellado used. The meeting was conducted in Spanish throughout. The word actually means council of four, but in Southwestern Spanish it means gang. The others could see for themselves that Maes committed the unpardonable sin. A Judas in their midst! Off with his head! Let him die that others may take warning should they be entertaining similar thoughts. Then, without further ado, he placed before the cuadrilla the vote of life or death. No clemency. No middle course. Death to the traitor. Completely innocent or totally guilty, Patricio knew he would never see another dawn. Silva stood up and said:

"Which one of you wants to go to the penitentiary?"

"Not I," came from all quarters.

The votes were collected. Every bean was a black one. The sentence: Death. Patricio was to be hung from the Gallinas bridge. By a remarkable co-incidence El Gavilan had a rope ready. El Moro made the noose. Maes went down on his knees and implored the men to re-consider. This is the fear Americans are fighting today. Huddled together as a mob, Maes was doomed. One helping hand meant more deaths. Individually perhaps some were in sympathy with the victim, but they dare not divulge it or they might suffer the same fate. The Iron Curtain long before Moscow brought it into play. Gavilan took a position on one side of the condemned; El Moro on the other. Each cocked a pistol against the head of Maes. The White Caps' masks were put on. The mumbled prayers of Maes were buried by the falling snow, both trailing away in the night as they made the death march to the bridge that separated both towns. Head bowed, countenance resigned, Maes offered no resistance. The place of execution reached, Maes lifted his eyes heavenwards only to have them burn from the snowflakes. He offered his soul to his Creator, once more pleaded for mercy—a vain plea—then asked mercy and pardon for his offenses. And with the mob were the three night policemen. Out of the bleak, gruesome, goblin-like darkness their eyes shone with brilliance at their power over life and death; three men who took an oath to rather lose their lives than witness this very happening. Silba and El Mellado placed Maes over the bridge. The rope slipped. With a deafening crash Maes fell into the waters below. Why didn't he escape? He couldn't swim. Sisneros and El Gavilan ran down, grabbed him and brought him back. This time they were more careful and successful. Snow covered their tracks and their deed as each one took his path to a loving wife, sleeping children, a warm hearth. Bold warriors resting after combat. And all the Las Vegas Optic had to say was: "Patricio Maes was taken by a mob early Saturday morning and hanged from the Gallinas river bridge at Las Vegas. The only cause assigned for the infamous murder is that the victim has published a card in the Spanish Republican paper that he had withdrawn from the White Cap party." (Raton Guard for October 27, 1892, as taken from the Las Vegas Evening Optic)

That morning bright and early, Silba was walking along the street on his way to open the cantina. Now the cantina was just off the plaza and his home was anywhere but in the direction of the bridge. No one seemed to bother asking Silba just how he chanced upon a body suspended from a bridge out of his way from home and place of business. How well he played the part. Aghast, he ran up and down the street yelling in Spanish: "There's a man hanging from the bridge." A crowd soon gathered. The authorities took over and cut down the body. No one could identify the corpse because it was covered with layers of ice and snow. It was carried to the coroner's house for a post-mortem investigation and to thaw out. A lot of testimony was taken but all vague. Finally, after some hours, the body was identified as that of Patricio Maes. After a few perfunctory remarks Silba was permitted to open his saloon. Nothing more was said until the District Court opened sessions on November 7, 1892.

But there was some one in Old Town who was not idle. Unsuspected by Silba, old Captain Esquivel, father of Refugio, was doing some investigation on his own about the goin's on at Monte Largo. He was not fooled for a moment. Even before Patricio's death he had enough evidence to hang every member of the White Caps. He suspected the cause of the hanging but had no tangible evidence. But this he knew: Horse-stealing was punishable by hanging so that Silba would come to the end of a rope in either case. At the trial the captain could not pin Silba down so tight was his alibi. But it made the leader of the lawless realize that the authorities were alerted. Somehow the finger would point to him so he took refuge in flight, hiding out in the Los Alamos area, and at times at Coyote. (Los Alamos is not to be confused with the more famous county near Espanola and connected with the history of atomic energy. Coyote is the present Rainsville above the village of La Cueva near Mora. Los Alamos at the time was a community of sixty-three families. It boasted a beautiful church, a school run by the Sisters of Mercy, several merchandise stores and laid out streets conforming to some hap-hazard plan. It was a farming community seven miles northeast of Sapello, behind the present Jim Whitmore ranch. Coyote is novelized in a book by Frank Waters entitled *People of the Valley,* which, while it is fiction, is not too far fetched as to the purpose behind its founding. The present name of Rainsville commemorates the family of Rains that helped settle it.)

Telesfora, Gabriel and seven-year-old Emma remained in Las Vegas. Silba's wife, refusing to see her brother mixed up with outlaws such as made a home of the saloon, had him discontinue his employment as bartender and gave him a place in the restaurant she opened up, for now she was without support of any kind and the day of the Welfare Department had not arrived. Emma was sent to the academy in Las Vegas. Just which I have not been able to ascertain since there are two under the auspices of two different religious groups in Las Vegas at the time. Vicente was informed of the activities of his wife which he interpreted as being against him and on the side of the law. He didn't place her beyond informing the authorities of his whereabouts had she known where he was hiding. By this time it was the consensus of opinion that he murdered Patricio Maes. His story stood too pat. And his discovery of the dangling body was comic.

Early in his career Silba came to rely on turning bad weather in his favor. For one thing it kept people in-doors; for another it slowed up deputies and policemen. On such days he took trips into Las Vegas, staying at the home of a very dear friend with whom he fancied himself in love. January 23, 1893, was such a day. Las Vegans remember it as the day the hurricane blew. It was no fit day for man or beast. Silba went to the academy in a buggy, had a compadre take Emma out of school on some flimsy pretext, then turned her over to another conspirator who drove her to Los Alamos. Why she didn't die of cold or fright is one of those unexplainable things that everybody talks about because they know nothing about it. Meantime Vicente returned to his home to visit Telesfora. Full of charm and endearment he explained to her that he took Emma out of school because he feared that the authorities would take her away from him since he proved such a notorious foster father. Neither he nor Telesfora could abide that. Some authorities seek to place Vicente and Emma in sordid light but this was not true. Silba took Emma from the school as part of a plan to keep Telesfora under his thumb. Emma was the stick the outlaw held over his wife's head. No mother loved a child with more tenderness than Telesfora for Emma. He promised that she should have Emma back after the rumpus quieted down.

Nevertheless he lived in constant dread of Telesfora. That she did not love him any more was an open secret. But she was faithful. She promised herself to him for better or worse and although it turned out for worse than worse, he was still her husband. She always had a way with him even though there was nothing attractive about her. There were moments he held nothing from her. For every such moment he now sweated a thousand. If she told all she knew just to get Emma back, Patricio Maes would have died in vain. He must be patient and in some way contrive to send her to meet Patricio. One other link kept her away. This severed, he could advance his plan. Her brother, Gabriel. This latter also knew all from his association with the members of the society at the cantina. He had such a love for his sister that he would do anything she told him. What if she sent him to the Justice of the Peace with the whole story. Gabriel alive would never do. He must join the ranks of the dead. On February 13, 1893, Silba returned to Los Alamos where he held a secret conclave with El Mellado, Dionicio Sisneros and El Lechuza. He told them that their safety depended on silencing Gabriel and Telesfora. Wouldn't any normal man have considered that their disappearance would have placed the blame on him the more? And what of the abduction of Emma? The juncta over, the buggy was harnessed and the horses guided in the direction of Las Vegas. El Lechuza went in to see Telesfora while the others waited outside. But the Owl found visitors in the house and decided to delay his message, much to the discomfiture of Silva. He was all for entering the house and killing her in spite of the company. But Manuel Gonzolez and Sisneros objected, saying that there was no reason to victimize two wholly innocent people to satisfy the mania of one blood-thirsty individual. Besides, the yells of the visitors would attract an audience they would rather do without. The plan was knifing for fear the sound of shots would stir the populace. How much more the yells of frightened women! Silba agreed that they were right. Sisneros and Gonzolez returned to Los Alamos.

Not too far away from Telesfora's house lived a woman whom we shall call Ramona. Another author has called her Flor de la Pena which was not her name either. She only fits into the story because of Silva's love for her. She had nothing to do with any of his crimes and stands vindicated. She was as unattractive as Telesfora but she could bear children. She knew more than Telesfora about the doings of the society but somehow Vicente Silba never for a moment suspected that she would go to the authorities. And she didn't. Upon occasion she ran into Telesfora on the plaza and the two had a sweet hair-pulling contest over Silba. Although her husband was the transgressor she placed the blame at the feet of Ramona. Or should I say the heart? She was duty bound to remind him of his obligations to Telesfora. Which of course was not the way Ramona looked at it. When Silba entered the latter's home on this particular day, she upbraided him for not obtaining a divorce from Telesfora. She was tired of Mrs. Silba's jealous fits. He told her that soon her worries would be over for brother and sister were going on a long, long journey. Then they could go to Mexico and be married there. A new life altogether! What a dream! And just as misty as far as Vicente was concerned. Ramona was just another tool in his hands. There was something fine about Ramona. An adultress, yes; murderess, never. She would never marry a man who killed his wife for her. But it was not for her that he was killing. It was for his own safety. No matter. She is supposed to have answered: "For the love of the child our passion brought into this world, never." Was this a dramatic touch? Had she really had a child? Old timers are evasive. They won't say yes; nor do they say no. Toss it up and divide by two. Silba remained hidden all day in her home. The three policemen came that night to draw up plans for the elimination of Gabriel Sandoval.

On the following day Juliano Trujillo met Gabriel in front of the Imperial tavern. They conversed for a while, saying nothing with many words. The policeman told him that as an officer of the law he and his two fellow officers would help to locate Emma for he was aware that Telesfora was very fond of her and would like to have her back, especially since Vicente ran afoul of the law. The officer told him that he would bring Emma to Ramona's house because he wanted no difficulty with Silva. Gabriel was now all ears, for the officer told him that he believed that he could have Emma back in Las Vegas that very evening, for he had inside information as to where he could find the child. Gabriel must tell no one. He was to meet them in front of the Imperial saloon at eight o'clock that evening and they would inform him as to their success or failure. Off to the side, peering into the tavern through the window, was El Lechuza taking it all in. His job in the gang was to see that the stolen horses and cattle got to Monte Largo. He was with Silva when Emma was taken from the academy, and some authors accredit him with the actual kidnapping. Gabriel turned and recognized him, calling him a thief, vagabond and kidnapper. He stepped over to strike him, but the policeman intervened, telling him that taking it out on Catallero would get him nowhere but would rather serve to hinder their plans. This calmed Gabriel, who quietly entered the tavern with the parting remark to Trujillo that he hoped to see him at eight that evening.

El Lechuza sauntered down National street to Ramona's house, found Silba, and told him all he heard, not suspecting that Silba and Trujillo had pre-arranged the whole affair. Silba told him to return to the tavern, order some drinks but to keep an eye on all Gabriel's actions. Silba and the three policemen met at the Gonzolez mill above town as appointed. All day long Gabriel was cheerful because he had faith and confidence in Trujillo's success. This convinces me that he was not as well informed about the society as Silva thought or he certainly would have recognized Trujillo as a member of the organization. He told Telesfora the good news and she insisted on accompanying him to the Imperial or at least to Ramona's house because she was afraid that once Ramona got her hands on Emma she would never return her merely out of spite. But Gabriel would have none of it. The Imperial was out of the question for it would mean that he talked; Ramona would not open her door to her. She was better off staying at home. Gabriel went alone. He was at the Imperial by eight. No officers. Sandoval was not worried. Perhaps some official business detained them. A half hour passed. No signs of Trujillo. An hour. At nine-thirty Gabriel decided to walk the streets in hopes of meeting up with the policeman. He found Trujillo at the Buffalo tavern. The officer told him that he would have to go to Ramona's house. They passed Our Lady of Sorrows church. Both crossed themselves. On up National street to Ramona's place, near which stood a solitary, sorry-looking, dilapidated Chick Sale house. From behind it sprung Alarid and Chavez, who pinioned the arms of the unsuspecting victim while Trujillo rained repeated blows on his head with the butt of his revolver, and stabbed with a knife. Gabriel fell on his knees and pleaded for his life. "Muere, ruin traidor, muere!" They cried. (Die, ruinous traitor, die) The Owl rode up on horseback, gazed at the proceedings, smiled and asked:

"How is everything going?"

"All according to plan," was the answer.

Silva came out of Ramona's house and together with Catallero held the arms while Trujillo took the feet and the body was thrown into a cistern on Moreno street. Chavez led the horse, the other officer holding the knives and guns. The body was covered with dung and earth.

Meanwhile Telesfora was pacing the floor, wondering what detained Gabriel. When he hadn't returned by ten o'clock she suspected foul play. But she hesitated to go to the authorities for fear Emma would be killed. On the following evening she decided to take her chances and went to Captain Jose J. Galindre, of the police, and reported Gabriel as missing. In the office at the time was Manuel Cabeza de Baca who seems to have been a police reporter for the Spanish newspaper in addition to his other work. He became interested. The captain commissioned him to find Gabriel. Manuel later wrote a book on Silba and his gang which ran through several editions in Spanish and one in English. Everyone agreed that Gabriel had no reason for disappearing. Something was wrong. Meantime Silba returned to Los Alamos. The funds of the society at this time scratched the bottom of the barrel. It was decided to stage a big robbery; then they would break up. While Silba's plans coincided with those of his men on this score, they reached over and beyond insofar as he would not rest until he could silence Telesfora, and he was safely in Mexico with Ramona.

At Los Alamos William Frank conducted a mercantile store that seemed to do a brisk business. Silba often wondered about it as to its possibilities. On April 6, 1893, El Mellado, El Moro, Patos de Mico, Dionicio Sisneros, and F. Medran went into conference with Silva as to the best means to procure the store safe. Silba gave Medran a twenty dollar bill and told him to buy something. When Frank went to the safe to deposit the large bill, Medran was to discover its contents and to estimate as best he could the value. He reported that there was at least three hundred dollars that he was able to see, and perhaps a good deal more hidden in other drawers. At eleven o'clock that night they drove a wagon to the store, unhitched the horse, got into the store by breaking a window, loaded the safe into the wagon, re-hitched the horse and sped away. They stopped at Sapello. They blasted the door away and were rather disappointed to find very little cash. On the books were debts to the amount of ten thousand dollars. They burnt the books with the idea that all obligations on the part of the debtors would automatically cease. This would induce the people to look upon them as other Robin Hoods. The safe, minus the door, may still be seen in the rectory of the parish of Our Lady of Guadalupe at Sapello. It houses the parish registers. When Frank recovered his safe he turned it over to the pastor at Los Alamos. Several years later, the community, too poor to support a resident pastor, was made a mission to Sapello, and the safe removed to the parish center.

Telesfora suffered in silence. Weeks went by without word from either Gabriel or Emma. One day the Owl appeared at the door with a letter he claimed was from her brother Gabriel. He handed her the letter and disappeared as quietly as he came. Evidently Gabriel knew how to write or she would not have been so gullible. But Telesfora did not know how to read. This explains why she could not identify the writing. A neighbor read it for her. It was addressed from Coyote and dated April 18, 1893. It told her that both Emma and Gabriel were safe and happy and well treated by Silva. The second letter was brought in by Florentino Medran. It was arranged that El Cachumeno would call for her to take her to Coyote to see her brother and adopted daughter. But she was not to go to the police. All the while Frank kept after the authorities to find the men who broke into his store. Los Alamos was in San Miguel county, of which Las Vegas was the county seat. It was up to the officials in Las Vegas to investigate. It was brought to the attention of the Territorial governor who posted a reward of five hundred dollars for the arrest and conviction of the thieves.

The same highway that led to Coyote also passed Los Alamos but one had to turn off near the present Whitmore ranch. Not being a traveler, Telesfora was not aware that the buggy made the turn. Silva and El Lechuza met the carriage at La Canada Pastosa about two leagues from Los Alamos. Five others waited at the hideout in the village.

The vigilance of the authorities was finally rewarded on April 10, 1894, when El Mellado was arrested in Las Vegas. Realizing he was a fund of information they impressed upon him how easy he could make it for himself if he turned state's evidence. His confession included Gabriel's murder. The body was fished out and given a decent burial. On the strength of the testimony the following were ordered under arrest:

El Romo
J. T. Montoya
R. Sandoval
Nestor Herrera
M. Maldonado
L. Polanco
G. Cabellero
P. Real
N. Gallegos
L. Maestas
H. Mares
M. Varela

Not found were: Silba, Pital, Sisneros. Just why the others were omitted has not been explained. Perhaps they dropped out after the hanging of Patricio Maes. Jose Chavez, hearing of the mass arrest, managed to elude the officers and escaped, but was captured in May 1895. He had been working under an alias as a sheep-herder near Socorro. His sentence was postponed until 1896. Alarid and Trujillo were finally captured and sentenced to life imprisonment. Judge Smith gave these two quite a tongue lashing before pronouncing sentence, for they were officers of the law.

In Los Alamos Silba showed his wife a letter written at her dictation in which she said she was going to the authorities to tell all. Both were aware that this letter was a forgery. But Silba wanted a pretext for his deed and this was as good as any. She told him that this was a ruse to get rid of her in order to marry Ramona. And as she had not obliged him by dying, and as Ramona would never consent to marry him while she was alive, he had to kill her. She begged him to let her go. Instead he stabbed her. How brave! The others entered. El Mellado took a look at her body and said:

"How deftly our chief handles the knife."

"Yes," replied one of the others, "He is an expert in the art."

Silba then gave each ten dollars and told them to dig a grave for "La Desgraciada" (The Faithless One). They dug a grave at El Campo de los Cadillos, about one-fourth of a mile south of Los Alamos, almost within sight of the Frank store. As they were digging El Mellado said:

"Mira, companieros—our chief—he does not stop with his wife. Perhaps one of us will be next. This is muy mal negocio. We are bandits, not wife killers."

The others agreed. As they dug they planned the death of their leader. The body of Telesfora was carried out and buried. They turned to go. About thirty steps from her grave, Patos de Rama, who was to the left of Silba, took out his pistol at a signal from El Mellado, and putting it to the head of his leader, shot him. The body was thrown into the arroyo and covered with dirt . This explains why Silba was not found when the case broke. The two were later dug up. Telesfora was buried in the Catholic cemetery in Las Vegas; Silba in Potter's Field.

(Note—While the name is Silva, in the Spanish Southwest, it is pronounced Silba, which is the spelling we followed.)

Poor Black Jack Ketchum. He became a legend even before his violent death. His grave at Clayton is a tourist attraction.

Book Seventeen

TRAIN ROBBERS, INC.

(Black Jack Ketchum)

Near the Texas border that separates Northeastern New Mexico one travels over the line to the little city of Clayton where they are confronted by large arrows pointing out the grave of Black Jack Ketchum. His story laps into the Twentieth Century. Tom Pickett out-lived him and was the last of the old frontier out-laws to pass on, Ketchum was actually the last to strike popular fancy. With the hanging of Ketchum came the line of demarcation. Following him men became racketeers, hoodlums, gangsters, mobsters and "shoot him in the back" types. No more "shooting it out," "draw" and the like. Those days are gone forever, although cattle rustling goes on to this day.

The Concho river in Texas offered good planting and grazing possibilities to the pioneer willing to break the virgin soil and gamble on stock raising. This the Ketchum family was willing to do. Shortly after Ketchum staked his claim, the Federal Government, anxious to break down prejudice resulting from the Civil War, and determined to protect the settlers against the inroads of the Comanches and other marauding tribes, built Fort Concho in 1867, when Black Jack Ketchum was but a year old. This fort was not too far from the Ketchum ranch. In 1875 the area was portioned off and named Tom Green county after a hero of the Texas Revolution who lived to win glory during the Civil War.

Old man Ketchum had three sons: Berry, Sam and Tom, the youngest. Some authors have maintained that papa Ketchum was a medical man which would not necessarily mean that he also could not run a ranch. The doctor who took care of Billy the Kid's wound was a cowboy and rancher. The two older boys pampered young Tom, who spent most of his time staring wide-eyed at the cowboys, rustlers, soldiers, Indians, mule-skinners, teamsters and desperadoes who milled about the fort as they came in and out of Dodge City, and rode the Dodge Trail. Whiskey and money flowed freely which impressed the lad as much as drunken brawls disgusted him. Throughout his life he never drank to excess. The power of money was an education to him. For the likes of him he could never understand why he had to break his back with work on the ranch when easy money could be made by sitting at a gaming table and playing your cards right. Jack attended school only because it was something his parents insisted on.

The frontier post took on expansive proportions and even after it was abandoned the place flourished and developed into the city of San Angelo. Had the youth been patient and invested in land he might have become a rich oil man and lived to this day. The Edwards Plateau in West Texas over-lapped Tom Green county from San Saba county. Here young Tom rode often with his older brother Sam and learned how to trail and read signs as well as any Indian. He was forever outdoors, which helped build up his huge frame, for he was a tall lad even in a country that grew tall men. The vastness of Texas appealed to him and he was forever entering feats that tested his strength and endurance. Schooling over Tom sought and obtained a job riding herd for L. B. Harris. Rain, cold, heat, hunger, thirst—he endured all, not because he believed in the survival of the fittest, but rather because he reasoned that if a horse became the symbol of strength by merely standing in the fields all day, then man could build up his strength by living in the open. In tracking down strays he came to know the whole Concho country as well as the Edwards Plateau area. His brother Sam was to his way of thinking also. The whole Ketchum family was agreed that Tom had the brains, which explains why he took over the leadership in running the male members of the household. Berry respected his brother's talent but would have no part of the lawlessness in which this talent was used. Later on Tom and Sam cowboyed for the Tabkersley outfit. Expert riders, they practiced for hours the use of Winchesters, Sharps, revolvers and pistols as they were definitely decided on easy money from the start.

Besides the range Tom came to know the schedule of the Southern Pacific. He studied every spot where the trains would have to slow up because of climbs, gradings, slopes, watering, sidings and the like. One day he entered San Saba and sat down to a card game. Before long he accused a player of cheating. A fight ensued. For the first time in his life Tom felt how uncomfortable a frontier jail could be. The experience only served to complete his plans for organized robbery. Again jailed for disturbing the peace in 1892, he now went all-out as a desperado. His first train robbery was at Stein's Pass. While it netted him less than he anticipated, the venture was successful and with his gang now fully organized he next stopped the train at Lozier. Sheriff Jerome S. Shields suspected that Ketchum was responsible for the hold-up and rounded up a posse to capture him. Tom and his brother Sam admitted their guilt and served a short jail sentence. No sooner out of prison than they planned the next hold-up.

Over at Richland Springs in San Saba county, Tom sat down to a game of cards. One of the players was Bill Powers, called "Jap" because he was sloe eyed. He was irritable and in a fighting mood. Ketchum obliged him by sending a bullet through him. He escaped the posse and rode up to the old Chisum ranch in New Mexico, where he worked for a time until he joined the L F D outfit near Roswell. Sam joined him here. They were good cow hands and well liked. They trailed herds and became quite popular with other outfits. Later they signed up with an outfit near the new railroad town of Clayton. Following a cattle drive, they took time off for a few days to ride over to Stein Pass for another robbery. A week after that they held up the train at Grants, then headed back to Texas. There they stopped the Texas & Pacific, then returned to Clayton as cow hands. Wanted in two states (actually New Mexico was still a Territory) not one of the cowboys they worked with suspected them as desperadoes. They had a suave, polished manner and were gentlemen at all times except of course when engaged in harmless pranks that produced hearty laughs from the rest of the boys who liked jokes as well as the next.

Tom Ketchum was of swarthy complexion and often wore a black broadcloth shirt or suit and the cowboys fond of nick-names named him "Black Jack." At Liberty, a cattle grazing area near the present city of Tucumcari, Levi Herstein kept a general store. Black Jack noticed that he was doing a rushing business and decided to relieve him of his money bags. But the merchant was of different mind. He reached for a gun, a foolish thing to do as the desperado had the bead on him. Exit Herstein. Escaping to Nogales, Arizona, the ill gotten gains were lost at the gaming table. Broke, Ketchum made an attempt to hold up the bank there but failed miserably. He was fortunate to escape with his life. His next venture was with some desperadoes equally as handy with a gun, but more blood-thirsty than Ketchum. They rode to the mining village of Camp Verde, held up the mercantile store there, killing two clerks as they made their getaway.

Again they made their appearance in the Pecos valley, riding herd from Roswell to Kansas. At the edge of the Texas Panhandle where Kansas and Oklahoma linked, an old buffalo hunter ran an eating establishment. Tom and the waitress lingered over the counter, for Ketchum was a heart-breaker if there ever was one and the waitress was flattered at the attentions of tall, dark and handsome. The proprietor thought the waitress should carry on the flirtation after business hours and told her so in very abusive language, in which he questioned both her virtue and her intentions. Ketchum came to her defense and the old buffalo hunter had more holes in him than the Swiss cheese he served. Kansas put a price on Tom's head although the lady thought he was Sir Galahad. Nobody in Kansas bothered to collect. Ketchum wandered into Wyoming, back-tracked into Oklahoma following a series of hold-ups. From Oklahoma he went to Roswell and Clayton. When the law at Roswell decided to pick him up for questioning he gathered his followers about him and headed for Socorro county.

There they hired themselves out to Captain William French, a rancher. He was well pleased with their work. One morning the cattleman noticed the bunk house shrouded in gloom. What could have happened to the boys? They were always up bright and early. Upon investigation he found the place empty.

"Sure beats me," the Englishman told a neighbor, "We got along so nicely."

"Black Jack might want to pull another robbery," said the neighbor.

"Black Jack?"

"Yes, sir. Worst blackguard this side of the Rio Grande. Wanted for more robberies than you can shake a stick at."

Sure enough the gang went to hold up the Santa Fe south of the little village of San Antonio near Socorro. The desperadoes escaped to the San Mateo mountains, rode to the Al Clemens ranch and took over. They forced Clemens to cook them a meal, took fresh horses from his corral and continued their flight. Rewards for their capture went temptingly high. Several posses made vain searches for the gang that always seemed to elude them. Every post office posted a picture of Black Jack with its demand: Wanted—Dead or Alive. Village belles would invariably sigh at the handsome man and wish that he could have been anything but a desperado. If Tom wished to be a gay lothario he had no time for it. Folsom, Springer, Raton, Raton Pass, Rayado, Clayton, Las Vegas, Cimarron, Santa Fe—up and he rode, striking here, rustling there—the terror of the Territory. If William Antrim had a special regard for Tom O'Folliard, Ketchum took for his pal one Bob McGinnis, the freckled, square-jawed, red-bearded horse thief who was death with a six-shooter.

There are a number of places in New Mexico that deserve preservation as permanent memorials of frontier days. One of these is the Don Diego Hotel, better known as Lambert's. It is to be regretted that the old bar has been converted into a dining room. No one seeking lodging at the old hostel can fail to conjure up ghosts of the past. These walls knew the voices of Clay Allison, William Bonney, Crockett, Wooten, Maxwell, Carson the Younger almost as famous as his more noted father,

Catron, Mills, U. S. Grant, General J. Pope and a host of others both nationally and internationally known. Lambert's also knew Black Jack. Here with Sam, McGinnis and Frank, Tom Ketchum planned the hold-up of the Colorado & Southern. No wonder he played poker with such reckless abandon. After he robbed the railroad he said to Henry Lambert, he would return for all the money he lost. Henry had better make sure it wouldn't be in his safe when he got back.

Three miles south of Folsom are Twin Mountain and Twin Mountain Curve. It was the steepest grade along the line of the railroad. Due to this fact the train was brought almost to a halt as it puffed up the incline. On September 3rd, 1897, the passengers of the C. & S. were suddenly confronted by a band of masked men calling out to them to remain seated and to place their valuables in the bag being passed for the purpose. The train had come to a halt and the engineer warned that if he wished to live he must leave his hand off the throttle until the last bandit was clear of the train. The conductor was Frank Harrington. He had no choice but to look on helplessly and hope that the railroad officials would not be too hard on him. Rings, watches, wallets—anything of value—all fed the kitty. A getaway was made in true Hollywood fashion. Harrington had the engineer back the train into Folsom, where he telegraphed the sheriff of Union county in Clayton and hoped the law could catch up with them before they got too far and shoot every last one of them. Storming at everyone in general and no one in particular he drew little crowds in Trinidad as he rehearsed the scene remarking that the officials were so incompetent and that if he were sheriff he would settle Ketchum's hash once and for all.

"The gall of the man," he would say, "Big as you please, and without the time of day, in he comes, mind you, to tell me to open the baggage room. And because no key to the strong box is forth-coming he opens it with a stick of dynamite. All the time his friends are having a holiday in the passenger cars."

"How do you know it was Black Jack?"

"How could I miss. A man six foot tall. Perhaps an inch

or two over. Black suit, black shirt. It was Black Jack, all right. I'd stake my life on that."

The trail led across Northern New Mexico close to Cimaron and on towards Taos. There Sheriff C. M. Forker lost it. Deputy Loce of Clayton studied the region and concluded that the gand had "dug-in" somewhere above Taos, possibly at Questa or Costilla. But nobody in these mountain homes saw the outlaws. A cave in any number of a thousand hills shielded them from the posse. Time alone would smoke them out when they got good and hungry. The sheriff would have to be on the look-out. How mistaken can you be? The gang was basking in the sunshine of Arizona. They gambled away at Camp Verde until they were broke and decided to replenish their resources. But Tom was uncertain.

"I have a strange feeling that it won't turn out right if we go into New Mexico now. Let's wait a little while longer. Call it intuition if you will, but to do now will invite disaster."

"What do you propose to do for money?" asked Sam.

"There is always cowboying."

"Not for me. I've done too much of the other to wait for wages."

"If you insist on going I suppose I can't stop you. But I don't like it."

"Nothing will happen. I'll be back."

So, off they rode—Sam Ketchum, Will Carver, George Franks, Bob McGinnis, Bob Hays, Bill Walters, Bronco Bill and Red Pipkin. Making it by slow stages at night and sleeping under cover in the day they headed for the Folsom area. Two years had elapsed since the first robbery and officials figured that Black Jack had gone off to Mexico. July 11, 1898. Same spot; same set-up; same conductor. Again dynamite was used. The haul was not as great as the first time, but enough to keep them going for a while. Again the backing into Folsom, and telegrams. One message was sent to Sheriff Ed Farr of Walsenburg, county seat of Huerfano county in Colorado. With a quickly assembled posse he rode south to Aguilar, Trinidad, Raton, Blossburg, veered west and south hitting the trail of the desperadoes in Turkey Canon nestled in the hills west of the city of Cimarron. The outlaws were making for their old hide-out in the Taos mountains. As luck would have it the outlaws were in a little opening cooking dinner. He yelled:

"We have you surrounded. Drop your guns and approach this way with your hands up."

The bandits fell flat to the ground. A shot went out in the direction of the sheriff's voice.

"We have all day and all night. You won't get out alive. Why not give up?"

Another shot.

"If it's fight you want, you've got it."

The posse opened fire. Sam looked at McGinnis: "Looks bad," he said.

"Yes."

"Guess Tom was right."

"Yes."

"No use lying here like dogs to die. Let's make a break for it."

They thought it best to ride straight towards where the sheriff was and shoot as they rode. It might surprise the posse into a moment's inactivity which would be enough for them. It did. But just for a moment. McGinnis was wounded, so was Sam Ketchum but not before he shot the sheriff. Another member of the posse was wounded seriously and several others slightly so. The gang dispersed into so many different directions that the posse was at a loss as to which one to chase, after which resulted in their going after none. Returning to cimarron the news was flashed to all the nearby towns. Hundreds of men organized in the biggest manhunt in Northern New Mexico history to date. No bush was left unturned; every foot of the canyon was searched as with a fine tooth comb. Several miles out of Cimarron they came upon a man trying to doctor a terrible wound.

"Grizzly bear," he said, but refused assistance. This aroused the suspicions of some of the men.

"We will take you to Cimarron anyway."

The wounded man had no choice. A wagon was hitched

up at the near-by Lambert ranch and the wounded man lifted into it. In Cimarron a crowd gathered. Excitement was high. The victim proved to be Sam Ketchum.

"Lynch him," yelled one.

"Remember Sheriff Farr," said another.

"Stringing is too good for him."

"Let's go. What are we waiting for?"

"Here's the rope."

Sam realized that this was his last day. Close to him lay a Winchester left there by some unthinking soul—or was it a very thinking body? Inch by inch he wiggled as the mob argued pro and con over his fate. In the crowd, George Crocker, brother of Frank Only Crocker, watched the bandit. He moved to the back of the wagon so that Sam would think that he was leaving the crowd. Suddenly he sprung just as Sam was in the act of lifting the rifle. Ketchum was carried to Lambert's where his wound was attended to, for the mob decided that it was better to let the law take its course. Later Sam was taken to the Territorial pen at Santa Fe, where he died of his wound. Considering his daring deeds, his should have been a more sensational finish.

Up in the Cimarroncito hills McGinnis was in agony. He must have been in dreadful pain for he tore off all his clothes. Eventually captured, he was also taken to Santa Fe where he mellowed with time and was given his liberty. He died several years later a respected citizen. Black Jack was soon made aware of his brother's fate. Sam died on July 24th, 1898. His younger brother made no attempt to recover the body. It is said that Tom robbed a store in Arizona about this time and placed two more murders to his credit. This has not been verified. Be that as it may, he was in New Mexico from October 19, 1898, to August 16, 1899, when the third robbery took place near Folsom.

It was warm that day in August when Jim Kent opened his cantina in Folsom, never dreaming that he would have as his guest that day the most wanted man in America. He wore a long, General Custer type mustache, black suit, white shirt. He had just returned from staking a horse near Twin Mountain. Here the animal would feed and bake in the sun until he was needed. All Folsom was agog as the tall outlaw walked boldly into Kent's bar. No one telegraphed for the sheriff. No one rode to Clayton to spread the news. He received the same treatment as any customer. Ketchum sat down to gamble. The roof was the limit. The men were agreed that Black Jack was not such a bad fellow after all. Kindly, considerate, easy going and cheerful, he joked about his losses. Every now and then he glanced at his watch. Thanking the boys for a good time he sauntered out of the bar and made for Twin Mountain Curve. Everything in readiness, he went back to Folsom.

There was no moon that night when the express stopped at Folsom. From the shadows of the baggage room a figure emerged. No one paid attention. Suddenly the figure disappeared. The engineer opened the throttle and the train puffed its way to Twin Mountain. Three miles out of Folsom Black Jack left his hiding place, Winchester in hand, to approach Joseph Kirchgrabber, the startled engineer. Casually he edged so as to reach for the barrel of the rifle.

"Better not."

Just two words but they had a paralyzing effect. Tom Scanlon, the fireman, opened his mouth to say something, choked the words back into his throat, snapped his mouth shut and went about his business. The plan was as daring as it was bold. I had occasion to talk to the assistant photographer from Raton who attended Ketchum's execution. I asked him, from what he saw of Black Jack's last moments whether he thought the desperado was a brave man. He said that he never saw a more scared coward in his life. Studying four views of the execution I could not agree with him. Wrong as it was to hold up a train, no one could possibly question that to do so single-handedly required the nerve of a man of daring or a fool. And Black Jack was no fool.

Tom Ketchum believed that there were two kinds of people in the world: good and bad—no middle ground. This is attributed to two worlds in the after life. He was convinced that hell was created for the bad. His way of thinking led him to believe that a man was born bad, lived that way and continued that way after death. While law courts were not to his way of thinking he would not change his mind in spite of law and order. The judge was only carrying out the sentence that was his fate from birth. The motivating force that steeled Ketchum to the very end was this warped conception of his destiny. When he refused the consolation of religion on the scaffold it was not affectation. He sincerely believed he had followed the pattern of life cut out for him. Doc Holliday knew no fear because he knew that a lung condition would eventually carry him off anyway. In a certain way he was a coward. He lived by six-shooter law in the hopes that a bullet would end his misery. Eventually he conditioned himself to face the end bravely and died a natural death. Ketchum lived dangerously because he believed he was born for hell. Whether he was right or wrong is not for us to moralize in this type of work; it will make a nice treatise for a theologian.

"Just you keep this train moving. I'll tell you when to stop. Then get off and cut the baggage car from the rest of the train and off we go to the exact spot of the last hold-up."

The conductor was Frank Harrington. Kirchgrabber and Scanlon got down, stalled for time in the uncoupling, trusting to Harrington's intuition to discover what was afoot. What fooled the conductor for a moment was the absence of a number of hold-up men. Always when the train was held up at least ten men took part in the robbery. The train was stopped but no one appeared with a six-shooter to inform him that this was a stick-up. But his curiosity was aroused. He reached for a shot gun and cautiously advanced to the front of the baggage car to ascertain the cause of the delay. The lights were extinguished. Stepping to the side, he pushed the door open with his foot, just wide enough to slip the double barrels through. Ketchum, impatient at the slow progress of the pair below, pressed into service Charles Drew, the baggage express messenger. Drew held a lantern. In the light of the lantern Harrington saw the figure of the bandit. Black Jack glanced up, bringing his rifle into play as he did so. Both guns went off simultaneously. The lantern flickered out. So did Black

Jack. Forty minutes later the train continued its journey, carrying a wounded hero aboard. Harrington saved the train's reputation. It would be jinxed no longer.

Only the darkness of the night hid the desperado's chagrin and the ground hungrily lapped up his blood as it flowed from the wound from the conductor's gun. Darkness also saved his life for the aim would have been deadlier. Forty-two pellets lodged in the arm. In Trinidad Harrington informed the authorities.

"I know I hit him. He can't be far."

A posse boarded a special train and the hunt was on. Five miles out of Folsom, head propped against his coat which served as a pillow; weak from the loss of blood, Black Jack watched the train approach. His condition made escape impossible. John W. Mercer, brakeman of the Pueblo-Texline run, was the first to sight the prone figure. Cautiously the posse approached. Precaution was unnecessary. The desperado had no fight left in him. Lifted into the train, he was taken to San Rafael hospital in Trinidad where the pellets were removed from his arm. Nothing more could be done. Four days later, under heavy guard, Ketchum was taken to the pen at Santa Fe. Whether he asked the guards about Sam's last moments no one has bothered to investigate. His arm gave him trouble. Dr. DesMarais of Las Vegas, prison physician, was called in. He decided to amputate. This struck the desperado as funny.

"The loss of an arm is not funny," commented the doctor.

"Nor the loss of a head."

The doctor looked at him a moment, bent down to his work.

"How about something to deaden the pain?"

"No, doc. When you start cutting I want to see what's going on—or what's coming off."

So he watched the skillful surgeon at work. He never flinched or moved. At last the arm was off. Ketchum took it in his free hand before returning it to the doctor with this comment:

"Let me know if I can do the same for you some day."

He got up from the table and walked to his cell under his own power. In Clayton movement was afoot to have the desperado returned to answer for his crimes. Attorney William B. Bunker of Las Vegas was appointed to defend Black Jack but he knew he was licked from the start. Jeremiah Leahy, brilliant district attorney of Raton, as severe in his demeanor as he was in his appearance, was selected to prosecute the prisoner. William J. Mills, Chief Justice of the Supreme Court, was the presiding judge. Ketchum was on trial for the last attempted hold-up rather than for the previous ones. The first witness called to the stand was Charles Drew. After the usual formalities he was questioned as follows:

Leahy: What is your name?

Drew: Charles Drew.

Leahy: Are you employed by the Fort Worth & Denver railroad (which it is to Texline; from there on it is the C. & S.)?

Drew: I am.

Leahy: What is the nature of your employment?

Drew: I am a messenger in the express and baggage car.

Leahy: Were you thus employed on the night of August 16, 1899?

Drew: I was.

Leahy: Tell the Court what occurred that night.

In terse, brief sentences Drew told the Court what transpired on that night.

Leahy, pointing dramatically to Ketchum, quietly asked:

"Is that the man?"

Drew: "It is."

Leahy: "You say the prisoner pounded on the door of the baggage car and demanded that you open it?"

Drew: "Yes, sir."

Leahy: "Did you open the door?"

Drew: "I did."

Leahy: "When this occurred what did the defendant say to you?"

Drew: "He pointed his gun at me and said: 'Fall out of here d—m quick.'"

Leahy: "What did you do?"

Drew: "I fell out mighty d——m quick. Isn't that what you would have done?"

At that the audience that packed the court room let out a roar of laughter. Judge Mills picked up his gavel and pounded for order.

"I guess I would," said Leahy. Turning to the amused Ketchum, he said:

"Is that true?"

"Bet your d——m life it is. He sure lost no time about it either."

Again laughter in the court room. Livid with anger, Judge Mills stood up and bellowed like a charging bull:

"This man is on trial for his life. This is no laughing matter." The disturbance subsided.

Leahy: "That is all. Shall we hear from the defense?"

Bunker: "The defense has nothing to say."

Leahy: "Next witness."

Frank Harrington was sworn in. He had completely recovered from his wound.

Leahy: "I want you to look at the prisoner. He is Thomas E. Ketchum. Is he the man you shot on the night of August 16, 1899?"

Harrington: "He is."

Leahy: "Did the defendant fire at you?"

Harrington: "He did."

Leahy: "Did the bullet he fired strike you?"

Harrington: "Yes. It struck me in the right arm."

Turning to Bunker the prosecutor said:

"Your witness."

Bunker asked a few questions about how positive Harrington was but there was no shaking the conductor. The case was turned over to the jury. Within a few minutes the foreman of the jury handed Secundino Romero, court clerk, its verdict. Romero handed the paper to Judge Mills, who read it and returned it to the clerk.

Mills: "The prisoner will arise and listen to the verdict of the Court."

Without hesitation Ketchum stood up.

"We, the jury consulting in the case of the Territory of New Mexico vs. Thomas E. Ketchum, find the defendant guilty of the charges in the indictment and fix his punishment at death."

Ketchum shrugged his shoulders and sat down. He was taken back to Santa Fe to await the date of his hanging which Judge Mills set as of October 4, 1900. But a delay was granted and the sentence was not carried out until April 26, 1901. In the register at the State Prison at Santa Fe you will find written: "No. 132, Thomas E. Ketchum. Received August 25, 1899—Committed by J. P. Victory, U. S. Commissioner, as U. S. prisoner—safe keeping. Taken out April 23, 1901, by order of W. J. Mills."

Black Jack remained in the Clayton jail for three days. The scaffold was then declared ready. The public was not invited to the hanging. The platform was screened from view behind the jail. Despite the fact that the public was warned to stay away, all roads led to Clayton that day. There was a slight breeze, not the strong wind that usually sweeps you off your feet in April. The blue New Mexico sky was cloudless. Off towards the horizon Rabbit Ear mountain was enveloped in a haze that gave it a picture post card look. Reporters from the various Southwestern newspapers talked in subdued tones as they grouped together in various corners. Several photographers adjusted cameras. Harrington, Drew and others were special guests. A Jesuit father from Holy Trinity parish in Trinidad was with Ketchum during those last moments he occupied his cell. Ketchum seems to have maintained to the end his fantastic philosophy of being born for hell. Whether the good father convinced him of God's Mercy during the few minutes they were alone together he never divulged. Whether Ketchum actually said on the scaffold that he had appointment to dance in hell or whether this was the embellishment of a newspaper man is a disputed question. It could have been a bravado on the part of Ketchum.

At one o'clock in the afternoon Sheriff Garcia of Clayton asked Black Jack if he was ready. He replied that he was.

Ketchum's last walk was from his cell to the scaffold. On the platform were the sheriff assisted by Sheriff Clark of Trinidad, Captain Fort of Las Vegas and two deputies. The Jesuit father prayed to the end.

"Are you ready?" asked the sheriff in his customary Spanish-American polite tone.

"Ready. Let her go."

Black Jack wore a white shirt, a white bow-tie, a black suit, shoes shined. The rope was placed about his neck and a black hood over his face. His right empty sleeve was pinned to his coat, the left secured to his back by a thin chain. He was the tallest man on the scaffold. The sheriff raised the hatchet, cut the rope that supported the trap. The trap door gave way under the weight of Black Jack's body which fell through with such terrific impact that the head was severed from the body. By one-thirty all was over. In the surrounding buildings a number of deputies put away their rifles. No one came to make a last minute stand for the desperado as predicted. The crowd dispersed. Gibbets that serve their purpose always disperse crowds. Some strike their breasts; others wag their tongues. After all the one who really got hurt for the crime that hung Black Jack was the desperado himself. He lost an arm. Funny he was never tried for murder.

The undertaker from Trinidad had come all prepared for a burial but not for sewing a head back on a body. This delayed the burial. Borrowing a large needle and some strong white thread, he worked for two hours. At three thirty a spring wagon drawn by one horse passed up Clayton's main street so that all the citizens could see the plain yellow pine box draped by a black cloth. Several of the more curious followed the casket to the grave. Captain Fort asked the undertaker to open the coffin before lowering it into the earth. Not a tear was shed, not a muffled sound was heard as the pebbles and dirt covered the mortal remains. Only the breeze hummed a dirge as it mournfully skipped towards Rabbit Ear.

Then began the "Remember when" and "I heard" tales. "I remember one day when Black Jack sat at the gambling table at Lambert's in Cimarron. . . ." "I remember one day in

Clayton when Black Jack walked into the hotel at Clayton...."
There is the story of how Black Jack decided to try out a new
.44-75 rifle, so he selected a Spanish-American riding the range
as a good target. He is supposed to have made a bet with one
of his cronies as to which side of the horse the man would fall
from. Such legends about Black Jack will grow as they have
grown about Billy the Kid, Clay Allison and others and nothing
you or I will ever do or say can stop them. Time incorporates
such legend as truth and more of the untruth is believed as
the truth is interred with their bones.

As a tourist attraction Clayton did very much with Black
Jack what Fort Sumner did with Billy the Kid. In 1933 a new
cemetery was opened one-half mile east of the old one. Ketchum
had been buried on government land. Hand bills were distributed and the public in general invited to witness the removal
of the remains. Over a thousand people attended the ceremony.
Sunday afternoon, September 10th, a prominent citizen well
coached for the affair told the assembled people the story of
Black Jack Ketchum. No church in New Mexico that Sunday
morning had as attentive an audience as that orator in the vast
blue-domed cathedral on the open prairie. The casket was
opened for the spectators to view. The black suit had turned
gray. The hair and mustache were now a deep red. Recently
Life Magazine ran a series of pictures of a mob of people about
the casket and body of St. Francis Xavier. The people who objected to such a public display should have seen this ceremony
at Clayton. Nobody seemed to object. And Black Jack Ketchum
was no saint.

Black Jack Ketchum—left hand chained to side—is prepared for the hangman's noose at Clayton, N.M.

The fellow with the loud cravat (tie to you) is dressed in his Sunday best. Black Jack almost held his head in his hand. His death evidently pleased these sheriffs.

Frank Harrington, whose lucky shot brought about the capture of Black Jack Ketchum. Railroad men, like Engineer Yoakley on the Denver and Fort Worth who rode with Harrington, tell me he was one of the most pleasant conductors ever to take up a ticket. That's saying a lot for a conductor.

BIBLIOGRAPHY

A. COURT HOUSE RECORDS

Hemphill County Criminal and Docket Records
    1887-1893—Canadian, Texas
Hemphill County Deed Book
    1879-1887—Wheeler, Texas
Colfax County Land Claims
    1869-1883—Elizabethtown, N. M.
Colfax County Criminal and Docket, Vol. 1
    1869-1875—Raton, New Mexico
Colfax County Criminal and Docket, Vol. 2
    1875-1880—Raton, New Mexico
Colfax County Criminal and Docket, Vol. 3
    1880-1884—Raton, New Mexico
Mora County Deed Book, Vol. A
    1869-1874—Raton New Mexico
San Miguel County Criminal Docket, Vol. A
    1882-1885—Las Vegas, New Mexico
San Miguel County Criminal Docket, Vol. B
    1885-1887—Las Vegas, New Mexico
San Miguel County Criminal Docket, Vol. C
    1887-1897—Las Vegas, New Mexico
San Miguel County Criminal Docket, Vol. D
    1897-1907—Las Vegas, New Mexico
San Miguel County Criminal Docket, Vol. E
    1907-1917—Las Vegas, New Mexico

B. NEWSPAPERS

Las Vegas Daily Optic, 1879-1900, All Issues
Las Vegas Acorn, 1875 Issues

Las Vegas Eureka, 1882 Issues
Las Vegas Chronicle, 1884-1885, All Issues
Las Vegas Republican, 1900, All Issues
The Lawrence (Kansas) Standard, May 21, 1880
Denver Republican, February 18, 1880
Las Vegas Gazette, All Issues
Santa Fe New Mexican, 1879-1888, All Issues
Santa Fe Gazette, All Issues
Raton Daily Range, All Issues to 1903
Raton Guard, All Issues
Raton Comet, All Issues
La Voz del Pueblo, All Issues
Las Vegas Herald Star, All Issues
El Sol De Mayo, October 9, 1892
Albuquerque Morning Democrat, October 6, 1886 to September 7, 1887
Cimarron News and Press, All Issues
Clayton Enterprise, All Issues
Woodward, Okla., Jeffersonian, April 21, 1895

C. PERIODICALS

Fulton, Maurice C., CLAY ALLISON
    Southwest Review, Vol. XV, Winter 1930
Knight, Alwyn W. & Hartley, W. B., ABLE TO KILL
    True Magazine, June 1948
Dobie, J. F., DON QUIXOTE OF THE SIX-SHOOTER
    New Mexico Magazine, May 1942
Upshaw, H. C., LUCIEN MAXWELL, DUKE OF CIMARRON, Ranch Magazine, June 27, 1940
    NEW MEXICO MAGAZINE, All Issues
    NEW MEXICO SUN TRAILS MAGAZINE, All Issues
    NEW MEXICO STOCKMAN'S MAGAZINE, All Issues
    THE CATTLEMAN (TEXAS) MAGAZINE, All Issues
    NEW MEXICO HISTORICAL REVIEW, All Issues
    THE SOUTHWEST MAGAZINE, All Issues
    THE SANTA FE (RAILROAD) MAGAZINE, All Issues

D. MISCELLANEOUS

Blandina, Sr., AT THE END OF THE SANTA FE TRAIL
   Milwaukee, Wis., 1948
Claussen, W. E., CIMARRON, THE LAST FRONTIER
   Santa Fe, 1948
Chase, C. M., AN EDITOR'S RUN, Lyndon, Vermont, 1882
Chabot, F. S., SAN ANTONIO AND ITS BEGINNINGS
   San Antonio, Texas, 1948
Dykes, J. C., BILLY THE KID—BIBILIOGRAPHY
   OF A LEGEND, Albuquerque, N. M., 1952
Burns, W. N., THE SAGA OF BILLY THE KID
   New York, 1925
Beebe, L., & Schmitt, M. F., HEAR THE TRAIN BLOW
   New York, 1952
Brown, B., & Schmitt, M. F., TRAIL DRIVING DAYS
   New York, 1952
Fergusson, H., RIO GRANDE, Glendale, Calif., 1936
Fergusson, E., NEW MEXICO, New York, 1951
Fergusson, E., MURDER AND MYSTERY IN NEW MEXICO
   New York, 1948
Fitzpatrick, G., THIS IS NEW MEXICO, Santa Fe, N. M., 1948
Forrest, E. R., ARIZONA'S DARK AND BLOODY
   GROUND, Caldwell, Idaho, 1936
Haley, J. E. V., CHARLES GOODNIGHT, Boston, Mass., 1936
Haley, J. E. V., JEFF MILTON, GOOD MAN WITH A GUN
   Norman, Oklahoma, 1948
Horgan, Paul, NEW MEXICO'S OWN CHRONICLE
   Dallas, Texas, 1937
Keleher, Wm. A., THE FABULOUS FRONTIER
   Santa Fe, N. M., 1948
Keleher, Wm. A., TURMOIL IN NEW MEXICO
   Santa Fe, N. M., 1951
King, Wm., WRANGLIN' THE PAST, Pasadena, Calif., 1946
Lambert, Fred, BYGONE DAYS OF THE OLD WEST
   Kansas City, Mo., 1948
Marshall, J., SANTA FE, THE RAILROAD THAT
   BUILT AN EMPIRE, New York, 1945

Marshall, E., THE STORY OF THE ROUGH RIDERS
   New York, 1899
Otero, M., MY LIFE ON THE FRONTIER, New York, 1935
McCarthy, J., MAVERICK TOWN, New York, 1946
Riddle, Kenyon, RECORDS AND MAPS OF THE OLD
   SANTA FE TRAIL, Raton, 1949
Scanland, J. W., LIFE OF PAT GARRETT,
   El Paso, Texas, 1908
Stanley, F., GRANT THAT MAXWELL BOUGHT
   Denver, 1952
Waters, L. L., STEEL RAILS TO SANTA FE
   Lawrence, Kansas, 1950
Cleaveland, A., SATAN'S PARADISE, Boston, Mass., 1952
Hamner, L. V., SHORT GRASS AND LONG HORNS
   Norman, Oklahoma, 1945
Thompson, A. W., THOSE WERE OPEN RANGE DAYS
   Denver, Colorado, 1946
Lake, S. N., WYATT EARP, FRONTIER MARSHALL
   Boston, Massachusetts, 1931
   TEXAS ALMANAC AND STATE INDUSTRIAL
      GUIDE, 1950

   ARIZONA STATE GUIDE
   KANSAS STATE GUIDE
   NEW MEXICO STATE GUIDE
   TEXAS STATE GUIDE

www.ingramcontent.com/pod-product-compliance
Lightning Source LLC
Chambersburg PA
CBHW021334230426
43666CB00006B/294